These
Are Our Lives

AS TOLD BY THE PEOPLE AND WRITTEN BY
MEMBERS OF THE FEDERAL WRITERS' PROJECT
OF THE WORKS PROGRESS ADMINISTRATION IN
NORTH CAROLINA, TENNESSEE, AND GEORGIA

The Norton Library

W·W·NORTON & COMPANY·INC·

NEW YORK

First published in the Norton Library 1975
by arrangement with the University of North Carolina Press

Books That Live
The Norton imprint on a book means that in the publisher's
estimation it is a book not for a single season but for the years.
W. W. Norton & Company, Inc.

Library of Congress Cataloging in Publication Data
Federal Writers' Project.
    These are our lives.
    (The Norton library)
    Reprint of the ed. published by the University of
North Carolina Press, Chapel Hill.
    1. Southern States—Social conditions—Case
studies. I. Title.
HN79.A2F43   1975   309.1'75   74-32212
ISBN 0-393-00763-4

Printed in the United States of America
4 5 6 7 8 9 0

Contents

Preface

SEVERAL MONTHS AGO THE WRITING OF LIFE HISTORIES of tenant farmers, farm owners, textile and other factory workers, persons in service occupations in towns and cities (such as bell hops, waitresses, messenger boys, clerks in five and ten cent stores, soda jerks), and persons in miscellaneous occupations such as lumbering, mining, turpentining, and fishing was begun by the Federal Writers' Project in North Carolina. This work has recently been extended to six other states, and a large number of stories have already been written.

The idea is to get life histories which are readable and faithful representations of living persons, and which, taken together, will give a fair picture of the structure and working of society. So far as I know, this method of portraying the quality of life of a people, of revealing the real workings of institutions, customs, habits, has never before been used for the people of any region or country. It seems to me that the method here used has certain possibilities and advantages which should no longer be ignored.

A large amount of material is already in print dealing with life in the South; but that portion which is fictional, excellent as it is as fiction, cannot be and has not claimed to be accurate in the sense indicated here. In works of fiction, the author may and usually does make his characters composites of persons he has known or imagined; and because of its composite or imaginary character fiction cannot be regarded as a transcript of the experience of particular individuals.

Popular non-fiction has not attempted the task contemplated here. Sociology has furnished the classifications and much of the information on the basis of which this work has been shaped and the stories in this book selected. But sociology has been content in the main to treat human beings as abstractions. Certainly, sociologists have used case histories, but for the most part their use has been limited to narrow segments of experience collected and arranged to illustrate particular points. Useful as such segments of experience are they cannot possibly convey as much information and real knowledge as a story which covers the more significant aspects of the whole life experience, including memories of ancestry, written *from the standpoint of the individual himself.* This principle has been recognized and applied in a number of sociological works dealing with special problems, particularly those of personal maladjustment, but never for the purpose contemplated here.

The life of a community or of a people is, of course, made up of the life of individuals, who are of different status, perform different functions, and in general have widely different experiences and attitudes—so different, indeed, as to be almost unimaginable. It would seem therefore that one important method of revealing the life of a people would be through life histories selected to represent the different types present among the people, with attention proportioned according to the numerical importance of the different types.

In writing the life histories the first principle has been to let the people tell their own stories. With all our talk about democracy it seems not inappropriate to let the people speak for themselves.

This volume is published only as a suggestion of what can be done with life histories. It is my hope that later separate volumes will be published on people in agriculture, in industry, in lumbering, turpentining, mining and in miscellaneous groups; at the same time it may be possible to choose typical communities and use this method to reveal their nature and workings. Until after a large amount of material has been collected and studied, it is not possible to know what is most important, most typical, or how stories should be classified and published in order to give the most faithful representation.

Twenty of the stories in this volume are from North Carolina, fourteen from Tennessee, one from Georgia. Stories have been written in Alabama, Florida, South Carolina and Virginia; but for various reasons I have had to decide not to include any from these states in this first volume. Among the more than 400 stories that I have had to choose from are life histories of baby-boarding house keepers, barbers, bootleggers, business men, carpenters, cigar makers, clerks, cooks, dairymen, doctors, dressmakers, elevator operators, farm owners, farm laborers, and tenants, fishermen and florists, boarding and lodging house keepers, housemaids, janitors, lawyers, lunchroom workers, mailmen, milliners, miners, workers in cleaning and pressing shops, nurses, midwives, ministers, old people, peddlers, policemen, railroad men, sawmill workers, shoe salesmen, shrimpers, stone masons, storekeepers, street car conductors, textile workers, tobacco warehouse owners, managers, doorkeepers, auctioneers, buyers and speculators, tramps, jailbirds and bums, truckers, salesgirls, sheriffs and deputies, shopkeepers, teachers, vegetable market men and women, waitresses, wash women, kept women and prostitutes, people on relief and people not on but who are in dire need.

I have chosen for this first volume stories which seem to me most typical and most important. I would like to have included at least one story each of fishermen, coal and iron miners and smelters, turpentiners, lumberers and miscellaneous factory and shop workers and especially of Negroes in these occupations. At present we have no life histories of factory owners and managers, and few of middle class people. I doubt whether any owners have ever spoken better for themselves than Kate Brumby and Smith Coon here speak for them; but nevertheless they should be given a chance to speak for themselves. I have not included in this volume any one of a number of extremely sordid stories which I think are of considerable importance, because space is limited and the stories here presented seem to me to deserve attention first.

My ideas as to what ought to be done and what can be done in the writing and publishing of life histories are subject to change. I have learned and hope to learn from this material things about people that cannot be learned by reading books written from other books, or books, however interesting, by persons with literary talent and fertile imaginations.

How authentic are the stories in this volume? I believe the best answer to this is to ask the reader to read carefully a few of the stories. If he does, I am convinced he will agree that real people here are speaking. Each story has been written after one or more interviews. When one name is given after a story the story has not been sent back to the author for revision and no revision or changes of any consequence have been made. Where two or more names are given, the names after the first one are of the editors, who have made cuts, suggested that additional material be secured, and made revisions generally. In all such instances the copy has been read and approved in final form by the author and, in some instances, by the subject of the story. All names of persons have been changed, and where there is any danger of identification, places also.

I have included in an appendix the instructions which have been given to the writers. These instructions have been amplified but have not been changed in any essential respect. In the stories here printed they have been carefully followed, and if the stories are not worth printing the fault is in the idea and the instructions, not in the persons who have carried it out.

To those who glance at a page and imagine they have absorbed its contents, to those who are fixed in their ideas as to how writing should be done, to those who are already certain how people think and feel, to those who are not genuinely interested in the rich variety of human experience, to those who cannot for a moment look at the world and people as if they were seeing them for the first time, pushing aside all patterns and doctrines that might be obstructive, this book will have no meaning. I ask only that the reader' take the time to consider and understand why and how it has been written. I shall appreciate greatly any suggestions or criticisms which might lead to improvement of the method used here, or to a better method of revealing the people as they are.

This is no trivial matter. The people, all the people, must be known, they must be heard. Somehow they must be given representation, somehow they must be given voice and allowed to speak, in their essential character. To accomplish this, many different kinds of effort on different levels will be necessary. Books of life histories can help with this job.

* * * * *

Here, then, are real, living people. Here are their own stories, their origins, their more important experiences, their most significant thoughts and feelings, told by themselves from their own point of view.

Here are John and Sarah Easton, farm laborers, one-time sharecroppers, past middle age, parents of five children all now away from home but two, living in a one-room filling station, getting jobs and wages when and how they can. In the cotton states in the last ten years there have been three-quarters to a million farm laborers living as they live, excepting that John and Sarah are probably better off than the majority in this group. How many families are dependent on farm laborers, how many people are in this group, no one knows with any exactness. This class shifts from town to country, from one farm to another, from working for wages to sharecropping.

The farm laborer and his family in the South are near the bottom of the social pyramid. Beneath them in economic and social status are only such groups as the down and out and almost hopeless unemployed not on relief, the derelicts, tramps, bums and criminals. No wage and hour laws protect the farm laborer; social security overlooks him, and likely as not he will overlook old age insurance if he does not die before he knows he is eligible. The proportionate size of this class is increasing because of the rapid introduction of machinery and rationalization of methods.

Here are Gracie and James Turner, Negro share-croppers, with their children, and their children's children, and Gracie's father, age 91. At the time this story was written the Turners were looking for a place to move. Gracie gives an account of the places in which they have lived. Her family has not moved as frequently as the typical cotton tenant family. Throughout the vast area from Virginia through Texas, tenants move, on an average, once every three years. This is probably the most severe handicap of this region, not without possible remedy, but nothing has been attempted by the states to correct it. In the story of the Turner family, as told by Gracie, we see the helplessness of the sharecropper, his awareness of his handicaps, and his inability to do anything to remove them.

Just how typical Irma is in "Get Out And Hoe" when Morrison comes home, after having run away with another woman, I cannot say; but when Irma says:

"I aint got no right to be mad now, Morrison. You had your fling and done come home. We need you awful bad. We got to get out and hoe in the to-bacco tomorrow. You better get some sleep,"

I feel as if I know Irma better than I possibly could from mere statistical facts concerning tenant farmers. I can assure the reader that Irma and Morrison are not unusual so far as those experiences of tenant farmers are concerned which have been counted, tabu-lated, and analyzed (except for division of crops four-fifths to tenant, one-fifth to landlord—which is un-usual) ; but this, which tells what kind of person Irma is, cannot be contained in any tabulation or subjected to any analysis. If we are to know the character of

Irma it is necessary that we be given this view of her.

The experience of Irma and her family and of the Turners is typical of that of about three-quarters of a million families, involving with children, three to four million people.

The Joe Fieldings, white share renters, are a little better off than the sharecroppers. The number of share renters, white and black, is slightly greater than that of sharecroppers. Tom Doyle and his family, Negro cash renters, are sturdy, self-respecting farmers, living probably as well as it will ever be possible for large numbers of people to live.

In the story, "Five Year Lease," the white cash renter, Martin, gives a good statement of one of the customs which make tenancy in the South so costly and destructive of both human and property values. His landlord, he says,

"—won't give me a five year lease and so I can't afford to make many improvements. If I was sure I could stay on, I could make over the house, fix up the terrace and clear off some more land. The trouble is that just as sure as the tenant makes the farm more productive, the owner boosts his rent."

In the Southern states there are about a quarter of a million cash renters, amounting with families to a million or a million and a quarter people. Tom and Martin, Negro and white cash renters, are probably above the level in prosperity of the majority of the group to which they belong.

Sally Reams, Negro woman, age 52, with her family, husband dead, faces her last chance to own a farm. She and her husband managed to acquire a farm of 50 acres and paid for it. Then they bought another

50 acres adjoining and were trying to pay for the additional 50 when two years ago George, the husband, was crushed to death in a road accident. Sally has not been able to make the payments on the additional 50 acres and fears she will lose the first 50 as well as the second. Sally is not bitter; she makes no charges of unfairness. From her account, she and her family were first fortunate but later, in recent years, have been victims of a series of misfortunes. George was killed by a careless driver:

> "The feller that was drivin' the truck wa'n't wuth nothin'; so we couldn't get no damages out'n him. They say he was put in the pen for five years. I don't know. It didn't do us no good; it didn't bring George back. Looked like I had a lapful o' trouble these last few years. A hailstorm destroyed the crop one year, my house and furniture got burnt up; my boy died of pneumonia; the land we paid for had to be mortgaged; I lost my husband. But I keep hopin' for better days."

Sally and her family in their ownership status represent roughly about a quarter of a million white and Negro families, or about a million people.

Sam Bowers, substantial Negro farm owner, "makes plenty." Sam and his wife are exceptional in that they have no children. Most Negro farms are well supplied with children. If we accept Sam's word, he is more prosperous than most Negro owners. In the South there are between one hundred and fifty and two hundred thousand Negro farm owners, comprising, with their families, six hundred to eight hundred thousand Negroes. In the corresponding white owner group there are about a million families or four to five million people. This group, white and Negro, comprises about one-third of the South's farm population. Not many small owners have as much cash income as Sam and it is doubtful whether cash incomes of this size will ever be generally earned by farmers in this group. Except for the size of his cash income a majority of Southern farmers could be as well off as Sam. The barriers to well-being are not in the land or the people. They are in certain customs and habits which can be changed.

What is to be done for the farmer and his wife who have worked, reared a large family, who now at an advanced age are too old and weak to work, children now grown and away from home, earning barely enough but not more than enough to support themselves? "Our troubles," says the farmer, who tells of first living on a place in western North Carolina, of exhausting the fertility of the soil there, selling out, moving to Tennessee, living on other places and wearing them out, "Our troubles," he says "is just because we've lived too long." The experience of this farmer is certainly typical of that of hundreds of thousands of others.

John Sylvester Hinson, white, son of a tenant farmer, worked hard for 19 years, saved his money, bought the place which his father had rented and is now a small landlord. Marsh Taylor, intelligent, humane, prosperous large landlord, tells the story of his family's fortunes and gives a picture of the community in which he lives: how some landlords are losing out and why, how others are gaining and why. Hinson and Taylor belong to a comparatively small group, less than 100,000, with their families amounting to less than a half million people. It is hard to understand how a country with people in it as vigorous and intelligent as Marsh Taylor can continue failing to find methods that will make chances better for the Eastons, the Turners, the Joe

Fieldings, the millions of members of wage laborer and tenant families. The interests that are involved are not only humanitarian, they are equally those of property, the preservation and creation of wealth.

Thus the eleven stories in the first part of the book give a picture of the life of the different groups of people in farming in the South.

The same method has been followed in portraying the experience of people in mill villages and factories, in service occupations, and on relief. The stories in these three parts have not been arranged according to status in the economic and social scale. The effort here has been only to represent different types and occupations as well as possible with the materials that have been secured up to the present time.

*　　*　　*　　*　　*

I owe thanks first of all to Henry G. Alsberg for giving me the chance to work on this job—a job which I have wanted to do for many years; to Frank Graham and Paul Green for active support and advice; to Mrs. Blanche Ralston of the Regional staff and Mrs. May Campbell of the North Carolina staff of the Works Progress Administration for intelligent interest, encouragement and support when these were needed; to Edwin Bjorkman and George Lawrence Andrews, Director and Assistant Director of the North Carolina FWP; to William McDaniel, and Samuel Tupper, State Directors of Tennessee and Georgia.

When the writing of life histories was no more than an idea and a nebulous one, Ida Moore started work and showed that the job could be done. Her first stories were used as samples. Her work included in this volume will speak for itself. I would have been severely handicapped without the assistance of James Aswell of the Tennessee staff and Walter Cutter, Assistant Regional Director. My wife, Elizabeth Calvert Couch (another example of exploitation—she is on no one's payroll), has read and edited stories, classified them, abstracted them, carried them back and forth for me, listened to me talk endlessly about them, and she is still my wife.

To the Board of Governors of the Press and to the University administration I am grateful for permission to help, on a part-time basis as Regional Director of the Federal Writers' Project, do the very important work that is being done under the able direction of Mr. Alsberg.

W. T. COUCH

Chapel Hill, N.C.
February 20, 1939

On The Farm

You're Gonna Have Lace Curtains

JOHN AND SARAH EASTON, WITH THEIR SIXTEEN-YEAR-old twin girls, live in a one-room filling station near Wilson. It was once painted white but now is a weather-beaten gray. The top bricks have fallen from the jaunty flue and the tin roof shows numerous patches here and there. The steps sag and the whole place looks neglected but clean. In the yard is clean bare sand but over on one side is a weed-grown flower bed.

"Oh, you brought Amy home," said Sarah, as she stood in the door. Then she added, "Do come in, I'm not ashamed of our house although it's the worst we've stayed in since we was married thirty-two years ago. The main thing is that we hope to do better after next year."

She is a pleasant-voiced woman, big and strong with the brownest eyes one can imagine. Her hair is heavily streaked with gray and there are many tired lines in her dark face. Her mouth has bitter lines as though she long ago screwed it the wrong way when she was inclined to laugh.

"The children are all low like their father except Jack. He is tall and rawboned like I was when I was young." She looked down at her plump figure. "I reckon they'll all be fat, though, when they git older like me and their father. Do have a chair. Have you ever seen such a change in the weather a day after

3

Thanksgiving in your life? I do believe we'll have a big snow before Christmas." She chatted on amiably about the weather.

The room was "pack-jam" full. It contained two beds, one iron and one wooden. One was painted sky blue, the other walnut. In the room also was a walnut dresser with a cracked mirror, a scarred white washstand with a dull mirror, two brown trunks which were new in 1880, an old sewing machine with a broken pedal, a small wood range, a cracked wood heater, a wobbly-legged dining table with a frayed white oilcloth, two long unpainted benches, a small table, and about ten straight chairs. The floor was clean and bare. On a rough plank shelf in the corner stood an eight-day clock and near it sat a grinning cat family. On the small table was a cracked blue pitcher.

"The pitcher's really no good now," said Sarah, "but it's too pretty to throw away. It ain't been cracked but a week. Last summer we kept it full of fresh wild flowers. We kept them in quart fruit jars, too, but we called the blue pitcher our Sunday vase. It's very little of pretty things we ever have. We don't have time to work no flowers so we have to use the wild ones."

She fingered the white scrim curtains. "I do wish we could afford some real lace curtains but I've done give up hope of that. I used to hope that some day we could have things but times gits worser and worser. We ain't never had nothing and we won't never have nothing.

"All of our folks before us was tenant farmers and that's all we've ever done. If you know anything about tenant farming you know they do without everything all the year hoping to have something in the fall. Well, it's very little they ever have, but it's a hope to live and work for all the year just the same. I was raised hard and so was John. We had plenty to eat and that was all. No nice clothes and never a cent to throw away. The first years after John and me got married was hard a-plenty but they ain't nothing to what we've had lately.

"We started off on a ten-acre farm, four acres of tobacco, two of cotton and four acres of corn. That didn't include the garden and the 'tater patch. We raised enough vegetables, hogs and chickens for us, and our money crop bought the rest—you know, sugar, coffee and a piece of clothes now and then.

"We worked early and late that first year and we made a good crop. In a little over a year after we married Lucy come, and as she come in August I won't worth much to John the whole year. He was good to me, too, and tried to keep me out of the field when I was so heavy.

"The next year I worked like a nigger and that fall John bought me a coat suit, come the time he sold the first load of tobacco. If he'd waited till the last load I wouldn't of got one because the last load got wet and we got just $35 for it when it was worth pretty near $200. The coat suit didn't do me much good that winter because I was in the family way again and it was the next winter before I could wear it. John bought hisself a suit of clothes, too, and he shore was proud of it because it was the first whole suit he ever had.

"Macy was born in March and I was pretty sick. John was mighty disappointed because he had his heart sot on a boy. He said that the younguns was coming too fast and that with more mouths to feed and me not able to work half the time we'd soon find ourselves starving to death.

"It just about got John's goat and he commenced to drink harder. He'd always drunk some but now he was like a hog in a bucket of slops. He suddenly got the notion that he wanted to git rid of me and the younguns and he'd raise hell and try to fight when he got drunk. He was mighty kind to us when he was sober but he worried about how to take care of us. Then I got big again.

"I would rather of done near 'bout anything than to had to tell him about it. There was a old granny woman in our neighborhood—she's dead now—and she told me to drink cotton root tea. She swore that that would knock it up, and it did but I liked to of died. John finally made me tell the truth and he cried and said that it was his sin instead of mine. He is funny like that. He didn't think it was wrong to cuss, drink, and work me to death, but he thought it was awful to git rid of a baby or to impose on a dumb animal. He would lie to me, too, but he thought stealing was the worst of all the crimes. Well, I was mighty slow in gitting well but he was good to me and didn't rush me to the field.

"He didn't say a word when I told him a few months atter that we was going to have another one. He just kissed me kinda slow and he said, 'God knows, Sarah, I love the brats but I'm worried about how to look atter them.' I told him that they'd be a way and he brightened up a little.

"Well, sir, when Jack was born John was tickled pink. For several months he didn't drink a drop but when he sold the last load of tobacco he found out that they won't going to be a cent left atter the bills was paid so he spent it all on a drunk and let the bills go to the Old Harry.

"He come home about midnight as drunk as a dog and as broke as a beggar." The big woman looked down at her knotted hands. "I suddenly took a notion that I could beat the stuffin' out of him, and I did. I got a barrel stave and I turned him across the table bench and I blistered his rump. I made him pretty sore but it ain't done no good yet 'cause he still gits drunk even in spite of the doctor tellin' him that it would kill him.

"When Jack was two years old the twins come. It had got harder to feed the new mouths and even if John had been mighty worried all the time I never did worry till Amy and Joyce got here; then I was in despair. We hadn't paid the doctor for bringing Jack yet and we still owed a little on Macy. He charged us double the usual price when he brought the twins and from that minute on ever' bill has doubled it seems like.

"Them was my last because before they was a year old I had appendicitis and when the doctor operated he tied my tubes so I couldn't have no more.

"John had his appendix cut out a few years atter that and all of them bills ain't been paid yet.

"It was lucky for us that our younguns was pretty healthy. They all had measles, whooping cough, chicken pox, and mumps and all the other diseases that younguns is supposed to have. The only things that won't perfectly natural happened to Amy. She was born with a crooked foot but she won't born with yellow fever. She had it though when she was five. We thought that we'd lose her then in spite of the devil but she got well. God bless the government—it had Amy's crooked leg operated on two years ago and it's as good as Joyce's now

"The county woman found out about her leg from her school teacher and she come to me about it. Well sir, I said right off that the child was a-going to git that chance but John was just as determined that she shouldn't. I finally won and we sent her off to Raleigh. It like to a-broke my heart that I couldn't at least go with her but we didn't have no money. We didn't see her for ten weeks but she could walk straight then. Since it healed we can't tell that it was ever crooked.

"All of us is in good health now and even if we don't have enough to eat all the time and nothing to wear but rags I am gladder of our health than money.

"We wanted our children to git a education because me and Pa can't neither one read nor write, and we know how not having a education can keep you out of a job, from teaching in Sunday school, and from 'sociating with good people. Me and John both went to school for a few months but that won't enough for us to learn nothing. We was too pore to help the younguns through high school. When Lucy got to the sixth grade we had to stop her because they was so much work to do, what with the farm work, the housework, the twins and all. She stayed home four years and helped me, then she got a job in a store in Goldsboro and went to work. I reckon she had been clerking about a year when she married a civil engineer and moved off to Raleigh.

"Macy finished the sixth grade the year Anne went to work so she had to stay home and help me. She got married when she was seventeen; married a farmer who won't worth his salt. She left him a heap of times but now he's doing pretty good. They've got seven young-uns. Jack quit school in the fifth grade to help his pa on the farm. He got married two years ago. Amy and Joyce is sixteen now and they can't go on in the ninth grade this year because we ain't got money to buy books and the stuff they need to learn to cook and sew. I wish we did have.

"We just played the devil by not farming this year. We thought that we'd make a whole heap more working out by the day but we found out different pretty quick. A heap of folks wanted work done but they ain't had no money on hand. A heap of them give us vegetables and stuff for our work. Some of them hired us on a-credit to chop cotton and barn and grade tobacco. When the boll weevil eat the cotton up they thought that we was no better to lose than them. When tobacco brought little prices they thought that we hadn't orter charge for our work.

"We are going to farm this land around here next year and so we don't have to pay no rent nor for wood we burn. It shore is a big help, too, not to have to pay for them things when gitting a little to eat's such a problem.

"We've got a 1924 Dodge sedan but it ain't much good no more, even if we had the money to run it. We made a good crop in 1924 and that fall John bought the car. He was drunk when he bought it and he bent a fender before he got it home. We ain't never had no radio. The house is wired for lights but we can't never afford it. We git water from the pump out there in the back yard. Our toilet is off there to the left and, if I do say so, it's kept clean. We take a daily wash in spots and every Saturday night we bring the big tin tub in and all takes a good hot bath. The girls bathe during the week sometimes when their pa goes off.

"Diet? Well now, I don't know. I always thought that just so a person eat a-plenty it didn't matter much what he eat. Of course I think vegetables, eggs, milk,

and butter is good for folks and I believe in plenty of
hot coffee in cold weather. Then I believe that corn
bread is better for a body than biscuits. We always
did have enough of something till the last year or so.
My worry's not diet but where to git any kind of rations
from.

"Well sir, it's been a good while since I thought of
religion. I used to belong to the Baptist Church but
I've always been used to cussing, drinking, and working on Sunday. I know a whole heap of times in the
busy season when we done our week's washing, scrubbing, and cleaning on a-Sunday and thought nothing
of it. I stopped going to church mostly way back when
the younguns was little. You see, I didn't have nothing
to wear for me nor them. It was a good ways to go and
John wouldn't go with me nor keep the younguns for
me to go. He never did care for churches nor religion
and way atter awhile the hard life took everything
outen me 'cept cussing, I reckon.

"I ain't never voted, but John's a Democrat. He
ain't never let me vote but he thinks it's a woman's
place to cut wood and stay all night in a mean neighborhood by herself. Two or three times I have had to
defend our stuff with a shotgun when he was away, and
he laughs and says that taking a man's place at home
is all right but a man's place in voting is all wrong.
There comes John now and I've got to cook dinner."
She bounded out of her chair and began building a fire
in the stove.

Just then John came puffing in with a small armful
of wood. He is extremely stout and low and has a
round jolly face. His hair is nearly snow white but he
does not look his fifty-three years. He has jolly brown

eyes, red cheeks, and wide mouth. Taken all in all, he reminds one of a fat and mischievous elf.

"Why howdy," he greeted his guest royally. "Just keep your cheer and make yourself to home. I thought I heard you hens talking politics as I come up." He continued briskly, "I'm a Democrat; I stand for the New Deal and Roosevelt. I am for the WPA, the NYA, the NRA, the AAA, the FHA, and crop control. I'm going to vote for control in December. We've got mighty little of the government money but I'm still saying that the WPA, CCC, and all the rest is shore doing a big part for North Carolina. The government shore give us enough when it paid for Amy's leg operation.

"I'm supposed to be one of the best farmers in Wilson County and I know that I'm going to make a good crop next year. Did you know that the best tobacco plants air raised on new ground land? They air, and the land's got to be burnt over for the best results. I usually fix it in the wintertime, that is, I clear the land up and burn the brush in December or January. I plow the land deep with a two-horse plow along about the first of February, rake out the roots and grass and plant the seed thick. I roll logs up to each side of the bed and pull the canvas tight across it.

"It don't need no more attention then till long about the middle of March or the first of April when the plants has to be thinned out and the weeds pulled out. Long about that time I break up my tobacco patch with a two-horse plow, harrow it good and run the rows. I want at least a half a ton of good guano to the acre and when I git it out I feel like I'm really starting to farm. 'Bout the first of May, if it's warm, or later if it ain't, I set out my plants. That's when my whole family commences to git busy shore 'nuff.

"We use good strong lightard pegs to stick the holes and one sets out about as fast as a feller can drop the plants. I want them about two and a half feet apart and I want the dirt packed tight to the roots. If it's real dry we water them with buckets and gourds.

"In about four weeks we go over and loosen the dirt around the roots with a hoe and then we plow it. We have to do this two or three times before time to lay by.

" 'Bout the time we git through chopping and plowing the first time, the worms commences to chaw on it and the little suckers start to grow. Them suckers and worms can ruin a tobacco patch pronto so we all gits busy killing them worms and pulling out them suckers. Man, that's some job! Atter we've gone over it two or three times it starts flowering out and then we've got to top it, too.

"Well, 'long in early July the lugs gits to turning yaller and we go out there and crap off the ripe leaves. The slides hauls it to the barn and the women and children and a few men hands it, strings it, and puts it in the barn. When all the racks are full or when we git all the tobacco crapped we quit for the day. Then we fire up and for several days we cure it. When the stems are dry, so they are brown and crack easy when broke, we take it out of the barn and pack it up in the packhouse or the house we live in. We go over and worm, sucker and top once more; then we barn the body leaves. Then we sucker, worm and top once more before barning the tips.

"When the curing is done we start to grading. The younguns takes it off the sticks while two people puts it in three or four grades. As many as wants to can tie it in bundles with another leaf of tobacco, and then the younguns puts it up on dressed sticks. The lugs, body and tips cured in each barn are kept in separate piles and sold that way. As fast as we git a barn graded I carry it off and sell it.

"Raising cotton is more trouble than tobacco but I always raise some. I break up the land in March and put out the fertilizer. I plant the seeds during April usually but we used to plant it in March. May's not too late, though.

"The first chopping is the biggest trouble because the plants has got to be chopped to the right stand. I like for them to be a foot apart. As soon as it's chopped it has got to be plowed. We do this about three times before July or August when we lay it by.

"We leave it alone until the bolls starts to opening in September, then we go out with clean guano sacks and pick that cotton. Did you ever pick cotton? Well, let me tell you, the burs sticks your fingers, scratches your hands and legs all over, and it ain't impossible to git stung by a stinging worm. When it turns cold, which it's apt to do before the last picking, your hands pretty near freeze off.

"As we pick it we put it in the packhouse and as fast as we pick a bale I carry it to the gin. Soon's it's ginned I haul it to the market and sell it. They ain't no money much in cotton no more.

"Corn's easy to raise. All you have to do is plant it in April and plow it a couple of times. 'Long about November, maybe in October, you have to gather it. Sometimes, when I have time, I pull my fodder or top it 'long about July. I need the fodder all the time but it comes off in tobacco barning time and we're pretty busy.

"Sarah will have a half a acre of sweet potatoes, a half acre of Irish potatoes, and a big garden always. Sometimes I fuss about it, but law, the vegetables comes in handy. She says that I'm a bad drunkard but she don't know nothing. She ought to have some men I know. I did git drunk the last load of tobacco year before last, and I spent $13 somehow. Shucks though, that ain't nothing; a heap of men spends the last cent they gits.

"I'll say it for Sarah, though; she has been a good wife through thick and thin and I don't know of none that's better." He looked at her affectionately. "She does raise a heap of hell sometimes, though."

He folded his stubby hands across his paunchy stomach and quietly said, "We don't always have enough to eat but me and Sarah both knows that times will git better. We've had depressions before and we've had to play the game a few times lately.

"What game? Well it's a heap of fun even if the belly is holler. You see, when rations gits slim we just have two meals a day or maybe we'll just have a cup of coffee for breakfast. While we drink the coffee we poke the fun at rich people and pretend that we are having just what we want. We ask each other polite-like to have toast and jelly and bacon and eggs and it shore helps.

"When we have cereal for breakfast or meat and bread we don't have no dinner at all and we have supper at four o'clock. As we set down to the table we play like all of us had been to dinner with friends. We ask each other what he had and we all make out we had turkey, chicken, cake, pie, and a heap of other fancy stuff. Sometimes when one's telling what he had somebody will say, 'That's funny, I had the same thing.' You'd be surprised how much that helps out.

"Lucy married right well off but she ain't got nothing to help us with because her husband's people lives with them and they try to put some in the bank. We had to help Macy till we got so we couldn't; now she manages without us. Jack is gitting a slow start but he can't help us none. The twins ain't got no jobs. They ain't got much clothes either, so when one goes a-visiting she takes pretty near all the clothes and the one that's left ain't got a half decent rag.

"I'm sorry my younguns can't git a education because that is the one thing a feller has got to have to git a job. Shucks, you can't dig ditches now unless you got a high school education and you can't put up a hawg pasture unless you got a college education. I wish things was back where they useter be when a feller just had to be strong and honest and have a little horse sense to git any kind of job.

"Sales tax is the biggest shame in North Carolina, especially when money gits missing from the Revenue Department and nobody can find out who took it. Well, I don't care much for the gas chamber at Raleigh either, but we have to have something I reckon.

"I'm proud of North Carolina, too, and I don't like for our President to call it no problem 'cause it ain't as much a problem as some of the other states what air running over with foreigner gangsters. The biggest problem I see here is the landlord that has a bunch of tenant farmers on his place. They work like niggers all the year and he gits rich. They can't even make enough to eat on through the winter. I've had some pretty good landlords and some pretty bad ones but I reckon that I'll have to put up with them all my life. I hate the thieving rogues anyhow, good or bad. I'm proud of our United States though, and every time I hear the 'Star-Spangled Banner' I feel a lump in my throat. There ain't no other nation in the world that would have sense enough to think of WPA and all the other A's.

"Oh, you want to talk religion too, huh? Well, I ain't much on that. I ain't never joined no church and I ain't been much either, but I told my family to go ahead. I'd be glad if they went to church. I ain't tried to teach them no Bible 'cause if I can't read how am I gonna know that what I hear is in the Bible?"

Sarah, who was calmly putting corn bread in a large iron griddle, broke in. "You set a pore example, John, and you know it. I did, too, for that matter, a-cussin' and swearin' and saying things I hadn't ought to. I always told the younguns, though, not to cast stones at people lest somebody throw bricks at them. I wanted them to be educated, kind, polite, and humblesome. I'm not disappointed; I'm just sorry we couldn't give them a better start."

"I maybe did set a pore example," John resumed, "but I shore didn't tell them to foller in my footsteps. Besides, I ain't altogether spared the rod. I'm right proud of them in a way. Of course, we ain't got but one boy but he don't drink and he ain't never been in jail.

"Speaking about money; well, I reckon we live on about four or five dollars a week now but it ain't exactly what you call living. I git a day's work here and yonder digging ditches or wells, chopping wood, or killing hogs. Some of them pay me off in meat or potatoes. Some weeks we don't have but a dollar or two and so we go in debt for groceries and have to pay it out of the next week's money. We've never had more than about twelve dollars a week to live on except in wartime and you know the high prices of everything then. I think we could do good on fifteen dollars a week and pay our bills good, don't you, Sarah?"

"I'd say so," Sarah nodded smiling. "We could live fine on that. Why we might even be able atter a while to buy some lace curtains."

John rebuked her gently. "It's no time to be thinking of lace curtains, honey, and us without half enough to eat."

"Oh," she said slowly, "oh, I'd forgot just about a minute where I was."

John coughed gruffly. "You're gonna have lace curtains someday, Sarah. Just as shore as God spares my life for a little while longer you're gonna have them lace curtains."

MARY A. HICKS
WILLIS S. HARRISON

Tore Up and a-Movin'

WE HAIN'T HAD NO CHRISTMAS HERE, NOT A APPLE or a nut or nothin': I told the chil'en not to look for no Santa Claus this year, but to thank their God if they had meat and bread." Gracie Turner folds her arms across her husband's brown shirt which she wears over her worn red dress for a sweater and leaves her wash tub in the back yard to show the way to the cheerless fire-place where green wood smolders.

"Dis here is my father, Sam Horton. He has seen
some years. He's ninety-one and in tole'ble good health,
except his 'memb'ance ain't strong and he can't eat much
grease. I've been takin' care o' him now for seven
years, best I could. For the past three months he's been
gettin' seven dollars and a half for de old age pension,
and dat's been a help here.

"Dat's Ola in de corner." Gracie indicates an attractive mulatto girl who looks almost dainty in spite
of her ragged clothes. Her feet are bare. "Ola is
twenty-four. Awhile back she married a drinkin' man,
but he scrapped so bad she couldn't stay wid him; so
she come back home to live. Dis girl is Amy, fourteen
years old. She's got bad kidney trouble; her leg swells
up big as two sometimes. Dr. Simpson started givin'
her treatments in de clinic, but she ain't had none in
some weeks now." Amy is also barefooted.

"De littlest boy is Raymond Farmer. Dr. Farmer
'fore he died named him for his brother, Judge Raymond Farmer. Stephen is de oldest boy at home. Sam
and Will belongs to my daughters, but I raised 'em.
Will, go tote in some wood and stir up dis here fire!
Will's mama married de second time, and I didn't know
how dat new man would treat de child. Wid my husband, James Turner, and Papa and me, dat makes nine
of us to stay in dese two rooms. Come on; I'll show you
over de house.

"Most of us sleeps on dese three beds in here where
we keeps de fire. In here is de kitchen. Mr. Jake
Anderson give me dat range; it's de one Miss Bettie
fust cooked on when she was married." The old stove
is coated with grease, but the kitchen is orderly and
fairly clean. At the table, covered with colorful oilcloth, are two long benches where the Turners sit to

dine. The bowl of cold collards gives off a penetrating odor even to the front door.

"Right across de hall is de other bedroom. Come on see dat too. De girls covered dese chairs and dis settee wid de flowered cloth deyselves. Dat victrola ain't no good now. We tries to keep dis room sort o' dressed up for comp'ny, but dey ain't no fire in de heater; so we better set in de fireplace room. Today's a cold day if you ain't about stirrin'.

"Now, 'bout de other chil'en: Hattie May lives on some island down here 'bout Portsmith—Hattie May Williams she is now. Her husband does public work and seems to be a right good man, but I didn't know where he'd be good to Hattie May's Will or not. May married Montgomery, and dey sharecraps for Miss Sallie Simpson over toward Benton. Edward's married and farms for Mr. Peter Ellis at Martinsburg. Lillian Turner—now I can't tell you 'bout her, 'cause I hain't heard from her in three years. Marcy works for rich folks in Philadelphia. She sent us a box o' old clothes 'fore Christmas, and dat's de onliest string we've had this fall. De rich folks is always givin' Marcy wrist watches and necklaces and things for presents. Dey sends her down town any time wid a hund'ed dollars to buy things for 'em, and she takes every cent back to 'em it don't cost. Dey has learnt to trust Marcy. I's tried to raise my chil'en to be trusty and mannerable, to mind dey mama and papa, to be honest. 'Show favor to your mother and father,' I tells 'em, 'dat your days may be lengthened on God's earth.' If dey does wrong it shore ain't 'cause I hain't tried to learn 'em right.

"Dey ain't been much schoolin' for none of 'em. Will's in de fif', and Lillian got to de ninth. None de rest got past de fou'th grade. Turner went to school enough to write his name, but he can't do no figgerin' to 'mount to nothin'. I never went a day in my life, can't write my name or add or keep track of our account on de farm. I want dese youngest chil'en to go long enough to do dat much.

" 'Tain't no while to say dis is de hardest year we's ever had. Every year's been hard, de forty-nine years I been here. Dat's all dey is to expect—work hard and go hongry part time—long as we lives on de other man's land. Dey ain't nothin' in sharecrappin', not de way it's run. My folks has always sharecrapped. Papa farmed round Gum Springs when I was a girl, and all I learnt was to work in de field. When I married Turner, we lived in Hawley, Virginia, 'bout six months. He done public work, railroadin' and sech dere. From Hawley we moved to a farm near Gum Springs, where we worked by de day for a year. From dere we moved to my brother's and sharecrapped for him five years. Den we moved to Mr. Calep Jones', where we stayed three years. Next we moved to Mr. Hughes White-head's and farmed wid him two years. Our next move was to No'th Ca'lina on Mr. Jake Anderson's farm at de Woollen place. We stayed wid him thirteen years. Den last year we moved here to de Willis place, dat Mr. Dick Henry rents from Mr. Bob Willis in Gum Springs, and here we is now. But we got to move somewhere dis next year. Another man's a-comin' here. I don't know where we'll go; houses is sca'ce and hard to find. Mr. Makepeace told Turner he'd help him all he could, but he ain't got no house we can live in. Plenty o' land everywhere, but no house! Turner has been huntin' a place for weeks, and every night when he comes home I runs to de door to hear de news. Every day it's de same tale: 'I hain't found no place yet.' I hates to move; nobody knows how I hates to move!"

"Yonder's somebody movin' now," Ola exclaims, looking out the window. All eyes turn toward the road. Over the deep ruts in the sand, wagon wheels grind slowly eastward; two wagons loaded with shabby furnishings wind around the curve out of sight.

"Dat's de way we'll be soon—tore up and a-movin'. I wish I could have me one acre o' land dat I could call mine. I'd be willin' to eat dry bread de rest o' my life if I had a place I could settle down on and nobody could tell me I had to move no more. I hates movin'.

"We left Mr. Jake Anderson 'cause he didn't treat us right. Me and him fussed de whole thirteen years we stayed dere, and I said if I kept livin' wid Mr. Anderson I'd go to de devil shore. When Mr. Anderson use to give de money to Turner, he'd tell him: 'Don't you give none of it to dat fussy woman.' I quarreled all de time 'bout him givin' money to de boys and chargin' it 'gainst our account. We always had trouble settlin' wid Mr. Anderson. One year I got me a book and ask him to set down everything he charged us wid in my book, so I'd have it in his own figgers when de year ended. But he said he wouldn't have it dat way; one set o' books was all he aimed to keep. So den I got to askin' him every week what he was chargin' us wid, and my daughter set it down. At de end o' de year we got Mr. James to add it up on de addin' machine. We handed it to Mr. Anderson when we went to settle, and it made him mad. He said we'd settle by his figgers or get off'n de place, dat nobody should keep books but him on his farm.

"Another time when we wanted a car, he bought us one over in Weldon, but made us put up the two mules we owned den against de car. De boys was in a wreck and damaged de car right smart. Mr. Anderson come and took in de mules and de car too. After he had it fixed up, we tried to get him to sell it back to us. He wouldn't, but went and sold it to another man. So we was lackin' a car and mules too.

"Mr. Anderson was all time orderin' us to get off'n his place. He's mighty fitified anyhow, and when somethin' didn't suit him he'd order us to move. One Christmas we ask him for fifty dollars for some clothes and a little Santy Claus for the chil'en. Dey was 'bout twelve of us den to take care of. Mr. Anderson said we shouldn't have de money and for us to move. We done it. Dey was a little house close to Maryton where we moved into, but 'twa'n't long 'fore here come Mr. Anderson orderin' us to move back. He finally offered us de fifty dollars, 'cause he knowed we was good hands. We was mighty slow dat time 'bout movin' back to his farm; he got uneasy 'fore we did go back.

"We never made nothin' much wid Mr. Anderson. De most we cleared was $179, after we'd paid out, two years. Most years it was fifty and sixty dollars after de account was paid. Every settlement day me and him had a round. I'd tell him he had too much charged against us, and he'd say I was de fussin'est woman he ever saw, and to go to de devil! De last year we was wid him we made 'leben bales o' cotton and three hund'ed bags o' peas. When we settled, we didn't have accordin' to his figgers but five dollars for our part o' de crap, nothin' to buy a string o' clothes wid, nothin' to eat but meat and bread. We left him. We had to sell de hogs we raised to eat to buy us some clothes. We hain't never got no rent money. I said somethin' to Mr. Anderson last time I saw him 'bout de rent. We needs

it for clothes and shoes; the chil'en's feet is on de
ground. It made him mad; he said he hadn't got no
rent. Turner went over to Benton and ask about it.
Dey said it wa'n't right, but Mr. Anderson was holdin'
de cotton and peas for higher prices dey reckoned; de
rent would come by 'n' by dey reckoned.

"When we started farmin' in March for Mr. Dick
Henry, he 'lowed us five dollars a week. On de tenth
o' June dey took him to de State Horspital, and Miss
Annie got her brother, Mr. Bates, to tend to de farm
for her. He owned up he didn't know nothin' 'bout
farmin'. Fust, dey started out lettin' us have $3.50
a week; den it dwindled down to two, den to nothin'.
Miss Annie said she dreaded for Sad'dys to come 'cause
we was lookin' to her for money for rations, and she
didn't have it. I couldn't fuss wid her, 'cause I knowed
she was tellin' de truth. Mr. Bates brought some hogs
here and told us to raise 'em on halves. I toted 'em
slops all th'ugh de summer and fed 'em co'n; here dis
fall he took 'em away from us, on our debt he claimed.
Turner traded his gun for a mother hog and three
little pigs, all we got now. De same way wid de co'n.
Mr. Bates commenced haulin' it away. I told him le's
wait and see what de cotton and peanuts 'mounted to
and den divide de co'n equal 'tween us. He said naw,
he wa'n't goin' to dat way. Cou'se I knowed we couldn't
make much, but looked like we was bound to have some
co'n for our bread. I went in de field and begun loadin'
me a one-ho'se wagon o' co'n, but he objected. So all
I got out'n de crap was a barrel o' nubbins dat I took
anyhow.

"Mr. Henry come home 'fore Christmas and 'pears
to be all right now. We hain't had no settlement wid
him yet, but he told us dey wouldn't be nothin' for us

this year, not to look for it. De account on de book 'gainst us is $300. How it got dat much I can't tell you. We raised 224 bags o' peas and 1800 pounds o' seed cotton on twenty acres. I knowed we couldn't make no crap, wid just twenty-four bags o' plaster 'lowed us to fertilize twenty acres. We was just about to get hongry here, with all de money cut off and no crap comin' in. Long as dey was cotton to pick or peas to shake some of us could get a day o' work now and then, enough to buy a sack o' flour and a little strip o' meat. Work has been sca'ce dis fall though. So Turner got him a WP and A job a-diggin' stumps. He's done had three pay days, $12.80 at de time, though he don't get but $12 'cause eighty cents has to go to Mr. Sickle for haulin' him to work. I makes dat twelve dollars do all it will, but dey's eight of us to live out'n it four weeks to de month.

"Turner ought not to be a-workin' wid de WP and A. De gover'ment's got no business a-payin' out relief money and a-givin' WP and A jobs to farmers. De old age pensions is all right for old folks dat's 'flicted and can't do. Take Papa dere; he can't work in de field now. He knocks up our wood to burn in de fireplace, but he's seen too many years to get out and work by de day. But able-bodied landers has got no business a-havin' to look to de gover'ment for a livin'. Dey ought to live of'n de land. If 'twas fixed right dey'd make all de livin' dey need from de ground. Dey ain't no sense in diggin' stumps for dollars to buy co'n and flour-bread and meat, when here's plenty o' land to raise 'em on. Every lander ought to raise his somethin' t' eat de whole year round and some to sell. Everybody's got to eat; dat's 'bout all wages comes to anyhow, somethin' t' eat. If I had de say half de land would be planted in stuff to eat; nobody would have to furnish me and overcharge me when settlement time come.

"I always tries to raise my meat and bread and lard, collards and sweet 'taters for de winter, and a gyarden for de summer. I keeps a cow. Milk and butter and biscuit is de biggest we live on now. I has to use butter in my biscuits for lard part de time. My collards hain't flourished dis year like usual. You see 'em dere at de front. Looks like hot water has been poured over 'em. De soil here don't suit collards; it's too pore to raise anything without plenty fertilize. Mr. Henry furnished de mule dis year and we de fertilize, but dey wouldn't stand for much; cou'se dey wouldn't sell it to us on our say. I believes de bugs dats eatin' up stuff now is sent 'cause folks is so mean. If dey don't do better, plagues is goin' to take de land. I tries to live a Christian, tell de truth, and be honest, but de world is full of dem dat don't. It ain't often I gets to church. I hain't been in over twelve months. Roanoke-Salem is where we 'tends, but I'm tellin' you de God's truth: I hain't had nothin' fittin' to wear to church lately; de chil'en neither. Amy had a print dress she could wear dis summer, but soon as cold weather come, she had to quit church and school both 'cause she didn't have no jacket to wear. I don't go nowheres, never been no-wheres, but to work. Picture show? I never saw one in my life. De onliest far ways I ever been was on a excursion one time to Portsmith.

"No, it's been nothin' but hard work for Gracie, and de boss man gettin' it all. I's known some good uns. Mr. Calep Jones was a pore man, but he was straight and fair in his dealin's. We got every cent we was due when we lived wid him. De years we was wid him we cleared $200, de most we ever made. Mr. Jones's dead,

but if he ain't in heb'n ain't nobody dere. Once Papa
farmed for a rich man, and he was good too. Every
Christmas dat come he give all de tenants on his place
a sack o' apples and nuts and candy."

Amy rises from her corner to warm her bare feet
at the dying fire. Gracie looks from the window and
sees the mother hog rooting in the front yard. "Sam,
go run de hog out'n de yard." She pushes her tin snuff
box more securely in the shirt pocket and leans her head
an instant on the foot of the bed. "My head's been
afflicted a long time; somethin' pops and rings in it
right constant. It ain't bad as it was once though; it
use to run corruption th'ugh my years, and I had to
keep 'em washed out wid salt water. Dey don't ooze
corruption now. Turner's health is pretty good; he's
'flicted with rheumatism, but he works as hard at sixty-
five as he ever done. I don't have de doctor much; dey's
old home remedies I tries fust, and if dey fails den de
doctor has to try his hand. Dat bottle o' castor oil up
dere on de mantel is de old stand-by here. When de
flu was goin' round so bad I mixed castor oil and turpentine and sprinkled a few drops on de chil'en's hair,
and not a one o' dem had de flu. Fluck is good too;
it's a weed I use for a purkitive. When de chil'en was
teethin' I use to tie fluck round dey necks. It costs
too much to send for de doctor. Right now we owes de
Roanoke Rapids Horspital $1.50 for Amy. She was
in a wreck up here 'bout Camp's store and got five teeth
knocked out and her legs bruised up right bad. Dey
took her to de horspital where she ought to stayed two
or three days, but we wa'n't able to pay, so we had to
bring her home. She gets in a quare fix some nights,
just lies dere and can't speak or move."

"It's de witches ridin' me," Amy announces casually.

"Do you reckon dey is sech a thing?" Gracie inquires earnestly. "I tells her it's de blood stops circulatin', how come her to have dem spells."

"How come I gets all right soon as I puts a fork under my pillow?" Amy wants to know. "Or a broom under my bed or a butcher knife under my pillow either?"

"I don't know. Dey's things can't be explained in dis world. When we lived in de Woollen house I use to hear strange things. One night I knelt to say my prayers, and I heard a woman walk in de door on high heel slippers. I looked round right quick, but dey wa'n't nobody dere. Another time after I was in bed I heard somebody take de chair settin' by my bed and move it crost de room. Somethin' was all time sweepin' de floors; you could hear somethin' like a straw broom go sweep-sweep, sweep-sweep, but you couldn't never see nothin', least I couldn't."

"I saw a little white boy standin' on de hearth one day; he had on overalls and was plain to me as my hand. Den he vanished," declares Amy.

"Some folks can see things dat others can't," Gracie admits. "Folks born 'tween de lights can see things. Amy was born 'tween sunrise and sunset, how come she sees things de rest can't. Most of 'em was born in de night time. I reckon it's her blood not circulatin' dat makes her have dem spells at night, not de witches."

"De witches use to ride me," old Sam speaks up from his corner. "I felt one hop on me one night, and I couldn't move or speak; I was pretty shore who, so next day I told her I was goin' to put a butcher knife under my pillow and kill de next witch tried to ride me to death. I wa'n't bothered no more. Dey was witches back den when I growed up. Dey use to jump out'n dey skin, and sometimes when folks found witches' skin behind de door dey filled it wid red pepper. When de witch got back into her skin she begun to holler: 'Slip, skin, slip; slip, skin, slip.' Folks put sifters under dey beds back den so de witches had to go th'ugh every hole 'fore dey could bother anybody.

"I was a slave on de Horton plantation up in Virginia. Old mistis and old marster was good to dey slaves, and I loved young marster next to God A'mighty. When he went off to de war, I stole away and follered him. He looked round and saw me comin' and hollered: 'You little devil, what you think I goin' to do wid you?' I stayed and waited on him at de camp till he had chance to go home and take me back. Den he slipped off from me and went back to de war. I stole away and follered him again. 'You little nigger. You can't stay here. I'm goin' to send you back home.' But I stayed on wid him when dey was fightin' round Richmond. Dey use to have big times in de camp, playin' and singin' and pickin' de banjo. I 'member dey sung 'Rally to de flag, boys, fight for freedom.' One night I looked out and saw de Yankees comin', and I woke young marster. De soldiers went away from dere. After dey'd been fightin' four days round Richmond, I looked down on de field, and looked like I couldn't see nothin' but blood. I fainted. But I wouldn't go home and leave my young marster till he moved away from Richmond. Den I had to go back home and stay.

"News come dat de Yankees was on de way to our plantation. Old marster sent de women to another plantation, and he stayed on and buried de silver and valu'bles out in de gyarden under de rose bushes. De Yankees got dere 'fore he could run where de women had gone; so he slipped out in de field and lay down flat between de rows. It rained and hailed on him three days, and he didn't have a mou'ful to eat.

"De Yankees broke in de smokehouse, brought big middlin's o' meat in de great-house, and throwed 'em on de fire whole. Dey cooked it a little on one side, turned it over, browned it on t'other, den dey eat it. Seem like it made me mad to see 'em eatin' our meat, and I stood watchin' 'em and wishin' de soldiers would come. One Yankee looked round and saw what I was thinkin' I reckon. 'You little devil, what you doin' here?' he said and slapped my face. Dat was de fust time I ever 'membered hatin' de Yankees; I knowed den how come dey was called dam' Yankees. I made up my mind if he hit me again I'd get de butcher knife and cut his th'oat. Dey ask my mammy if any silver was hid round dere; she told 'em not as she knowed of. Dey went to de gyarden, dug up de rose bushes, and found all de treasure old Marster had hid. You couldn't hide nothin' from dem Yankees. Dey could track worse'n dogs.

"Den dey went to the cellar where eight barrels o' 'lasses was settin'. Dey knocked de barrels open; de cellar was waist-deep in 'lasses. Next dey set de house on fire and burned everything up at de great house 'fore dey went on to de next plantation. When old mistis come home she ask us where was old marster. We told her de last we saw o' him was when he was slippin' crost de field. All hands went out to look for him. We found him lyin' 'tween de rows so near froze to death he couldn't move. We brought him to de quarters, built up a big fire, and laid him before it. Soon as we thawed him out he died. Dem was hard days back den."

"Dey's still hard." Gracie droops dejectedly in her

chair and covers her face momentarily with her hands. "Farmin's all I ever done, all I can do, all I want to do. And I can't make a livin' at it."

"I reckon I soon farm as anything else," Amy observes.

"I rather go in service. I want to be a cook or a maid for white folks," Ola adds. "I can cook some already and I could learn more."

Gracie raises her head, but she remains downcast in spirit. "Dis year has been so hard we've had to drop our burial insurance. We enrolled wid de burial association in Ga'ysburg some years back. All it costs is twenty-five cents when a member dies. But dey don't come many twenty-five centses in dis house.

"Every night I prays to de Lord: 'Please keep death off till I get out'n dis shape.' Dey ain't a decent rag to bury me if I was to die right now, and I hates for de county to have to put me away."

BERNICE KELLY HARRIS

Get Out and Hoe

No, I don't mind tellin' you about me and Morrison and the young'uns. Won't you sit down. Ollie! Bring out another chair. We got company. People don't come around so often. Sometime Uncle Hank comes from across the creek to see us. We get sort of lonesome. I'm mighty glad to have some-body to talk to. I use to tell Morrison our lives would make a good true story—like you read in the magazines and hear on the radio—Ma Perkins and the others. Oh, yes! We got a radio—a battery set. You see, we ain't got no electric power. We listen to all the good stories and string music. Sometimes we buy things they sell on the radio . . . medicine and other things.

"I guess we been hard luck renters all our lives, me and Morrison both. They was ten young-uns in my family, and I was next to the youngest. We had it awful hard—I reckon my father was about the meanest there ever was—he used to beat me and run me out of the house, but I'd come back when he cooled off. It was his hot-headedness that ruined us. They was a neighbor, Sam Hicklin, that lived near us. His farm run next to ours, and one day he come over to the house and told my father that he was plantin' corn all the way over on his land, and he had better put up a fence and watch out. My father told him to tend to his own business and this made Sam mad. Next day, when my father went out to work, he saw a big ditch cut right down through the middle of his corn-field. Old Sam was settin' on a fence watchin' him. They started cussin' and in a minute they was throwin' rocks at each other. Well, both of 'em got lawyers and took it to court. The judge divided the land halfway between the ditch and the end of the cornfield, but this didn't do any good, because when the case was settled, the lawyers' bills was so big they couldn't pay it. The lawyers got the farms and left Sam Hicklin and us without anything. The lawyers sold our farm and we had to move out. That was when I was nineteen.

"We went to Yadkin County and rented an old run-down farm for a share of what we could raise. The crops wasn't any good that year, the landlord came and got what we had raised and had the auctioneers come and sell our tools and furniture. They was a bunch of people at the sale that day from all around. I was standin' there watchin' the man sell the things when I saw a good lookin' man in overalls lookin' toward me. He watched me all during the sale and I knew what he was thinkin'. That was the first time I ever saw Morrison. I reckon he fell in love with me right off, for we were married a few days later. Morrison didn't have no true father. His mother wasn't married, and he was raised up by his kin folks. Then we moved to a little farm near Shortridge, about ten miles away. The owner said we could have three-fourths of what we raised. The first two years the crops turned out pretty good so we could pay off the landlord and buy a little furniture . . . a bed and table and some chairs. Then the first baby came on. That was Bernhard. He's out in the field workin' now, suckerin' tobacco. By that time, we was able to get a cow, and that came in good, for the baby was awful thin and weak.

"After that, things didn't go so good. Another baby come on and we had our hands full takin' care of the two children and lookin' after the farm work. When the second baby was four years old, he started gettin' pale and thin. We put him to bed one day because he looked so sick we thought he was goin' to die. We didn't call a doctor for a long while. You see, we didn't have any money then, and we'd heard that the doctor up in town wouldn't come unless you had the money ready. But Morrison said he didn't care, so one night after dark he started walkin' through the woods toward the highway. He caught a ride into town and about two hours later, him and the doctor drove up in the yard.

"When the doctor finished lookin' at the baby, he turned around with a worried look on his face and said he had meningitis. That was some kind of ailment that got in his back. The next, he got awful sick and when the doctor come again, my little boy had a stroke of infantile paralysis. He died the next day. After we had buried him up at the church cemetery, we went on with our work. There wasn't much we could do but try to forget about little Sammy. But we did love him so much. I go to his grave and put flowers on it every Sunday.

"The crops was comin' in and we had to work hard to get the tobacco suckered and cured before the market opened, or else we couldn't pay the landlord his share, come fall.

"Bernhard was only six, but he could help a lot, pullin' and tyin' the tobacco, and helpin' hand it in the barn. We got out more tobacco that year than any other, but when we took it to market in Winston, they wasn't payin' but about twelve cents a pound for the best grade, so when we give the landlord his share and paid the fertilizer bill, we didn't have enough left to pay the doctor and store bill. We didn't know what we was goin' to do durin' the winter. Morrison had raised a few vegetables and apples, so we canned what we could and traded the rest for some cotton cloth up at the store so the children would have something to wear that winter. Morrison got a job helpin' build a barn for a neighbor, but it didn't last but two days. The neighbor gave him two second hand pairs of overalls for the work.

"That was one of the hardest years we come to. Next spring another baby was born. That made four. You

see, we'd already had another one, a girl, before little
Sammy died. This one was a boy. He was the strong-
est and healthiest one we'd had yet. I loved him so
much, because I thought he would take the place of
little Sammy. Just before he was one year old, Morrison said we ought to bake a cake for his birthday. I
was in the kitchen bakin' the cake and some pies, when
I heard little Tom start cryin'. I ran to see what was
the matter, and he was layin' on the floor, all pale and
sick lookin'. I put him in bed and ran out toward the
field and called Morrison . . . he was hoein' corn.
When Morrison looked at Tom, he said: "It looks like
a bad spell. I'm goin' after the doctor.' I'll never
forget how scared I was while I waited for Morrison
to come back. I sat there beside little Tom holding a
wet rag on his head, and prayin' he'd get well. I recollect how I prayed that night. I said, 'Oh, God, please
don't let him die like little Sammy. He's the only baby
I've got.'

"Morrison and the doctor came; little Tom was awful
hot. The doctor looked at him a minute then turned
around to me and Morrison.

" 'He's been dead half an hour.' I guess he must've
died while I was prayin'.

"Next spring when we was plantin' tobacco, Morrison got to leavin' home every night, and comin' in
about midnight. I didn't know what he was doin' till
one of the neighbors that lived up the road tole me that
he had seen Morrison goin' up to the Carson house every
night. The Carsons didn't have any children but a
girl named Amelia Carson lived with them. She was
some kin to them. Amelia was sixteen years old and
pretty, too, but she had a bad name. A month after
Morrison started goin' up to her house, they ran off

together. That was the first time I started gettin' relief from the government. They was a government woman that come around and gave orders for food and clothes, and sometimes we got a little money. I needed it awful bad, because with Morrison gone, they wasn't any way to feed the two children. I had to do most of the work in the field that summer, and sometimes I would go to the neighbors' house and wash for them for a piece of meat.

"Then, about two months after Morrison and Amelia ran off, the sheriff down in the sandhills, in the eastern part of the State, found them livin' together. They brought Amelia back home but they didn't get Morrison. A month later, I was settin' in the kitchen sewin' when Morrison walked in. He looked kinda' bad like he'd been hungry for a long time. He sat down in a chair in front of the fire, like he was awful tired and said to me:

" 'I been a damn fool, Irma. That crazy woman didn't want nothin' but my money. You ain't mad at me, are you, Irma?'

"I said: 'I ain't got no right to be mad now, Morrison. You had your fling and done come home. We need you awful bad. We got to get out and hoe in the tobacco tomorrow. You better get some sleep.'

"About six months later, Amelia had a baby. Right off, she blamed it on Morrison. When she took it to court, Morrison denied it—said it was just as apt to be somebody else's baby. But the judge said he was guilty and told him to pay Amelia fifty dollars. Morrison didn't have any money then, so he went to jail and served twenty-one days. Accordin' to the law, he had paid his debt. That was the fourth baby Amelia had . . . all of 'em born out of wedlock. Only two of 'em are living now. She had two by one man. I still can't believe Morrison was the father of one of the children. Anyway, that's all in the past now, and today there's no better man than Morrison. This year he gave a week's labor on the Methodist Church at Center. That was when they built a new part to it. All the men in the neighborhood that can't give money help on it. Morrison has always give his share.

"Things are a lot better for the renter today than in the past. It used to be we couldn't get enough to eat and wear. Now we got a cow, a hog, and some chickens. Morrison bought a second-hand car and every Sunday afternoon we ride somewhere. It's the only time we ever get away from home.

"The landlord gives us five-sixths of what we raise, so we get along pretty good when the crops are fair. Of course we have to furnish the fertilizer and livestock. This year we had seven barns of tobacco and four acres of corn. Wheat turned out pretty good, too. We raised forty-three bushels, and I hear the price is going to be fair at the roller mill. I canned about all our extra fruits and vegetables. I reckon we still got about a hundred cans in the pantry.

"We never owned any land, but Morrison and me just bought a house. It's the old school house down the road about two miles. We bought it from the county for $270. We only got $150 paid but we can pay the rest after next year's crop. They's only one thing bad about it though. It's right next door to where Amelia Carson lives—with her children. It's goin' to be hard to face her after what happened between her and Morrison. It'll take a lot of courage, I guess—more'n I've got. I don't think she'll attempt again, though. He's learned his lesson.

"Some day we hope to own our own land as well as the house. It might be a long time, but with the grace of God we'll get there. It seems like that man in Washington has got a real love for the poor people in his heart, and I believe it's due to him and his helpers that the poor renters are goin' to get a chance. We've got more hope now than we ever had before.

"I'm mighty glad you stopped to see us. Won't you come again? We'll be livin' in the new place then, I reckon."

CLAUDE V. DUNNAGAN

Some Sort o' How

A ND HE WALKS WITH ME AND HE TALKS WITH ME,
And He tells me I am His own—"

So the radio is blatantly declaring to the world, and the Joe Fieldings are listening, consenting, with relish. The headlights of the automobile pick up the bush of red roses lush and beautiful under the artificial glare, the group of white lawn-chairs, the small trees with yellowing leaves, the outlines of the five-room white cottage.

"And the joys we share as we tarry there—"

The car lights are switched off. Suddenly it is like waiting for the footlights, for the curtain to rise. It is unreal, almost theatrical, when Joe Fielding, like a Carolina Playmaker made up to play the role of a share-cropper, steps into the parlor in his sock-feet after receiving his curtain call. A soiled tan shirt both sleeves of which are torn from the elbow down, as though some meticulous costume director had added that touch just before the cue-line, and a pair of blue denim overalls cover the tall lank figure. Long stringy hair grows down his neck and over his forehead. A slight deafness which necessitates a frequent "Mo'm?" a cast in one eye that gives the effect of a twinkle, a chew of tobacco in one cheek, a slow hesitating drawl, and—enter the Southern sharecropper.

But Joe Fielding is not a sharecropper. Born of a family of renters in the Concord community sixty years ago, Joe has rented practically all his life, has never owned any land, never owned a home, and does not see a farm home very clearly in his future. He tells his story after drawling out a few answers to questions, which he doesn't hear very well.

"My mammy died when I was just a little thing. We was raised over on the Mallard plantation—your husband's daddy named me. We was renters as fur back as I know anything. I was sick for eighteen months when I was a little feller; they thought shore I'd die. If I had it would o' saved me a many a step." He walks over to spit tobacco juice into the cold tin heater. "Mo'm?—All the learnin' I got was in a old-field school: two months free and two months at a dollar a month. I went through the blue-back speller. I've needed learnin' a many a time, how come I to try to keep my younguns in school. My younguns ain't never done me a speck o' good. They've always been in school times the work had to be carried on; so I've had to do

it all myself and hire it done, together; they do pick a
little cotton evenin's after school.

"I've raised eighteen younguns—thirteen of my own
and five o' somebody else's. The five was mostly my
wife's kinfolks. Dell in yonder (Dell is sticking to the
radio—'He speaks and the sound of His voice, Is so
sweet the birds hush their singing'—Joe glances a little
wistfully toward the closed door.) belonged to my
brother that's dead. They didn't have nowheres to
go; so I took 'em in. I can't stand to see nobody suffer.
I knowed I'd take care of 'em somehow. Ain't none of
'em been hongry as I know of. Two of us is dead, four
has done finished school, and four is in school now. Annie there just started this year and likes fine; she's my
baby one."

Vivian, who stands by the door throughout the visit
instead of going into the other room for a chair, says
that she has no plans except just to stay at home. She
took the commercial course at the Wayboro school two
years ago, but because of a change of teachers in mid-
season she claims the course did her little good. Tonight she wears a neat print; on her arm there is a wrist
watch. Ernest, nine years old, has on a white shirt
and overalls hanging by one suspender. The three
children in the room are strikingly pale. Joe's brother
died of tuberculosis, and several of his children tested
positive. Mrs. Fielding is inquired after, but she does
not appear. For eleven years the Fieldings have lived
just outside Wayboro; they go to the Baptist church
where several of them are members, where I am a member. Yet Mrs. Fielding is a stranger. I don't even
know how she looks.

"Johnny kept messin' round after he left me till he
got a right good job in Roanoke Rapids; he married a

nurse, and she stays in a job o' work 'bout all the time.
Arnie and his wife is sharecroppin' for Mr. Little, and
Raymond and his'n for Mr. Roddy Olds.

"Mo'm?—No'm, I never sharecropped much; two or
three years for Dr. Kimball was all. Me and him got
on good together, but when he died and Thompson, the
doctor's son-in-law, took holt we didn't get on in no
sort; so I started back rentin' like my folks always done.
You come nearer bein' your own boss thataway. Four
times is all I ever moved—once at Doctor's, once up
yonder side the railroad, once on the Bill Mallard farm,
and here on the Holdford place. I been rentin' this
house twelve year and land wherever I could get a-holt
of it. The Holdfords is good folks.

"I run a three-horse farm and good years make about
eighteen bales o' cotton. I rent for four bales and some
money. This year I won't get over one bale. My peanuts is right good, but it'll take my whole crop to pay
my rent. There won't be no cash money from this
year's crop, and the whole crowd's needin' shoes and
clothes. They can't wear their old clothes, 'cause they're
wore out. I'll get by some sort o' how. I been lookin'
for my little rent from the gov'ment for thirty days.
The younguns is hard on shoes; they have to look sort
o' somehow, goin' to school. No, they ain't never helped
me none, cost me that's all. They ain't a one I could
do without though.

"I can't hardly get by on no less'n a hund'ed dollars
a month, and I can't make that even good years. I
been carryin' insurance for twenty-seven years, but
looks like I'm goin' to have it to drop. Don't reckon
old Santy Claus can get around this year; he ain't failed
yet, but this year—" Annie who is looking at pictures
in an old magazine glances up with wide-eyed interest

and a hint of alarm. Joe's eye twinkles, and she turns back to her pictures.

"Mo'm?—They's ten of us lives here. Course I raise my smoke-house meat and chickens and garden truck and sweet potatoes. We got no orchard. I buy apples and peaches off'n them trucks that comes down from the mountains and several bushels o' pears where I can get 'em to preserve. It takes it here!"

A little figuring showed that one hundred dollars would provide each member of the family ten dollars per month. At ten cents per meal or thirty cents a day for rent and food, one dollar would be left for clothes, medical attention, school supplies, dental care, insurance, electric bill ("And He walks with me and He talks with me" is not without benefit of the Virginia Electric and Power Company) newspaper, gas, car repairs, church, cold drinks, trips—or a total of twelve dollars per person per year.

"Long as I can work I'll get along somehow. I love to work. Yeste'day I plowed up seven acres o' peanuts and kept ahead o' ten hands that was shockin'. No, if the gov'ment give me a pension tomorrow I might lie off a little while, take a trip maybe, but then I'd be right back at work. I couldn't stay out o' the field. I done a little bit o' everything in my life. I carpenter when there's a chance—ain't no expert at all—cut out meat for folks when they kill hogs; you might call me a expert in that line, many thousand pounds o' meat as I've cut out. I've worked on the roads; as foreman I kept time and paid off the force. I love to pay off. Sometimes o' evenin's now I have a pa'cel o' little school children pickin' cotton for me, and when I finish weighin' 'em up nights I get me a sack-ful o' change and pay 'em off. I enjoy that."

Joe arose from the davenport to spit in the tin stove. "Five hours' sleep is all I need to get along on. Summer time I rise anywhere around three o'clock, feed up my mules, and start to work before good day. My younguns ain't done me no good, cost me that's all. I've had five operations in my family, two for appendicitis. Raymond's was the highest. It cost me five hund'ed dollars in Norfolk. The rest went to the Jane Linton Hospital. Ernest here got knocked down by a car and cost me right sharp. 'Nother one had diphtheria in the windpipe and cost me a big bill at the Jane Linton. I've spent between six and seven thousand dollars on doctors and hospitals. When I look back I don't see how I done it. But there's always a way. Heap o' times when I was in a tight, Henry Bowman— Henry's a good feller; they ain't nothin' 'gainst him but his drinkin'—he endorsed for me to borry maybe fifty or twenty-five dollars. And I never asked Whit Bowman for a dollar in my life he refused. I can say I didn't owe him nothin' when he died last June. I try to pay my debts, and I never got a penny dishonest.

"Me and my folks before me was all Democrats strong. Roosevelt is as good a man as ever lived. If things was carried out like he wanted, the country'd be better off now, farmers and all. He's shore for the common class o' folks. If everybody was as 'true' and honest as him— But some folks wants it all. I heard Mis' Relia Fuller say—course this ain't got nothin' to do with the conversation—but I heard her say one time if she had all the money in the world but one dollar she'd want that one. Now she's gone, and all her dollars won't do her no good now. I ain't thataway. I'd like to see it divided up so nobody won't suffer. I hate to see anybody suffer. I never could stand to look at the sick lyin' sufferin'.

"No mo'm, we don't go much. Two year ago I bought me a old Ford, aimin' to take a trip to the mountains. But times got too hard; we had to give it up, for the old purse wouldn't stretch to the mountains. Once or twice a year we go to Norfolk. The children gets to the movies once'n awhile. (Joe, according to the men down town, likes his drink once'n awhile!) We still get the Norfolk Virginian-Pilot.

"What I rather have than anything is a home and a farm o' my own. I wouldn't care about a big one, just so it was mine. No mo'm, I can't say I see one ahead. Long as I keep my health I'll get by somehow though. I always have."

The white plastered walls of the parlor, showing here and there black pencil marks, are broken in patches, one whole section of plastering having fallen near the window. The ceiling, doors, floor, and woodwork are unpainted; a linoleum rug is on the floor. Coarse lace curtains hang over the fringed window shades. On the table are an electric lamp with a tan shade, a miniature cedar chest, and a fancy upright calendar. By the tin heater is placed a bushel basket of chunks of rotten wood, though the October night is too hot for fire. An overstuffed davenport and matching wing chair of embossed velour in taupe and blue and a rocking chair are in the corners. A magazine rack full of old papers sits by the davenport. There are five enlarged pictures on the walls.

"Mo'm?—That's old Mr. and Mis' Jacob Reeves, my wife's mammy and daddy; that un in the soldier suit is her brother that was killed in the war. Yes mo'm, Johnny does favor him some. That's four of the younguns when they was little—Johnny, Arnie, Raymond, and Vivian. And that un—" he pointed to a synthetic oil in "natural" color, framed in "gold"— "that's old General Pash. Mo'm? Why, old General Pash that took our boys acrost the waters! I paid eight dollars for it, a fool, and now I need that eight dollars for shoes. That's me and the old lady when we was 'long about thirty. I was a man then; I wa'n't nothin' else but."

A man, *then?* Yesterday at sixty he plowed up seven acres of peanuts ahead of ten shockers; with only one bale of cotton in prospect this year and four bales of rent due, with no money in sight with which to buy shoes and clothes and hats for his family of ten, he enjoys paying off the little cotton pickers out of a sackful of change; wanting more than anything to own a farm he can call his, he keeps tending somebody else's land, resolving to pay his rent, believing "there's always a way"; he has provided funds for five operations and fed and clothed altogether a family of twenty —fifteen of his own and five of somebody else's.

Almost one believes that He *has* walked with the Joe Fieldings, in spite of the appendectomies, the broken plaster, and the mountain trip that has never been taken.

BERNICE KELLY HARRIS

I Has a Garden

A ROCKY CHUNK OF A MAN, TOM DOYLE SAT STOLIDLY in his cane chair and talked in a soft clear voice. He seemed a part of the land, patient and enduring. The gray workshirt, opened comfortably at the throat exposed a thick-columned neck. It had to be thick to support his huge head. Tom is black, and the blackest of his features are large liquid eyes; their look is simple and direct. Tom's overalls are stoutly made, unpatched, and his brogans thickly soled.

Dusk was falling. It was almost dark beneath the oaks that tower over Tom's small frame house. He brought a chair from the porch to the yard, swept clean in country style with a stick broom. As he talked his eyes wandered contentedly over the neat peanut stacks in his fields, with the land showing soft brown between them. Down the wagon road two dim figures made their way toward the house.

"Them's my boys," Tom said proudly. Already it seems that the five-room house can hold no more. By count it shelters twelve, from the eighty-year-old uncle of the second wife to the lastest arrival of last year.

The boys came into the yard, two tall healthy fellows about twenty years old. They stopped by Tom's chair and told him of the day's work. They had been helping a neighbor harvest his peanuts and each will receive a dollar when the crop is sold.

45

The wife was sitting on the porch, a quiet figure in solid blue cotton dress with a white collar. The boys stopped and whispered to her, then passed on into the house to make ready for supper. Feet dangled from the edge of the porch, but the uncle never lifted his bright old eyes from the ground. His back was bent and his mouth hung open.

There was a little chill in the air. Tom turned to the uncle, "Hit's gettin' cold, old man. You'd bettah go on in." The old man, his thin knees punching bags into worn bottle-legged trousers, tobacco drooling down an incredibly wrinkled face, tottered to his feet with the aid of the wife and went indoors. The woman returned to her seat on the porch. She was friendly and interested, but silent while Tom spoke. She leaned forward with her chin resting in her palm, her buck-teeth and half an inch of gum exposed in a grin.

"He's the third old pusson I'se taken care of," Tom said, referring to the uncle. "Fust there was my step-mammy. Then when I ma'ied that woman"—nodding at the woman on the porch—"she brung her uncle to live wid us. The one before that was ninety year old. His name was Toby Neal. No, he wasn't no kin to me. Just said he'd rather stay wid me than anybody he knowed. I tole him I was a pore man but if he wanted to live wid me I'd be glad to have him."

"Tom's got a good heart," the second wife interrupted in a low voice.

"I was bo'n in '89. I'm what they calls a off-child—my mother wasn't ma'ied to my father. She give me to her daddy to raise, then she took off up Nawth. I ain't heerd of her since. I don' know if she's livin' or dead. The man who was my father got ma'ied. We didn't have nothin' to do wid each other. He jus' died about a yeah ago and lef a three-hoss farm to his chillun. My gran'daddy went by the name of Allen Doyle; my name's Thomas Doyle but everbody calls me Tom.

"My mother didn't have no education and my father just had a common one. He went up to the third grade in school and got to be a deacon. My gran'daddy was a tenant and he didn't have no education neither. Hit was funny 'bout him, he couldn't read his name if hit was writ a foot high 'gainst the side of the house but he could figger as good as the next man. One day goin' acrost the fields he dug out a big bunch of peanuts and carried them up to the house. That night he set down befo' the fire and counted off a hundred. He taught me to count wid them peanuts. I remember hit as good as if hit was now. He made me go thru the fourth grade too. My step-mammy—that's what I called my gran'mammy—was as good to me as she could be. She didn't have much of a education neither and her father was a tenant.

"Gran'daddy died when I was fourteen. Step-mammy went to live wid her sister. I went to work to make 'nough to keep her up. I hired out to Mr. Jim Bascum, a white man, for eleven dollars a month and boa'd. I sent mos' of the money to my step-mammy. She was a slave woman and never had over a dollar and a half pair of shoes in her life till I bought her a better pair. They cost me three dollars.

"She died too a few months atter I started workin' for Mr. Bascum. I had to borrow forty-five dollars from Mr. Bascum to bury her wid. It kept me in the hole all the rest of the year payin' for that casket."

Tom was silent for a moment, staring out across the fields. "Hit were a lot of work jest to put away a

woman. But I never minded it nary bit. She was a
mighty good woman.

"When I was nineteen I left Mr. Bascum and went
to work for Coy Blake, a colored feller what owned a
little farm. I worked for wages and stayed wid him
a year. He give me eleven dollars and fifty cents a
month and boa'd and then threw in a acre-and-a-half
of peanuts so's I'd have somethin' toards the end of the
year.

"Mr. Bill Bunting, a white gentlemun, went halves
wid me on some of his land. He give me eleven acre of
good land and paid me fifty cent a day to help him
when I wasn't workin' on my crop. He give me a fifty
dollar order on a town store. Mr. Yates who run the
store charged ten percent in trade; he let me trade
forty-five dollars wuth wid him and I paid him fifty
dollars at the end of the year. His goods costs high.
When we sold the corn 'n peanuts 'n cotton off that
piece and I paid my half of the fertilizer and pickin',
I cleared a hundred and twenty-seven dollars. It was
the fust time I ever had a hundred dollars. I like to
a-shouted.

"Me'n my wife felt pretty good. I had got ma'ied
to a gal nineteen year old and she was pretty smart.
We had a little two-room house that was right com-
f'table.

"That next year Mr. Bunting give me thirteen acre
and a dollar a day widout boa'd when I was workin' for
him runnin' the peanut bagger, fifty cent a day when
I was plowin'. My wife worked wid him too when he
had need of her. That was beside goin' halves wid him
on the thirteen acre and it come in mighty handy 'cause
I made from a dollar and a half to three dollars a week
sometime for workin' wid him.

"Somethin' else I did. I took that twenty-seven dollars and paid out'n it for my share of the fertilizer, and I didn't run no account at the store. It sure opened my eyes when I seen how much cheaper you could buy things for cash. That yeah I cleared two hundred dollars. In them two years we had one chile, a boy chile, and we had the midwoman. Midwomen only charged five dollars and the doctor would'a charged twenty-five dollars.

"The next year I quit Mr. Bill Bunting and went back wid Coy Blake. I 'greed wid him to rent nineteen acre of ornery land for fifty dollars and then I went down to Mr. John Bales and paid fifty dollars for a blind mule. Everthing went along all right until my wife come down wid another chile.

"The midwife got the chile out all right. It was another boy. But my wife was young and strong and she wanted to he'p me so she went out too soon and worked in the field. She took sick. I had the doctor and did everthing I could but she died with buth cold. She weren't but twenty-two year old. I didn't think nobody that young could die. Hit was a funny feelin' 'thout nobody to cook 'n wash 'n look atter the chillun. Hit was kinda lonesomelike.

"The doctor bill took more'n I had and when I give him all the money I had left out'n that two hundred dollars—it was 'round a hundred and twenty-five dollars—I still owed him eighteen dollar and a half. I told Coy Blake he could take the crop and the mule if he'd square me wid the doctor and bury my wife. He give me forty dollars to bury my wife wid but he wouldn't square me wid the doctor like he say he would. He got the crop and the mule.

"I went to Belhaven and got work with a big sawmill. They paid me a dollar and a half a day. I wouldn't stay at the camp. Nossuh, I got me a room in a colored hotel. It took most of what I made to live wid and send money back to my wife's father. He was keepin' my chillun for me.

"I stayed at the sawmill for six month then I come back and got ma'ied to that woman yonder. I rented twenty-five acre from Mr. Glass and moved out wid my two chillun and that woman's two chillun. She had two gals. That year I got off sixty-four dollars. You see, I got started so late I didn't have no time to raise food for my mule and my wife and the chillun. I had to run a account wid the store. My wife did have a mule that she got from her firs' husband and that cut down on hit a little. Nossuh, you know I didn't ma'y that woman for her mule! Well, Mr. Glass charge me a hundred dollars for rent and the store charge me three hundred dollars for what I got so I come out bad sixty-four dollars. That woman had a boy. We used a midwoman. I alus' uses a midwoman.

"The next year wid Mr. Glass I rented twenty-eight acre of land, I bought another mule, and I cleared three hundred dollars. All together I stayed wid Mr. Glass eight year. I had some off year, but I regular made from two hundred dollars to three hundred dollars. That woman had four chillun during them eight year. Mr. Glass come back to farmin' hisself and I moved here with Sheriff Dunne. I been here ever since, seventeen year.

"I started out wid seventeen acre but now I rents sixty-five acre of land off him and lets my ma'ied boy have part of the crop and use one of my mules. I got four mules. They's twelve here in this house and down my son's place they is five. I pays Mr. Dunne four

hundred and eighty-five dollars rent. I spends two
hundred and fifty dollars for fertilizer and the store
run me 'bout three hundred and fifty dollars a year.
The store is for my son's family and mine too; 'bout a
hundred and fifty dollars of hit is for clothes and the
rest for food and things about you need. I has a garden wid collards 'n' cabbage 'n' tomatters 'n' I raises
my own meat. Want you to see my hogs in a minit.
Reckin you better see 'em now 'fore it gets too dark."

Tom led the way down to the pen and proudly displayed eight large hogs. "They're Berkshire and
Poland China," he explained. The pen was grounded
with pine straw as was the shelter. He sprays them
with disinfectant. In a field in the woods he had other
hogs. Asked if he used the county agent much, he
replied that he heard from him about once a week.
Sometimes he does what the agent suggests, then sometimes he doesn't, depending on how the advice looks to
him.

On the way back through the neat barn, Tom took
to task one of the smallest of his numerous offspring for
throwing the harness on the floor. He also detoured by
way of the hen house. "The hogs is mine and these
here chickens is that woman's." In the house were about
a hundred fat hens, barred rocks and other straight
breeds. "She makes about three dollars a week offen
the eggs of these here chickens," Tom said. Other
sheds house tools, a V-8 and model A Fords. The latter
belongs to his oldest son.

Back at the house, Tom opened the door of the living
room. A lamp had been lit and a fire made in the
silver-painted tin stove. Faded paper covered with
tiny pink roses covered the walls. On one side of the
stovepipe was a colored picture of Joe Louis sparring

with a white man. Tom went to New York to visit "that woman's" oldest daughter last summer and brought back the picture as a memento of a place he wouldn't live in. There was a carpet on the floor and a two-piece living room set, upholstered chair and sofa. Several assorted chairs were in the room. There was a battery radio and a winder phonograph. On the side table were a few china figures of the kind given away as pitch-penny prizes at the fair.

Tom doesn't vote for presidents or sheriffs. He did vote in the crop-control issue presented to the farmers. He doesn't mind government control, thinks it would work all right if everybody would cooperate. He complies with all the regulations, he says, and that ought to show he believes in it.

If his interest in politics is little, Tom makes up for it by religious fervor. He is a deacon in the Missionary Baptist Church. Not only a deacon, but he is the treasurer of the church as well. Every Sunday he drives there with as many of his family as his '35 V-8 will hold. (In 1934 Tom had his most prosperous year and cleared one thousand dollars. Six hundred and fifty dollars of this he devoted to the V-8). His son follows behind in one Model A with the rest of the family. Tom doesn't drink, doesn't gamble. Dice? "I don't know the game!" He isn't in favor of movies, has never been to one in his life, and won't allow his children to attend. Neither has he ever been to dances. He won't sing John Henry now. He used to when he was a sinner, but church folks don't approve of reels. Regarding drinking, Tom says, "I doesn't drink before my boys and I doan want them 'round me drinkin'."

He isn't interested in amusements. A tobacco farmer has to work all year. Tom rises every day at sunup and labors until sundown. He plants corn and cotton in April, peanuts and tobacco in May. He cultivates these crops in June and July. In August he harvests the tobacco; September, the cotton; October, the peanuts; and November, the peas. In December he starts getting his land in shape for another crop, making manure and "suchlike" things. In January and February he continues that work and plants his tobacco beds. In March he breaks land. When he comes in from work and eats, the family sits around and talks and when they get sleepy off to bed they go. Sometimes he walks down to the highway to hang around the filling station for a while. His sons take the car off to fill dates with their girls sometimes and the family goes visiting occasionally. But the real day is Sunday, when they all go together in style to church to see all their neighbors.

"Education only hurts a fool," says Tom but he doesn't care if his family does no more than finish high school. Tom does think they ought to know enough to look after their interests, to "figger" and keep accounts so nobody can take advantage of them. Only one of his children has finished high school—"that woman's" oldest daughter, doing housework in New York. The boys went no higher than the seventh grade.

Life in the country is the only life for Tom. It isn't like life in town, all cluttered up. He can get his wood and his water free on the farm. He wouldn't live in town.

He doesn't think the owners he's worked for have done as well by him as they might have. The houses they have given him weren't as good as they could have provided. The sitting room is the best room in this house. He had to paper it himself. The other rooms, some of them, leak pretty bad and he has to repair them. His chief grievance is that they haven't given him sheds to put his tools and machinery under or his cars; he has had to build them. He owns a hay baler and rents other machines. He also thinks they charge him too much rent for the land.

"What does I want? I got a option on a farm now. I'm hopin' the government's gonna help me get it. The county man's already been out and 'proved it. Guess I've paid eight thousand dollars rent these last seventeen year and I don' own a foot of land. I want 'bout a hundred acre of cleared land, 'nough for me and all these chillun of mine to work on. I want it good land and I want a good lil' house on it.

"Chillun? I wouldn't ma'y a woman unless she give me some chillun if I was a young man. And I ain't but forty-nine year old now . . ."

WILLIS S. HARRISON
EDWIN MASSENGILL

Five Year Lease

MARTIN WAS ON ONE END OF A SAW AND HIS TWENTY-two-year-old son, Rufus, was on the other end when I met them.

"I cut down this pine because it was so near the house," Martin told me. "It's. green now but mixed with a little dry wood will last a long time. We burn it in a heater in the family room. This tree was in our pasture. If it was my farm or if I could get a five year lease I would cut out the underbrush and sow it with 'lepserdeser.' Then the cows would have good grazing eight months in the year."

"Do you work on the farm all the year round?" I asked Rufus.

"No, I am a senior in the Five Forks High School. I work afternoons and Saturdays as well as during vacation."

"Rufe ought to have been out of school seven years ago," Martin said. "But I had to have him on the farm some of the time. He missed some because of illness. He will soon be through. All three of my children are fortunate enough to have a high school education."

"They probably got more schooling than you did," I suggested. "No, I finished two years of college at High Point. Wife and I were neighbors as children. We both finished the county schools. There was a private academy near me and I studied there before going to High Point College.

"I think too many boys and girls are going to college. They go just because they think it is the best thing to do. Every pupil ought to know what he wants to do before he leaves high school. Unless he is from a wealthy home he should begin preparation at once for his vocation. I think all ought to go through high school. But the country schools are preparing their pupils for college rather than for life. Only a small percentage will ever see a college. Why so much French and Latin? They do have an agricultural course at Five Forks. But neither of my boys could estimate how much lumber it takes to lay an ordinary floor. Boys on the farm ought to know these things. They should be trained as brick-layers, carpenters, plasterers, mechanics. Industrial training is what the country boy needs. The country girls ought to be taught 'poultry,' dairying, canning, and how to run a country home successfully and economically.

"I was talking with Professor Woods the other day. He teaches math in our high school. He has a little farm too, mostly a poultry farm. He gets about four hundred eggs a day during the winter. I have a lot of confidence in him. He tells me that there is no use for me to spend several hundred dollars sending Rufe to college unless he is sure he wants to do something that calls for college training. Even if he goes to college, two years will be enough in all probability. Then he can study the thing he wants to do.

"Our eldest boy wanted to go into the industrial field. He got a small job in Richmond so that he could earn enough to go to night school. He studied mechanical drawing. They got him a job with a steel firm. One of his superiors draws the plans and my boy assigns each task to one of the workers. I call him the 'placement man.' They started him at a low salary but are promoting him three times a year. Each promotion of course brings an increase of salary. He hopes to work up to forty-five dollars a week in a year or so. He married last year and feels like moving the world. I consider him a success.

"Our daughter is twenty-four. She doesn't seem in a hurry to get married. Wife hopes she won't marry too soon. She will probably marry a farmer as she has no desire to live in the city. We haven't much of a house as you can see. Four little rooms, two little discouraged looking porches—all begging for paint.

"After I left college, I bought a farm near Ledford. Wife helped me save and we had it paid for. Wife and I were both in the hospital off and on for several years. So we lost our place. We moved into Ledford where I got a job clerking in a hardware store. Later I bought the store and had it paid for when the depression hit us. Everything went up like smoke. We began then to rent a farm near Ledford. Nearly everybody in Ledford owns a farm or two and we couldn't sell much of our produce there. So we moved out here near Durham. Durham is a good market for vegetables, fruit, chickens and eggs. You see we have started a house here for our biddies. We are going to compete on a small scale with our good friend, Professor Woods. Farmers depend too much on one or two money crops, both coming to market in the fall. That system is slavery. A successful farmer must work fifty-two weeks in the year and have an income all the year. Some are blaming their poverty on the war, some on the tariff and some say it's 'an act of God.' I say it's laziness, mental and physical laziness.

"We've got to plan as though all depended on planning. We've got to work as though all depended on work. The Lord helps those who help themselves. Some farmers act as though they expected the Lord to work a miracle for them. There are months in the year when many farmers don't do a thing but feed and water the stock, milk the cows and get in a little wood, a day's supply at a time. They do all this in the rush months on top of a real day of work. There are a few geniuses who stumble onto success. Usually success comes to the worker, the man who is at it early and late, 'day in and day out,' 'year in and year out.' I have seen a few farmers who were broken in health before they were fifty, all due to overwork. That is unwise. They were succeeding and they could have let up on physical labor and given more time to management. These are the exceptions.

"Most of the farmers I know are getting fat. They sit around half the year doing nothing and eat enough for hard working men. No wonder there is so much sickness in the country. I believe that's the reason so many who go to the city return to the farm. It is true that they like the independence of country life, but they also like its leisure months. They say they want to be their own boss, but the only time they boss themselves is in the spring and fall. Most of them work hard those months because they have to work enough in six months to run them a year.

"I rent this place from Mrs. Pearson. That large house out on the road is her home. She and her husband started out poor and they finally got to be rich as farmers go. Mr. Pearson was a hard worker and a good farmer. Mrs. Pearson held close to the money. They ran several sawmills and paid for several large farms. They also invested in several houses and lots in Durham. Mr. Pearson died five years ago and as the three children are married this left his widow alone. My daughter spends the night with her each night except Saturdays and Sundays, and on these nights she finds her social life. Mrs. Pearson visits her children or they come to see her on week-ends. I cultivate twenty acres and pay a standing rent of one hundred and twenty-five dollars a year.

"Mrs. Pearson won't give me a five year lease and so I can't afford to make many improvements. If I was sure I could stay on, I would make over the house, fix up the terrace and clear some more land. The trouble is that just as sure as a tenant makes a farm more productive, the owner boosts his rent. The only way most of us can make any improvements is to buy a farm."

I asked if he planned to buy another farm. "Yes," he said. "Just as soon as I can find the farm I want and get the terms that I can handle I will buy. I think it is fair for the purchaser to pay down the equivalent of a year's rent so that the owner will be assured of that much for his property to start with. If men could buy a farm without a down-payment, many of them would cultivate the land one year and then move without paying a cent on it. I tried to buy a farm last year but the owner wanted five hundred down-payment. I told him I couldn't pay that much and have any left to buy my fertilizer and run my family through the first year.

"If everybody was as fair as Mr. Seward over on the old Fayetteville road, it would be easy to pay for a farm. I suppose you know Mr. Seward. Mr. Prince says he walked all over the place before he bought it. Mr. Seward wanted to get three thousand dollars for the place, but Mr. Prince was willing to pay only twenty-eight hundred. After they returned to the house, Mr. Seward said, 'Mr. Prince, we have talked for hours and I have not heard you use any rough language. So I have decided to let you have the farm at your own figure.'

"The first year Mr. Prince had bad luck and Mr. Seward volunteered to let him off from paying one-half the first note, adding to the other notes. The next year he again volunteered to extend the time for payment if this were necessary to enable him to buy his fertilizer for cash and carry his family on a cash basis.

Mr. Prince sees his way out. But many owners would have taken the place back as soon as he failed to meet a payment and he would have lost all he had put into it.

"I could borrow enough from friends to make the down payment but they charge too much interest and want to be paid back before I could get my notes for the land paid.

"I could borrow from the government-controlled land-banks but they insist on you making more improvements than I can afford. If I were to borrow from the land-bank in buying this place, I would have to underpin it with a new foundation, put on two coats of paint and enlarge the porches. I can't make these improvements, make the large down-payment the land-bank requires and meet the notes coming due each year. I shall have to find someone like Mr. Seward who will let me off with a small down-payment and be patient and fair with me about extensions when times become hard."

Rufus broke in to say, "Mother and Sister have just gotten back from town. Probably you would like to see them." So we went in to the living-room. "You probably notice that our furnishings are better than our house," Mrs. Harris assured me. "But we have had a better house and hope to have one of our own before many years. We like the farm better than the city and if we fail one time we can come back. I am glad you came to see us in this little house. When we get a home of our own, I hope you will be close enough to come to see us again. We haven't been here long, but we go every Sunday to the Bethel Baptist Church and work just as though we belonged. We know all the neighbors for several miles around and are fond of them all. Mrs. Pearson is our only close neighbor.

She is plain spoken but as good as she can be. She wants every penny you owe her and if she owes you anything you are sure to get it. We can't get her to make any improvements because she watches her money too closely. She often says, 'We made our money by hard work and I am holding on to it the same way.' She's getting old and won't live long. I don't know what the children will do with the place when she is gone. But one thing is certain—they can't be any more honest than she has been. We will probably stay on here as long as she will let us or until we buy a place of our own."

W. O. FOSTER

Last Chance to Own a Farm

EXCUSE THE WAY THINGS IS SCATTERED ROUND IN here. I opened up this trunk here a-Monday mornin' to pick over and patch all the old clothes that would stand mendin'. I tries to keep things neat in my little house. They ain't much furniture, but I likes to keep stuff picked up and in place best I can. Every stick o' furniture, all my bed cover, and every thread o' clothes we owned got destroyed here four years ago when the house was burnt down. After the fire, Shepherd's in Minton sold us ninety-nine dollars' wuth o' furniture on time, and it's all paid for but $13.50. It'll take squeezin' and schemin' to make ary payment this year. Mr. Makepeace built this five-room house back in place o' the other one. Le'me show you the room across the hall."

Sally Reams opens the door and exhibits the room across the hall. It is neat and attractive with its soft blue fiber rug, its overstuffed blue tapestry three-piece suit, its crisp white curtains, its subdued wall paper.

"Them is pictures Frederick drawed. Take one. Which you rather have? He won't care; he'll be pleased you took it. I've got four children with me now. This girl is Annie Lee Reams, eighteen years old. Then there's Woodrow Wilson Reams, twenty-two years old; Dora Bryan, twelve; Frederick Reams, seventeen—all single."

Annie Lee—dressed neatly in brown skirt and green sweater, with straight black hair and with surprisingly pleasant soft voice and nice enunciation—takes a chair near her mother, who continues her story.

"George Faison Reams is married and works at the Three Forks sawmill. My second oldest daughter married Sim Tyler, and they own a one-horse farm. My oldest girl lives in Pittsburgh, where her husband works on automobiles and she keeps house. Arthur died three years ago when he was 'leben years old. I've been the mother of eight, one by my first husband and the others by my second. My children has been a great help and comfort to me.

"I was born fifty-two years ago. My father was George Andrews. My mother died when I was twelve years old. As I was the oldest girl, I had to take charge o' the house and the little children the best I could. My father never owned no land; he rented and share-cropped round in the neighborhood o' Walnut Hill far

back as I remember. My first husband was Timothy
Jones. He died two years after I was married to
him, and George Reams started goin' with me. Mr.
Makepeace built a house for George, and on the second
Sunday in June we was married right here in the
house that got burnt up. I remember a crowd o'
neighbors come in and had a big supper cooked up for
us.

"Me and George worked hard and tried to have
somethin'. Some years back we bought fifty acres o'
land from Mr. Makepeace and started tendin' our own
little farm as well as sharecroppin' for Mr. Makepeace.
We wa'n't satisfied to let well enough alone; so we
bought fifty more acres in the hopes o' ownin' enough to
put our children through school and all of us livin'
better. Mr. Makepeace required us to put up our
fifty acres that was done paid for in j'opardy for the
fifty-one in the other farm we owed him for. We was
to pay $1000 and the interest, the payments to be a
hundred dollars a year. We made some payments,
but they all had to go for the interest.

"Then two years ago George got killed by a peanut
picker. He was parked on one side o' the road when a
truck come along, run into the pea picker, and turned it
over on George. It mashed him to death. We couldn't
hardly get George's body untangled from the machinery without tearin' him all to pieces. The feller
that was drivin' the truck wa'n't wuth nothin'; so we
couldn't get no damages out'n him. They say he was
put in the pen for five years. I don't know. It didn't
do us no good; it didn't bring George back. Looked
like I had a lapful o' trouble these last few years. A
hail storm destroyed the crop one year, my house and
furniture got burnt up; my boy died o' pneumonia; the

land we paid for had to be mortgaged; **I lost my** husband. But I keep hopin' for better days.

"When George died we was tryin' to school Woodrow Wilson. He had one year at Shaw University and was studyin' to be a teacher—"

"He was majoring in science," Annie Lee adds in her pleasantly modulated tones.

"But soon as his father was killed he had to come home and take holt o' the farm. We don't see no way ahead for Woodrow Wilson to do nothin' but farm the rest o' his life now. Faison had to quit school in the seventh grade and go to work. Frederick is in the tenth grade at Ga'ysburg now and hopes to finish high school next year. He says he rather be a farmer than anything else, but he'd like to learn how to make a good one. I think farmers ought to have schoolin' like other folks, so they can keep up with their business. Frederick wants to study drawin' too; what he does he just picked up of hisself. My baby, Dora Bryan, is in the sixth grade at Faithful Band, the schoolhouse down the road from here. Annie Lee, tell about your schoolin'."

"I went to school three years in Pittsburgh, staying with my sister during the time. Then I came home and went to Durham, where I stayed with a friend of mother's. I finished high school in Durham and worked as a maid for Mrs. Henley there awhile. I liked it. Since I've been home I've tried to get enrolled in the NYA and go to Brick's, but I haven't had any success yet. I rather be a trained nurse than anything else; next to that I'd like to teach. If I could get a job as maid I'd be glad of that."

"If George had lived we was goin' to try to school 'em all," continues the mother. "I had to become the

mother o' my brothers and sisters when I was twelve;
so I never got much learnin' myself. They wa'n't no
grades when I come along, but I went through the
fourth reader. I can read better than I can write, but
the children can do my writin' and figgerin' for me.
What I'm afraid of now is that we're goin' to lose the
fifty acres o' land we paid for when George was livin'.
All that's been paid so far had to count for interest,
and this year we still owe seven hundred—no, we owe
the thousand dollars and sixty more for interest this
year. It's hard to keep straight. Mr. Makepeace hain't
said nothin' to us yet, but we're expectin' it any time.
I stay scared all the time. I know this is our last
chance to ever own a farm. That's what we all want
more than anything, to farm for ourselves. If we lose
then, it's our loss; if we make, it's ours too.

"Mr. Makepeace's a good man to work for. We've
been with him twenty-seven years, ever since me and
George was first married. This year has been a failure
with us like it has everybody else. We tend a two-
horse crop for Mr. Makepeace, and all we made was
one hundred and thirteen bags o' peas and one bale o'
cotton weighin' 535 pounds and three hundred pounds
o' seed cotton left over. We got half o' that. On the
farm we call ours—the fifty acres we put in j'opardy
for the fifty-one—we hoped for three bales o' cotton
and didn't get but fifty pounds o' seed cotton. We
hoped for sixty bags o' peas and got thirteen. We
wa'n't able to fertilize it with nothin' of course, but the
main trouble was that the cotton and peas was
drownded.

"The income from the crop is all we got to look to.
That's how come me huntin' old clothes to patch up this
mornin'. We sure can't buy none this winter. I

thought I could piece some together that would do to work in. Woodrow Wilson has tried to get a job to help out this winter. He put his application in at Freeman for gover'ment work, but ain't heard nothin' from it yet.

"Mr. Makepeace don't furnish us so much money a week like some landlords. He's got a store, and we go there and get what we need. He don't complain about our account, but books it as we buy. We've done had our settlement with him this year; our account was $375, which included our food and fertilizer and the labor for pickin' peas. We liked $220 payin' out. So we've got to start out the new year with that debt starin' at us, besides the debt on the farm and the mortgage.

"We own our own team, two mules, our wagon and plows; Mr. Makepeace pays the fertilize bill, but the expenses of the peanut machine and labor has to come out of us, for our part and Mr. Makepeace's too. Looks like a hard year like this the landlord ought to mark down some of the loss for hisself too, but still if a big landowner like Mr. Makepeace done that he'd have too big a loss. I can see that. I can't complain about Mr. Makepeace. He's a right good man. We got the rental off our own place, five dollars, but the check from our half with Mr. Makepeace hain't come in yet.

"Some years has been right good for us. The most we ever cleared was four and five hundred dollars, on a two-horse crop. The average runs around $200, clear, but that's a livin'. I've worked hard, 'oman, tryin' to get somethin' ahead! If I had dollars for all the backaches I ever had wrastlin' with the grass I'd be rich. I love to work. The farm suits me exactly. No city life for me. I went to Pittsburgh to see my daughter twelve years ago, and I certainly did enjoy the visit. But it seemed good to get back to the country. It's too crowded in Pittsburgh.

"I've had to drop our burial insurance. Woodrow Wilson's is paid up, and so was Arthur's when he died. We got a hundred dollars to bury him with. We hated to drop the insurance but that fifteen cents a week counts up too fast when no money's comin' in. If we was to buy from all the agents that comes along we'd be handin' out money all the time. They comes through the country sellin' everything. Why, the Watch Tower woman thought she'd sell me a book anyhow. Last fall a white man come through sellin' holy stones for luck. He said I had enemies, and all the bad luck and trouble I'd been havin' would be changed to good luck if I bought a holy stone from him. Lots o' white women has been through sellin' stuff like that. One come in and read the Bible to me awhile before she started her sellin' speech. I don't believe in nothin' like that. I wouldn't buy it from strange women from 'way off if I did—"

"Most of them say they're from Oklahoma," Annie Lee smiles.

"They'll have to sell their conjure 'mongst folks that believes in such mess. I know they ain't no such things as ha'nts and spirits and conjuration. White folks is just tryin' to make money temptin' them that's weak.

"I manages to keep up with my church dues one way or 'nother. When time comes to pay my two dollars a year, I sells chickens or eggs enough to cover what I owe and gets that off o' hand. I wants to carry my part. We all belongs to the church. It's too far to walk, but we usually catches a ride on a neighbor's wagon or on our own. I goes every preachin' Sunday, which is once a month, and the children attends Sunday school reg'lar the other Sundays. We got a fine preacher.

"As for our somethin' t'eat, we won't suffer there. We raise hogs so they'll always be some meat in the smokehouse. I have a nice chance o' chickens, and my hens lays right good. They's plenty o' collards and turnips to boil, and we got a nice hill o' sweet potaters. I canned up fruit and vegetables last summer, so when we get in a tight we can open up a can o' fruit. We put up them peach pickles there at the bureau. I brought 'em in here to keep 'em from freezin'. In the summer time I always keeps somethin' to eat in my garden. We've got a cow; so milk and butter's on hand all the time. Elizabeth is a good hand in the kitchen; she likes to fix up little dishes extry."

"We don't have exactly what you'd call a balanced meal, like we study about at school, but we have some of the things we ought to eat every day almost. For breakfast we have eggs, butter, preserves, and biscuits, sometimes canned fruit; at dinner we boil greens or turnips and cook a chicken sometimes, maybe pie or cake; we usually have cold vegetables and fried meat for supper. Milk and butter help a lot." Annie Lee drops her head in her hand.

"One way we've been blessed a lot," Sally continues, "is in health. We've been right well all along. Annie Lee is havin' trouble now with her head though. The pain over her eye is so bad sometimes she can't hold her head up. She's been havin' toothache too lately. I know she ought to go to the dentist and have her mouth seen to, but they's no money to go with. Some of the other children complains o' toothache too, but we has to suffer it out——" Sally herself has three gold teeth in front.

"The only operation we've had in the family was mine, for appendicitis, in Portsmouth twenty-two years ago. They charged us sixty-five dollars, and we made payments every year till we got it paid off.

"We don't get about much. They's no way to go except walk or ride on the mule and wagon. We owned one car in 1925, but we ain't been able to buy another one. I'll tell you the truth: we found out we wa'n't able to run a car. Before our car wore out, we set it aside when we found out it was eatin' up all our change. I wouldn't own a car, that's the truth, not unless we was abler to run it than what we are.

"The children goes to parties sometimes, 'specially on holidays, and they visits round in the neighborhood and sees their friends at Sunday school. They seems to enjoy stayin' home nights more'n most children, readin' and playin' games together."

"*Grit* is the only paper we take." Annie Lee raises her hurting head and supplies politely. "It has a good story section that we all enjoy. Sometimes we read and study our school books. I really like to read. Frederick drew that checker board behind the bureau, and we enjoy sitting around the fire playing checkers and telling jokes and working puzzles."

"Santy Claus brought some fruit and confectioneries Christmas, and the children seemed to enjoy it. I spends most o' my time durin' the winter makin' quilts, patchin' and mendin', tendin' to my chickens and cow and pigs, and cookin'." Sally pokes the fire.

"When night comes I miss our organ. It got burnt up in the fire four years ago, and we hain't been able to re-place it. I think music helps the feelin's of a home."

BERNICE KELLY HARRIS

We Makes Plenty

FIVE MILES FROM THE POINT WHERE BUIES CREEK empties into the Cape Fear River is the home of Sam Bowers, a Negro farmer.

The farmhouse in which he lives is a frame, ceiled structure with four rooms. It is low, only eight feet from floor to ceiling. In the kitchen is a small stove flue which extends from the ceiling rafters through the house. The house is not painted and, as it was built fifty years ago, looks weather-beaten, although the lumber used was of such good quality that the building is in fine condition. The roof looks moss-grown but the heart pine shingles have not rotted.

There are several trees in the yard and enough flowers and shrubs to give it a pleasing appearance. The farm is near a dirt road, and a quarter-mile driveway leads from the main road to the house.

A car shed, a barn and a hog and cow lot face the house on the north. The house is surrounded by a forest consisting principally of hardwoods.

With the exception of Sundays and holidays or when attending to important business in town, Bowers is always found on his farm. Planting, tilling and housing his crop keeps him very busy.

"My father's name wuz James Bowers an' my mother's name wuz Mary Bowers," he began after I told him the purpose of my visit. "Dey wuz both slaves an' wuz set free by de Confederate War. Dere wuz nine chillun in our fambly, seben boys an' two girls. Ma had two miscarriages. I'se de younges' of de chillun. I is fifty-seben yeahs ol'. I wuz born July de sixteenth, 1881.

"My father died in October, 1913. He wuz born in 1843. My mother died in 1922, on July de third. She wuz eighty-six. My mother an' father stayed wid de marster atter de War fur a long time, den went to a home my father built on twenty-five acres of land he bought wid money while he worked fur his marster atter de War.

"Pa believed in big famblies an' farm work. He wanted all his chillun to have a fair eddication, but he thought a colored chile otta go to work an' quit school atter dey learned to read an' write an' figger enough so people couldn't beat 'em out of what dey made.

"Pa made a lot on his farm. Fack is, he made mos' of what we et, an' him an' his boys always done de work. Some of his ol' marster's chillun wuz always callin' on dem to do things, an' no matter if Pa wuz busy he tried to he'p 'em out. He kinder had a habit of he'pin' his white friends out in every way he could. Ma wuz a mighty good cook, or dat's what de white folks said. Some of dem wuz atter her every week or two to go stay wid dem, 'specially when dey had a new baby in de fambly. Ma never grannied a youngun but she wuz good at nussin' atter de youngun got dere.

"Ma knowed mo' 'bout home remedies dan mos' anybody. She made medicines out of herbs, shrubs, roots, sassafras tea, mullein tea an' catnip tea. Dere's one thing she could do dat a baby wuz crazy 'bout. Dat wuz makin' sugah tits. She jes' kinder conjured

dem a little wid her teas an' dey would eat an' eat, an'
when you tuk it 'way from dem dey'd cry fur mo'.

"Mos' of de white folks in dis section wuz glad to see
Pa or Ma comin'. De white chillun wud run out of de
house an' say 'Yondah comes Uncle Jimmie,' or 'Yondah comes Aint Mary,' whichevah one it wuz comin'
to see dem. Ma an' Pa wuz thought well of by de white
folks. De chillun knowed Mammy wud cook dem good
things to eat, an' Pappy wud tell dem funny stories.
Pappy laughed an' joked a lot. He had a lot of funny
sayin's. When he didn't have much to eat he et it an'
den he'd say, 'A short hoss is soon curried.' Another
thing he told de white folks dat tickled dem a whole
sight wuz dis: If dey wanted him to do some bad job
of work an' he didn't want to go do it he'd say, 'I'll
send my elect; if dey cain't do it fur you I'll come ovah
an' do it myself.' Pa called we chillun his 'elect.'

"Pa always told us to 'tend to our business an' let
other people's business 'lone. Pa'd say, 'Now boys,
don't take sides wid any of de white folks in any fuss.
If you hear dem talkin' 'bout somebody, don't say a
word.' Pa always said fur us to be honest. 'Don't
never steal nothin',' wuz what he told us. He said fur
us not to take a watermelon or a apple dat b'longed to
somebody else. Pa said if you begin takin' little things
you'll soon take big things.

"We chillun played wid white folks mos' of de time.
Dere wuz nobody else fur us to play wid. We had a lot
of manners. Pa an' Ma seed to it dat we wuz polite.
We 'spected white folks an' dey wuz good to us. Mos'
of our company wuz white folks. Some of de white
people used to talk 'bout we chillun an' called us
Jimmie's white niggers. Another thing dat he'ped us
out wuz Mammy made us keep ourselves clean an' she

kep' clean clothes on us. We dressed as good as de
white boys but we kep' our places. We always remembered dere wuz a diffrunce. We didn't furgit we
wuz black.

"I think I'se been he'ped by keepin' white folks'
company an' I think de fusses an' bad blood 'tween de
races dat happens sometimes is jes' de fault of both
niggers an' white folks not havin' a good understandin'.
My pa believed in big famblies, but I don't. No sir, I
don't. No gang of chillun fur me. I married Bessie
Kelvin, a school teacher, in Febawary, 1911. She wuz
teachin' den an' she's still teachin'. We don't have no
chillun. If we had a-had chillun we couldn't a-got nowhere. It wud have tuk it all to put on de chillun. We
bought dis home in 1918 an' it's paid fur. We can pay
our debts widout de white folks dunnin' us. We make
a-plenty to meet our promises to de folks who sell us
things an' have plenty fur clothes an' to buy de extra
rations we needs. If we wants a doctor when we is
sick we has de money to pay him. I has spent $15 a
month fur medical cures ever since I wuz twenty-one
yeahs old. It wouldn't a-been dat much but I has been
to de hospital three diffrunt times. I had a sore on one
of my legs dat wuz mighty hard to git rid of. Den I
had 'pendicitis an' den hem'rhoids. I'm well now,
though. We don't owe no pressin' debts now but if
we had a lot of chillun we'd owe everybody we could, I
reckon.

"When I started out to work fur myself I worked at a
sawmill. I got twenty cents a day an' one meal. I
worked fur Mr. Mack Morris. My Pa give me de other
two meals. Next I went an' worked at a mill b'longin'
to Mr. J. C. Stone. He paid me fawty cents a day an'
I boarded myself. I stayed wid Mr. Morris two yeahs

an' wid Mr. Stone two yeahs. Den I went to work on de railroad section. Dey paid me fifty cents a day an' I boarded myself. I saved up some money, too, but at Christmas one yeah I jes' had sich a good time; I spent mos' of it. I bought good clothes an' presents fur my folks. I got off from my work fur two weeks an' by de fust of de yeah I wuz broke. I had a good time, but I started out on de new yeah broke. Den I went to savin' agin. Soon dey raised me to sebenty-five cents a day. Ol' Cap'n Peters of de Durham an' Southern Railroad wuz my Cap'n an' he pulled fur me. I stayed right on an' saved my money. My next raise I got a dollar a day. All de time dey furnished me a shanty to live in an' I boarded myself. By 1911 when I wuz married I had a right good fist of money saved up. We rented dis place from Mr. Will Johnson de fust yeah we wuz married an' we finally bought it.

"I likes farmin' bettah dan anything else but no matter what I done, sawmillin' or railroadin', I tried to do my work as good as de other man done his, or bettah.

"I didn't go to school so much, 'bout fo' months a yeah, an' I won't graded. I learned to read, write, spell an' figger. I guess I 'bout finished de fifth grade when I went to work fur myself. Pa didn't believe in much eddication fur a nigger boy. I'm mighty glad of what eddication I has. I think everybody otta git a eddication. My wife teachin' he'ps us out a lot 'cause it's ready cash in a season when de crop has all been sold. It gives us money to run on through de spring an' summer months.

"Soon as I got married I begun thinkin' of ownin' a home fur myself an' wife. I worked fur dat wid it in mind day an' night till I bought it.

"My next mind wuz to buy a car. I saved up money

an' bought one. I paid cash fur it. It wuz a model T Ford. I kep' savin' an' when I could I traded fur a Buick car, de one I has now. I don't believe in goin' in debt fur things much. If you can git on widout 'em it don't pay. Dere's no 'parison 'tween what I makes now an' when I fust started to work. I made twenty cents a day den an' one meal. Now I makes 'bout $3,000 a year—from two to three thousand, countin' what my wife makes. We makes plenty to meet our needs an' keep buildin' up our place.

"We has some money fur lux'ries an' to give to de chu'ches an' other good organizations. We is satisfied wid life. We think ownin' our home an' makin' mos' of what we eat on our farm an' havin' money left over is somethin' to be thankful fur. I never 'spect to go back to public work ag'in.

"Me an' my wife is both Republicans. I think everybody should vote as dey want to vote while I don't think much 'bout politics or care. I think Mr. Roosevelt sho' knows his bizness. He's done mo' good dan any of de rest of 'em but Pa wuz a Republican, so I is too.

"In religion I'se of de same mind I is 'bout votin'. I thinks a person otta find de chu'ch he wants to jine no matter 'bout de 'nomination. Me an' my wife b'longs to de original Free Will Baptist Chu'ch. Pa an' Ma b'longed to it, too. I don't mean de Holy Rollers either. I thinks it jes' makes anybody bettah to go to chu'ch even if he ain't a membah. Dere is sumthin' in bein' in God's house an' I thinks everybody otta go to chu'ch an' Sunday School. It hurts me to see how keerless some people is 'bout 'tendin' meetin'. Dey ain't mo' den half as many at chu'ch lately dan dere wuz befo' de World War. I thinks everybody otta give all dey kin to 'ligion, 'cause when dey gives to de chu'ch dey is givin' to God.

"My wife knows how to cook an' what to cook. We makes our collards, turnips, beans, peas, okra, an' mustard an' in summer we has plenty of green corn. We also raises a lot of 'maters. I likes melons an' we raises a lot of watermelons and mushmelons. My wife puts up a whole heap of fruit an' grapes. We has two scuppernong vines.

"We raises a lot of chickens so we don't have to eat jes' a thing or two all de time. We make our hog meat so you see we kin change our eatin' when we git ready. We has a cow fur milk an' butter.

"Our work is like mos' of de rest of de people farmin'. In de plantin' season we work from sun to sun 'cept a hour we rest at noon. Through de growin' season hits de same 'cept we rest two hours 'stead of de one at dinnertime. Since I been raisin' 'backer, in housin' time we works mos' all de time 'cause when you is curin' 'backer de fires has to go all de time, night an' day.

"At layin'-by time in July we gen'ly has some time off but since we been makin' 'backer dis is not always de case. De time off depends on de condition of de 'backer an' it's been happenin' de las' few yeahs dere wuz no time off till it wuz all cured 'way long in September. 'Course den dere is cotton to pick, fodder to pull an' peas to pick. Fack is, dere is always work on de farm.

"Our 'musements, if you call it 'musement, is goin' to chu'ch an' visitin' a little. We 'tends de meetin's of de Good Will Society an' Parents' an' Teachers' 'Sociations. My wife 'tends de Mother's Club which she b'longs to. We tries to do de best we kin fur all de clubs. We b'longs to de burial society. I thinks everybody otta have some kind of inshuance so dey kin be put away when dey dies widout puttin' de burden of it on dere folks."

T. PAT MATTHEWS
EDWIN MASSENGILL

Lived Too Long

O NCE I WAS ALWAYS SO HARD AT WORK THAT I DIDN'T have much time to talk. It's different now. I like to talk. It helps to pass the days away.

"Sometimes I wish I was young again. I wouldn't go galavanting about the country like the young boys do hereabouts. I know it's hard to git work, but it seems to me that the young generations don't like to stick to a job these days. They just throw their money away when they git it. But on behalf of them, they's a big difference between now and when I was a young man. Then a man could hope to buy his own farm. Now a young man's got no hope at all of gitting a farm of his own by his own hard work. What he can make from wages will never buy him a farm. Maybe after all is said and done, we can't blame the young men from spending their money without aim. Sometimes I just can't figger out what this weary old world is coming to.

"Yes, it was different when I was a young man coming

up. Oh, money was hard to git. We had to work long hours for it, so we appreciated it when we got it. But land was cheap then and most young men could git up enough money to buy a farm if they just worked hard enough.

"Now, I was born in North Caroliny, in old Madison County, on a little farm that had been in the family for many a generation, and away back in the mountains. I was a come-after child, born three months after my father was killed at the Battle of Gettysburg. Just before he died he had his chum, another soldier from his home district, promise to take care of my mother when he got back home. What the soldiers in the Confederate War called a chum was the same as what the soldiers in the World War meant by their buddy.

"Anyhow, my father's chum got back home after the surrender. He come to see my mother. I had just been weaned a few months, and it wasn't long before my father's chum kept his promise to take care of my mother. He married her himself. He always told it around in the neighborhood how he had kept his promise. He was as proud of that as he was of his record in the war. He was a good step-father, but he was stricter on me than he was on his own boys and girls. He sent me to school whenever they was a chance. But it seems like they wasn't any too many chances. As soon as I was big enough to work, I had to do all sorts of jobs on the farm. I hoed corn when I was eight. I cut wood when I was ten. When I was thirteen I begun to plow. I worked in the tobacco field and tobacco barn as far back as I can remember. I don't know how young I was when I begun to help my mother by toting water from the spring. I couldn't have been over five. Children hereabouts of that age do that now.

"So my schooling didn't amount to much. But I suppose it was as good as any of the other boys in the district got in those times. I learned to read real well by the time I quit school. I could always figger fine. I could figger better than the last teacher I had. I only learned to write good enough so that other folks could read it. I don't think I would have done any better in life, or made more money if I had more learning. I had enough for a farmer and they wasn't no chance to be a doctor or a lawyer. Guess I had enough education to run a store, but I didn't never have a chance to run a store, though I've always kind of wished I could have, somehow.

"Well, by the time I was sixteen I was doing a man's work. I easy got a job at a sawmill. Made seventy-five cents a day. It was a small mill according to what they have these days, but we thought it was a great big mill, and it was owned by a big lumber company that owned thousands of acres of mountain land. Pretty soon I was working in the woods with the teams hauling logs to the mills. By the time I was nineteen I was a boss man in the woods. The other boys did not stick at their work regular like I did and I soon knowed more than they did. The Yankee superintendent took a fancy to me. I guess because his people had killed my father in the war he thought he was due me something that was not due to the other Madison County boys working with me. He sure was a kind man and a good man. He tried to get up a Sunday School class at the mill. The boys never was interested much and he finally give that up. But during the week days he could sure drive hard and I tell you we had to work to make our money. The no-count boys was caught pretty soon. They never could git a job at the mill again. They was too many others who wanted to work for wages. The super-intendent could pick his men.

"So the superintendent took a liking to me. He found out I could figger right well and he taught me how to figger lumber. I hadn't learned how to do that at school. That man could handle figgers faster than any school teacher I ever saw. He was a fine one to estimate standing timber. He teached me how to do that. One thing, though—he couldn't tell the different sorts of trees any better than I could. He learned that he could not tell them as well, for he was raised in the northern country, which didn't have near the different kinds of trees our mountains has. I was raised up in the mountains and can tell at sight any tree that grows in the Smokies, and how they're different from any other trees. By the time I was twenty-one I was es-timating for the company. They sent me traveling all around and inspecting timber they was on a trade for. I got two dollars and a half a day. It was big money in them days. I had already saved nigh two hundred dollars. So after working a few months, I picked out Lady Jane—the finest girl in that part of the country —and we married. We lived at her pa's home for a while until I could git a home of my own.

"Well, I picked out a farm of two hundred acres with five acres of bottom land along a creek. They wanted a thousand dollars for it. It took me just two years to pay that money out of my wages. I was doing fine. My own boughten land, a pretty little wife, and me only twenty-three. So I quit my timber job. I cleared and fenced a field and built us a log cabin and we moved in and got down to work. The children started coming along. Pretty regular once a year, Lady would make me a daddy again. I worked hard.

They wasn't much in the way of recreation for us. All I can remember in that way is setting on the front step along about after dark and listening to my dogs off on the ridge running a fox. I was too tired to run with them. Just set and listened, and it was a mighty pretty sound.

"Yes, it was hard work, but times was good and I felt I was gitting ahead.

"I farmed for many years. Busy all the time. The months and the years just slipped me by and I didn't notice them. In the winter months, when they wasn't much to do at home, I would estimate timber for wages again. I had hard luck as a farmer in one way. All my first five children was girls. It was a long time before the boys come and grew up big enough to help me.

"We had fourteen children in all. Ten is still living and all married but the youngest boy. My oldest daughter died when she was eighteen from typhoid fever. The fever run all through the family but she was the only one that died. Then I lost a boy when he was twenty-two and already married. He died of consumption, the only one in my family that ever had any signs of that disease. He got pneumonia fever when he was working in a coal mine up at Duggersville. Soon after gitting well of that, he got the consumption. He went pretty fast. One of his sisters was working in Chattanooga. She went up to see him and seeing how bad off he was she had him brought home here. We did all we could for him but he died within three months after gitting back home. The doctors hereabouts have told me that this boy didn't git the right treatment when he had the pneumonia, or he wouldn't got the consumption afterwards. They say that when a person is about well of the pneumonia, the doctor should draw the pus off the lungs by sticking needles through the ribs into the lungs. My boy had the coal company's doctor and he didn't drain his lungs. The company doctor didn't know his business, if the doctors around here are right. If my boy had had a good doctor, I believe he would be living today. All his five brothers is living and in good health. It seems to me that a coal mining company ought to have men at the head of it who have sense enough to hire a good company doctor.

"The only other two children we lost was the twins. They died five days after they was born. I don't believe we would have lost them if we could have got to a doctor. I could see that they was weakly as soon as they was born. We didn't know what to do for them. We just used the home remedies for sick babies. Guess we done something wrong. They was only one doctor in that end of Madison County then, and the snow in the mountains was awful deep when the twins come. I sent for the doctor. He didn't git my word until three days later. Seems he was away from home with the sick, and by the time he was found three days had passed. It took him two days more to git to us after he got the word. The babies was dead and put under by that time. Sometimes I think what the twins would have been like if they was spared. But it's not good for a man to study too much about those things. I try to keep from it.

"I tried to do the best for my children as they was growing up. They got all the schooling they was in the neighborhood. But most of them got no better schooling than I got. The schools was just about the same as when I was a boy. I made all my children, boys and girls, learn to work and do useful tasks as soon as they was big enough. I never let their work keep them from school when the school was running. We all sort of doted on our youngest daughter. She'd come along between the boys. She's the third youngest child. She got the best education of any of the children. She got a diploma from Gordon Collegiate Institute at Rushton. When she finished, one of her sisters, who was working in Chattanooga, put her through a business college. She got a job at seventy-five dollars a month as a stenographer in Chattanooga. But she didn't work much more than six months before she married a town boy.

"It was along about the time our ninth young one was born that I got dissatisfied. I thought I could make better if I left North Caroliny and come to Tennessee. I'd done some of my timber work in Tennessee and I knew I could git land cheaper over here. I sold my farm for three thousand dollars in cash and we said farewell to Madison County.

"The roads across the mountains in 1897 was just terrible. We come in three big wagons loaded down with farm tools and furniture and provisions and children. We come through the Smokies along the French Broad River, through Hot Springs and Newport, and we rested a while at Knoxville. When we felt like it, we went on to Rushton and up a little river to Tick Bush Cove. We'd traveled a long way but we'd been doubling around on our tracks. We come to rest in Tick Bush Cove just thirty-five miles crow's flight across the mountain from where we'd started from in Madison County.

"I soon found a farm with a house and barn already on it that suited me. The owner was willing to sell for cash. They was some pretty good land already cleared and I soon had my crop in. I bought about five hundred acres of land in this trade and it cost twenty-five hundred dollars, or about five dollars an acre. It was what I'd paid for my smaller North Caroliny place. I had to pay that much for it because it was a small place. The big lumber companies buying large tracts was gitting their lands for two dollars an acre and less. All they wanted was the timber. Of course they bought much rougher land than would be good for farming. But when these big companies sold their uncut acreage to the National Park they wanted thirty dollars an acre. Their lands may have been worth that much for a park, but a farmer in the mountains can't pay more than five dollars an acre because his lands washes out so.

"In this mountain country cleared land for a crop washes and leaches out no matter what you do to stop it. Yes, I know all about running the plow across the slope and not up and down. The furrow across a slope on a level helps to hold the water back. I hear that some city folks say that we mountain farmers are so ignorant that we plow up and down a hill and that this causes the top soil to wash away. Not a bit of truth in that! I never plowed my land that way. Never heard of anybody else doing it that way. Them that thinks we plow that way are pure down fools. They ought to know that a horse can't pull a plow up hill and a man can't hold a plow going down hill.

"Us mountain farmers know all about terracing land to stop it washing. But it takes a team to throw up terraces and ain't many farmers up here owns more than one head of stock. Another trouble is that the land is so steep that you can't hardly control a team to throw up a terrace. Because most of the land in a cove is steep, one horse walks higher than his mate in throwing up ground for a terrace. The horses don't pull together, the harness gits broken, and a man trying to terrace soon spends a day at it and gits nowhere. No, terracing just ain't worth a penny on a mountain farm. The soil of the coves is rich, but loose and leaches bad. New ground will produce ninety bushel of corn an acre the second year. But even with the best kind of farming, doing all we can to save the top soil, it gradually washes away and that ninety bushel is made no more. Crop gits less and less each year. In ten to twenty years so much top soil is gone that it don't pay to work it. What a man has to do then is to clear a new cove. So I bought five hundred acres when I first come to Tennessee so that I'd have plenty of new land to clear later on.

"Up in Tick Bush Cove I bought a grist mill that would grind five bushels of meal an hour. I farmed and run my mill. Did it for about five years. The children could help me lots on the farm and because the mill was right close by to my house, I could go to it and grind whenever a turn of corn was brought.

"I made money from the mill. Then Lady made me sell it. The trouble was I fell into temptation at the mill. Many of my customers was moonshiners that made good pure liquor with some of their meal. It was the only way they could git any real cash money in those days. Them moonshiners give me plenty of liquor. I had drunk liquor like most mountain boys since I was a youngster. I could drink it or let it alone. I could drink and still go right on with my work. But at the mill I drank too steady and it begun to tell on me. So Lady made me sell out, and talked me into moving out the neighborhood to git away from the crowd I had been drinking with. Besides, they was no schools up there and my children was growing up in ignorance.

"So I sold out and bought this home and farm down here. It was about a mile and a quarter from Drooping Elm where they had a school that run pretty regular, a grist mill, blacksmith shop, stores, and a Baptist church. Yes, we're Baptists but I never paid much attention to religion. I don't understand much of the Bible when I read it, so I leave that to the women folks and the preachers. They claim they know all about it. Lady reads the Bible while I read the newspaper. She taught the children about religion. Of course, I've got no objection to religion. I really like a good sermon. But they's few preachers that can preach a real good sermon—at least hereabouts.

"Well, this was a good farm when I bought it. This frame house, the first one I ever lived in in all my life, was already here. They's about three acres of good bottom land along the creek, but the rest is all mountain land. I bought three hundred acres but sold off part of it little by little until now I own less than two hundred acres. We've had to do here just as we did in Tick Bush Cove—clear out fresh land when the old got wore out and had to be turned into pasture or back to new growth of timber.

"For many years we got along fine. I made a good living on the farm. During the winter I estimated timber. Wages rose and I got as much as five dollars a day for inspecting timber. I made trips into Kentucky, West Virginia, and all around in East Tennessee. My children got grown. They married off and left home. My winter work inspecting timber gradually fell off because most of the virgin timber had all been bought by the big lumber companies. In fact, about the time

I moved here most of the buying was by one company from another. They gradually quit trading altogether as they cut the timber out. Then I give all my time to farming. Winter meant no rest. I had to keep clearing land to take the place of what was wore out. Plowing is hard work. But I never minded work. I've worked from the time I was just a little boy.

"Well, I've farmed on this land the best I knowed how until it is about to give out just as I am about to give out. Ten year ago I cleared the last cove that was fitten to clear. I don't think a young man could make a living on it now. I don't make near the corn I used to make on the same ground. I can't make enough to feed a horse all the year and have corn for bread too. I swap work with neighbors to git my land plowed. If I had a horse it wouldn't help me much. I'm too old and shaky to plow these days. I'm gitting right deaf too. I can't stand the cold like I used to. Even five year ago I could work in the open with the cold at zero and not feel it. But the doctors say my circulation is bad now and my hands and feet git too cold in the open when they's frost on the ground. I can still read all right with glasses but I can't walk up the hills easy like I used to. The doctor says my heart is too weak for hard work any longer. Once I could lift a two hundred pound hog and swing it. Now I can barely tote a turn of corn to the mill. Even five year ago I would take a bushel at a turn. Now I can't tote but little more than a peck.

"Lady has give out too. She's seventy and was all right until that cancer in the breast hit her. Our doctor here told us what was wrong. But he couldn't do a thing about it. She had to go to the cancer clinic in Knoxville. The clinic doctors told her the cancer come

from nursing too many children, and that they would
have to cut it out right away.

"Now, what seems funny to me is that God would put
a cancer on a good mother because she brought too
many children in the world, if the clinic doctors are
right. We don't think we had too many children. We
love every one of them just like he was the only one. I
guess if we could live our lives all over again, knowing
what we know now, we would have just as many children. What I read in the papers about the city folks
having birth control seems plumb sinful to me. Don't
the Bible say that man should multiply and replenish
the earth?

"When this cancer trouble come up, I borrowed two
hundred dollars on this farm, the first mortgage I ever
give on any of my land, and all the money was spent on
Lady. The doctors at Knoxville said the operation was
a success. We hope Lady is all right now. But they
had to cut so much flesh away and so high up on her
right arm that she'll never be able to work her garden
any more. We had to give the cow up because neither
one of us could milk her. You know butter and milk is
half the living on a farm. They take the place of meat
when the cured meat runs out, and in the last few years
I didn't make enough corn to keep enough hogs to give
us all the meat and lard we need. About all the money
we can git these days comes from Lady's chickens and
eggs and from my tobacco. But I only make enough
tobacco to pay the taxes. The chickens and eggs buy
our salt, sugar, soda, soap, and coffee. This house
needs repainting and a new roof. I can't git up the
money to buy the materials. If I was younger I could
split enough boards to put on a new roof, but I can't
do that work now. We're not making enough on the

farm to live on now and we can't work any longer. So
I guess we will have to sell out. The only reason I can
git sixteen hundred dollars for the place is that a
Rushton man wants it to build up a tourist camp here.
It's off the main highway so the tourists would be free
from the noise and the dust.

"None of our children is in a place where they can
help us. They've got children of their own, lots of
them, and not yet grown. And their first duty is to
their own children. Besides, all of them are poor.
None of them except the youngest daughter had much
of an education, and a man has to be educated to make
money these days. A man can't make more than a
bare living on a farm. And the wages a man gits from
public works, such as building roads, in the coal mines,
and at the lumber mills, ain't much more than enough
to keep body and soul together.

"Mountain farmers haven't got no future—none at
all. Most of the land is give out, and they ain't no more
new land. Even the bottom land along the rivers and
creeks in Rush County is gitting poorer and poorer
every year, no matter how much care is taken to keep
the soil up. There's Mr. Hilton on the river near
Drooping Elm with two hundred acres of bottom land.
He's always had enough money to farm well. He
rotates his crops, uses fertilizers, and his land don't
wash away like these steep hillsides do. He's always
tried to take care of his land. Up to ten years ago he
always made fifteen bushel of wheat an acre or more,
but for the last ten years the wheat has dropped to
twelve bushel or less. All the land in Rush County is
gitting poorer and poorer each year.

"The farms can't keep up the big families like they
used to. Not near so many folks can live on the farms

and work the land and make a living as a generation
ago. The young folks have got nothing to look for
ahead on a farm now as I did when I was a young man.
Plenty of land then. We thought the price of five
dollars an acre was high, but we didn't appreciate what
we was gitting according to prices now.

"When these farms wear out, I guess the National
Park or the National Forests will take them over and
let the timber grow back. The old folks will die about
the time their land is give out, just as mine has wore out.
The young folks will have to live on wages from the
public works or go to Chattanooga and git jobs in the
mills. It may all be for the best. I don't know and
can't seem to figger it out.

"I've lived a long time and I've worked hard, and I
don't worry none about the future of the country. Now,
I think the country ought to take care of Lady and me
until we're gone. I would give this farm to the State
of Tennessee, if they would let me and Lady live in this
house as long as we live and give us enough pension
money to buy the things we have to eat and wear that
we can't raise. It wouldn't be much money, less than
the thirty dollars a month they are talking about. And
the State wouldn't have to pay that long. We are
both plumb wore out and about done.

"They's old age pensions in the State and seems like
me and Lady ought to git one. But they tell me at the
courthouse in Rushton that Lady and me are what they
call ineligible for the old age pension. I don't know.
Maybe it's because we own this worn out farm. The
man at the county court talked mighty fast so I never
could git no clear notion of what he meant. Them
politicians sure are mighty glib talkers. You think
they's told you all you want to know. Then you study

it out and you find they ain't told you a thing. Just a
lot of high sounding talk.

"Nothing comes out the way it looks like it ought.
Life don't work like a job of work. You study out how
to do a job and do it. It works pretty much like you
thought it would. But when it comes to living, they's
not any way you can plan it and have it go according.

"I don't know. I guess, though, that when all is
said our troubles is just because we've lived too long."

DEAN NEWMAN
JAMES R. ASWELL

I Saved My Money

I'LL TELL YOU THERE'S A LOT OF THINGS HAPPENED IN
my life since I wuz born," said John Sylvester
Hinson. "I wuz born in December, 1881. My father's
name wuz George an' my mother's name wuz Ellen.

"There wuz nine children in our fambly, seven boys
an' two girls. I wuz the fifth child. My mother never
had a doctor when any of us wuz born 'cept when she
had George. He wuz the third child. She had old
Dr. R. T. Alexander then. All the rest of the times
when she had a youngun a granny-woman done the job.
She never had a miscarriage in her life.

"Ma died when she wuz eighty. Pa died at eighty-
four, twelve days 'fore my mother's death. Pa shore

loved Ma if ever a man loved his wife. Ma loved him jest as good. I'll tell you there ain't many sich couples nowadays as they wuz. No matter what happened, I never heard Ma complain in my life. Pa never slept anywhere but with Ma from the time they wuz married 'till he died, unless he wuz away on business. Ma had been down helpless for a year when Pa died. All that time Pa slept with her. Pa seemed to be well durin' Ma's sickness up to the day of his death, an' he refused to leave her durin' this time. In the mornin' of the day he died he eat shad for breakfast and said he felt good. All he talked 'bout for a month 'fore his death wuz that he wanted to die first. He said over an' over again that he didn't want Ma to leave him. Pa went to bed early the day he died. It wuz 'bout seven o'clock in the evenin'. He wuz complainin' then of bein' weak. A doctor wuz sent for. Before the doctor got there he raised hisself up in bed, an' restin' his head on his elbows, he looked around over the room an' said, 'I shore do feel good.' In a instant he fell back on his pillow, gasped a few times, an' wuz dead. Ma died twelve days later. Pa died of a heart attack an' Ma died of heart drapsy. Her health wuz good 'till she wuz took sick before her death.

"My parents wuz tenant farmers. My father never owned a mule or horse 'till the youngest child, Henry, wuz seven years old. We moved from place to place an' farmed with steers. We had always cooked, eat, an' slept in a one-room house 'till Henry wuz born. We had been livin' at that place nine years. It belonged to Raymond Willington, the man we farmed with. Pa farmed, worked turpentine, an' made turpentine barrels. He also made shingles.

"We moved from this place to a house on the farm

of Bill Chance near Lane's Creek where Ledford College is now. The house had one room, but there wuz a little kitchen forty yards away which we used to cook an' eat in. In them days kitchens wuz built away from the other dwellin' so that if one burned the other wouldn't be destroyed. They wuz called 'Big House an' kitchen.'

"We stayed at the Bill Chance place one year then we come to Mac Jameson's place. It wuz called the 'Mac Place.' The big house had four rooms downstairs an' two porches an' a upstairs attic. The kitchen part, which wuz fifty yards away to the west, had three rooms an' a cellar beneath. We farmed there seven years.

"Rob Williams' water mill an' cotton gin wuz a half mile from this place. While livin' there we worked at the mill through the fall an' winter all our spare time. Pa wuz ginner an' I helped bring cotton to him an' put lint in the press. I got fifteen cents a day for my work. Pa wuz paid fifty cents. He gimme my board an' with the money I made I bought my first suit of store-bought clothes. I paid $3.50 for a suit, shoes, shirt an' hat. I remember it as well as if it wuz yistiddy.

"When we left the 'Mac Place' we went to Durham an' worked in a cotton mill two years.

"Pa's next move wuz back to Williams' Mill in Parsons County where we worked 'fore we left the 'Mac Place.' There wuz a twenty-five acre farm besides the land which the pond, dwellin' an' mill buildin's covered.

"The fambly broke up when Pa moved from Raleigh. Three of the children come back with him and six kept workin' in the mill. I wuz one that stayed on in the mill. Mill work wuz too confusin' to Pa an' the hours wuz too long. We worked from six o'clock in the

mornin' 'till six o'clock in the evenin', with thirty
minutes off for dinner.

"I went to see him in 1900. While I wuz with him a
desire come over me that wuz so strong I cut my visit
short an' went back to my work. It wuz a desire to buy
the place. I'd always liked it. I didn't tell nobody
'bout my feelin's, but I saved my money an' nineteen
years later I bought it for cash an' own it now.

"Pa teached his children to be honest an' pay their
debts. He wuz mighty honest hisself. He made us go
to church an' Sunday School, an' he wouldn't let us
hunt or fish on Sunday.

"My parents done all they could to educate us. All
of us could read an' write an' figger good enough to do
business.

"If Pa owed a penny when he died I never heard of
it. He had enough to pay his an' Ma's burial expenses.

"Pa wuz never arrested, never a juror, never a witness, an' wuz never called to a courthouse for nothin'.

"I married Annie Huntington of Durham in 1909.
I wuz workin' in a cotton mill there then. I wuz a
weaver, makin' what wuz considered good money at that
time. I wuz paid $10.50 a week for sixty-six hours'
work. I paid $2.50 a week for room an' board. I left
mill work when I bought this place.

"While workin' in the mill I dressed well, pressed my
own clothes, shined my shoes an' done all my patchin'
an' mendin'. I made sacrifices to git ahead. Durin'
this time I wuz offered better jobs but my education
wuz so little I couldn't take the work.

"I've got four children but I don't believe in big
famblies. I think birth control is all right. Big
famblies costs too much, an' they ruin a man's chance
of savin' money. I don't believe in 'em.

"I fully believe in education an' our modern schools, but I think there's too much entertainin' plays at the schools. They take too much time off the children's books.

"The county agent's an' farm talks over the radio helps me. They know more 'bout farmin' than I do, so I follow what they say. It shore has helped me to make more an' take care of my place better.

"My income now is ten to one better than when I first went to work for myself. Now I have cars, stock, clothes an' food aplenty an' I'm not in debt. I make 'bout $4,000 a year an' I have five in my fambly. I think a man an' wife should have $2,000 a year to live on.

"I have one boy jest moved off. 'Fore he moved off I bought him a home an' give it to him. That's cut my fambly down one an' makes me think how old I am.

"Outside of the birth of my children I average 'bout $5 a year for medicine treatment. Mill work hurt my health an' I never have fully got over it.

"Farm work has never hurt me in any way. I have made money sawmillin' since I settled here but the timber got so scace I quit an' sold my mill. I made money with my grist mill, too. It went down in Hoover's Administration an' I won't able to repair it so I sold out, rocks and all.

"I have tenant farmers on my place. I try to treat 'em right an' give 'em a chance if they show they want to better theirselves.

"I believe in morals an' religion. I think a moral man is better than a man who don't have none. A religious man who is in earnest 'bout it is what we all should be. I'm a member of the Missionary Baptist Church, but sometimes I think I ought not to belong to it 'cause I don't live right.   I've told 'em to turn me out a time or two.

"Sometimes I have a party an' drink a little, 'fact is, I get drunk now an' then. The boys used to git a lot of cider or corn whiskey an' then steal a lot of chickens an' have a big party. We called 'em 'functums.'

"When the boys went to a house to steal chickens for the 'functum' some would go in an' talk with the owner while the others went to the hen house after the fowls. Sometimes as many as fourteen chickens would be stole an' eat in one night. These things has died out. There hain't been one in this neighborhood in five years.

"Times is changin' fast. When I wuz a boy people courted at home; now young people court in automobiles. People don't visit like they used to noway. People don't visit the sick or take part in burials either like they done when I wuz a boy. Now when a man dies the fambly an' a few close friends is 'bout all that attends the buryin'. The churches around here jest 'bout has no crowd unless it's at the Sunday services, an' then there ain't more'n a fourth as many at preachin' as used to be thirty years ago. Movin' pictures, dance halls, an' jest ridin' 'round in automobiles is where you'll find most of the young folks. The old folks stays home, listens to the radio, an' talks. Times has shore changed.

"The first thing I remember wuz the cyclone that killed Mrs. Nellie Hogan an' six members of the Mansion fambly who wuz at the Hogan home that night. That wuz a sight. Dead people, horses, cows, chickens, geese, dogs an' cats wuz blowed to pieces. Everybody wuz skeered mighty bad an' today people in this county is 'fraid of clouds, 'cause it's been talked so much an' signs of it can still be seen. Big bent-over trees is still green. Stumps, where trees wuz wrung off, is still standin', showin' how terrible strong the wind wuz.

"The next thing I remember that wuz skeery wuz the earth shock. People wuz runnin' all over the neighborhood, cryin' an' prayin'. I went under the bed hollerin'. I thought the world wuz comin' to a end.

"There wuz a man, John Mullins, who wuz bad fur cussin'. He wuzn't a bad man, but he liked to talk, cuss and make a mountain out'en a molehill. He made out he won't 'fraid of nothin', not even darkness, storms an' varmints. He said there wuz no sich a thing as haints an' ghosts an' he won't 'fraid of things he could see or could not see. Well, when the shock come he wuz jest skeered near 'bout to death. You never seed sich a sight in yore life. He prayed or tried to pray. Some sed when it wuz all over that he wuz skeered so bad when he tried to pray he forgot the Lord's name.

"People gathered 'round in the neighborhood after the earth shock an' had prayer meetin's two an' three times a week. It skeered folks a whole lot worse than the cyclone. I remember Pa, Ma, and we children all went to Aunt Bonnie Tompkins' house, to Pete Willson's an' to Hal Smith's to prayer meetin's.

"Pa an' some of my older brothers carried hand lights. These lights wuz made of light'ood pine splinters. 'Bout six or eight of the splinters wuz bundled together an' lit at the end. They give a good light. Sometimes I got me some splinters an' carried me a hand light, too. The splinters wuz put out when the house wuz reached an' if they hadn't burnt up 'till they wuz too short they wuz lit and used on the return trip home after prayer meetin' wuz over. Most everybody carried fresh splinters along for hand lights in case the ones lit wuz burnt up 'fore the house visited wuz reached.

"Men always done the talkin' in meetin's then an' the
women done the shoutin'. I never heard a woman talk
in meetin's 'till I wuz a grown man an' I never seed a
man shout 'till I wuz a grown man. It won't style then.
You see styles change, even in religion. There shore
wuz a difference in it then an' now. Another thing,
when the meetin' wuz over an' all the younguns would
be asleep, when women told them younguns to git up
they got up. If they begun to cry the women give 'em
somethin' to cry for. They took 'em behind the house
an' spanked 'em good an' hard.

"Most couples had big famblies then. They knowed
nothin' 'bout birth control, an' they had 'em like rabbits.
It wuz nothin' to see a poor renter livin' in a one-room
house with a fambly of ten or twelve children an' sometimes more.

"Another thing I noticed back in them days wuz bad
winters. Jest let a bad, snowy cold winter come that
wuz so bad the men'd have to stay inside the house most
all the time an' you might look out. Most every woman
in the neighborhood would get bigged and there'd be
the biggest crop of young babies you ever saw in a year's
time.

"There's a lot of folks gittin' on to keepin' from
havin' too many children. I believe in it but I guess
the single women will be affected by it as they will shore
learn the trick an' half the girls has stayed ladies 'cause
they wuz 'fraid of gittin' bigged, I reckon.

"I acted as midwife for a woman named Susan Hardy
when I wuz nineteen years old. I passed a home on a
back street in Raleigh an' heard a woman hollerin' an'
callin' for help. I had had two or three drinks of
whiskey an' I wuz brave, so I went in.

" 'What's the matter with you?' I asked.

" 'I'm goin' to have a baby,' she said.

" 'Well, who do you want me to git?'

" 'There's no time to git anybody now, you help me yourself. Don't you leave me.'

" 'Well, what do you want me to do?'

"She told me to fix a sheet 'round the foot of the bed an' give one end of it to her. I done like she told me. She pulled an' pulled, an' the baby started out, movin' a little every time she pulled. Every time she pulled she grunted, an' after 'bout a hour the baby just popped out all covered in the nastiest lookin' stuff; looked like thin skin. She grunted an' said, 'What a relief!' That wuz after the baby come out. He wuz still tied to her, so she told me to git the scissors. She wuz bleedin' an' it kinder skeered me. She showed me where to cut the cord. There wuz several knots on it. She begun fixin' it back in herself.

" 'Git that afterbirth off'en the baby,' she told me.

"I got it off an' the baby breathed kinder quare-like, opened his eyes an' begun to squall. I mean he raised Cain. I got some warm water off'en the stove an' a lot of bandages an' things out'en a bureau drawer. She put a band 'round him an' fixed him up. I helped all I could. I put the baby down by her side an' put the cover over her after I had fixed a rubber sheet, so she lay on it without it hurtin' her.

"She then thanked me an' told me to go two blocks away an' tell a nigger woman to come up there. The nigger went at once, an' I went on home. This woman wuz a whore, an' she had nobody to care for her. But she lived all right, 'cause I seed her on the streets after that.

"I never seed a toilet in my life 'till we moved to Raleigh in 1897. I wuz then 'bout seventeen years old.

Nor had I used one. I had heard of backhouses but had never seen one nor had I seen a well pump. There wuz no sich things as backhouses and water pumps nowhere in the country where I'd been. I wuz a full grown man 'fore I tasted ice cream or Coca-Cola.

"People toted their corn to mill on their shoulders from a distance of three miles sometimes when they had as many as two rested horses in the stables. We'd never used a barn 'till we moved to the Mac Place. The buildin' we put our corn in at housin' time wuz called a crib.

"Many of the houses of the landowners wuz so full of cracks you could stand inside the house an' look through the cracks an' see people passin' by on the road. Strangers goin' through wuzn't charged for a meal an' a place to sleep 'cause their company wuz appreciated so much.

"The farms, the roads, the streams an' the forests has changed since I wuz a boy. The farm is cleaner now of briars, shrubs an' broomsedge; the roads has been repaired an' many of 'em concreted an' asphalted; the streams has been bridged, an' the timber in the forests has been cut an' made into lumber. In lots of places where there wuz pine thickets when I wuz a boy, houses now set an' the land 'round 'em is a fine farm. We air makin' progress an' in twenty more years, if it keeps goin' on as fast as it is now, this neighborhood will be a town itself."

T. PAT MATTHEWS

Marsh Taylor, Landlord

WILLSPORT IS A QUIET LITTLE TOWN. THE ONLY source of amusement for most of the townspeople is the one small movie which shows pictures "after they've travelled and seen the world," as one caustic citizen put it. Occasionally a merry-go-round and Ferris wheel with accompanying pitch-penny and throw-at-the-doll games are put up on a vacant lot to get a whack at the crowds from the country which throng the county seat on Saturday. There is little industrial activity—several sawmills and the tomato cannery in season. Five blocks in all make up the business section. The stores are mostly designed to supply farmers. A few cater to town trade. There are two drug stores, two hotels: the rest are holes in the wall—Negro shops, pressing club, barber shops, tiny stores.

With it all, there seems to be an air of prosperity, as witness the fine houses which line the best of its four paved streets. The town is old; it was settled long before the Revolutionary War and it has been the home of the county's wealthiest landowners and merchants for generations.

Close to the old brick and balconied courthouse there is an equally old two-story structure which houses the office of the town clerk, the Williams Company and, upstairs, the county hospital. The hospital has a porch which extends over the sidewalk, giving the Williams

101

Company's quarters an even dingier atmosphere than
the arrangement and kind of stock it carries would
produce. In the windows of the store are plow lines
and sacks of beans and the long interior is lined with
dark shelves up to the ceiling with an old running
ladder alongside for the convenience of the clerk. In
the back is an arched passage to the other side of the
store which lies behind the town clerk's office and houses
feed and flour. The store is obviously intended for
farm trade and no attempt has been made to arrange
merchandise for sales effect on the passersby. The
people who buy here will buy anyway and there is no
need to attract them with window and counter displays.
They will buy staple articles and so nothing fancy is in
evidence.

Past the Williams Company, past the courthouse and
the artesian well on the corner there is the block on
King Street occupied altogether by the Williams heirs.
In the right front corner of the block stands the Confederate statue on a triangle of ground given by old
Mr. Ben Williams. The courthouse was right up on
the street and when the county commissioners yielded
to the salesmanship of a New England company and
bought the soldier, they had no place to put him until
Mr. Ben came through with the little plot.

First in the block is the big house in which live Mr.
Ben's widow and his second son, J. B. It is white,
turreted, and circled by a high porch on two sides. Its
turret room is higher than the top of the courthouse.
Before it are two huge magnolia trees whose branches
touch the ground. Behind the Big House are three
weathered, unpainted bungalows occupied by the Negro
house servants. Next door is a two-story white house
occupied by Ben Williams, Jr., his wife and child. It

is a common sight to see their little boy, affectionately
known as "Whiskey," in tow of a Negro servant's child:
a little black girl peddling a high tricycle with the little
white boy running along behind.

The last house on the block, a large brick residence
with colonial entrance, belongs to Marsh Taylor and his
wife, Nancy Williams, the only daughter of old Mr.
Ben. It sits well back from the sidewalk in a beauti-
fully kept yard: green lawn fringed with purple
crape myrtle and split by a cement walk lined with
small box bushes.

A white-haired woman was working in the yard, bend-
ing over plants with a trowel, loosening the roots. She
is tall and slender, her figure well-preserved. When she
looked up, the face beneath the white hair appeared
surprisingly young. Her forehead is lined and her
whole expression is that of a woman who must have
known tragedy. Near by in a little wagon, his eyes
staring vacantly before him, was a boy of about seven
years—seemingly an idiot.

Mrs. Taylor said that Marsh was around somewhere.
Her smile is ready and her blue eyes friendly. Laughing, she said that he had been riding up and down the
street on a motor scooter which an enterprising salesman was trying to sell to local merchants.

The door behind her opened and Marsh came out
into the yard. "Why didn't you come on and ride,
Nancy?" he laughed.

"You can break your neck if you want to, Marsh
Taylor, but I'll never get on one of those things."

"I only want to put you in the delivery box and give
you a free ride . . ."

There was a sputtering roar and the little red motor

scooter charged up the street with a bespectacled and very sedate man astride the seat.

"Ride her, Tom, give her the gas!" Marsh yelled at the leading deacon in the Baptist Church. "Don't be scared, give her the works!"

At this challenge to his courage, the deacon, coat streaming behind, gave the scooter "the works" and with a roar it charged down main street.

"I declare you act more like a child every day." Nancy looked provokedly at her stocky husband who listened calmly and puffed away at his pipe, grinning.

He has to look after some business but he will be glad to furnish any information about his way of handling farms tonight; that is, anything except his financial affairs. With a glance at the boy in the wagon, he climbs into the Model A Ford sedan and drives away.

Mrs. Taylor looks after him with a twinkle in her blue eyes: "Marsh really is just like a small boy. He'd rather drive that Ford than a heavenly chariot. He wouldn't take a thousand dollars for it. Only a few months ago he had a new motor put in. I imagine it really is useful to him; he uses it to go all over the farms—ditches, fields and everything. When he was having the motor put in he had to use the Buick"— nodding at the new Buick Road-Master on the street before the house—"and you would have thought someone had asked him to travel in a *wreck*.

"He was laughing this morning about the funny names colored people call their children. He saw some little boys in the pecan orchard stealing nuts and turned the Ford off the road and went tearing across the field to the orchard. They saw him coming and started running, with him right behind them. When he caught them he said that they were the three most frightened little colored boys he's ever seen.

" 'Nossuh, Mistah Taylor,' the oldest said, 'us weren't stealin' no pecans. 'Twus Jugbelly dare.' He was pointing at the littlest one of all and that one started bawling. The sight of little 'Jugbelly's' goings-on tickled Marsh so much he gave him a nickel and let them go. Said if he caught them again he'd skin 'em alive."

A red Ford zoomed by and honked at somebody on the opposite sidewalk.

"There goes Mary and that good-for-nothing Jim," she said, trying not to appear interested. "That's all he has to do, ride around and hunt and loaf in general. I don't see how two brothers could be so unlike. Marsh hasn't any patience with him. No, he doesn't live here; he's just visiting us for a few days. Marsh wouldn't have him around any longer than that. As for Mary, I never see her any more. She hasn't showed her face in this house since she left college and married that John Martin. Oh, yes, she did come back once when I wasn't in to get her clothes. She didn't want them or pay any attention to them before. I reckon she's found that she needs everything she can get now that she's married John. I never liked any of the Martins. My father used to tell us never to trust them any farther than you could see them. You know she won't be happy. He hasn't got any education to speak of and just barely makes a living in the trucking business. He certainly won't inherit much from his family. Of course Mary will get what her grandfather left in trust for her when she's twenty-one, but that wasn't so much. It won't last forever—and Marsh and I won't feel like doing as much for her as we would have.

"Marsh and I can't travel and do things and I wanted her to do and have all the things we can't. She had every opportunity in this world and the little fool threw it all away. I wanted her to finish at Queen's-Chicora and then go to Europe and travel for a few years. She could have done that and come back and gone to one of the big Northern universities. She used to tell me that was one thing she'd never do—get married secretly. Then she left school and married that John Martin without telling me a word. Physical attraction, that's all it was. I could spank her."

She looked wistfully at the little boy, then: "Ann—that's my cook—told me that Mary told her that she was smoking too much. We never let her do that. I suppose she feels that now she's married she can do anything."

For a moment she said nothing, then brightened and began to laugh over a prank of her college days at St. Mary's. Night was falling. The nurse had gone and the little boy stirred, the first movement in hours.

"I must take Henry in," she said.

Marsh himself opened the door that night, standing there in the light looking very much like pictures of an English squire throwing wide the doors of his manor. He lead the way to the living room, crossing polished hardwood floors, through French doors into a long wide room which extends the length of the house, with windows at both ends, a wide fireplace in the center and doors on both sides of the fireplace leading into the sun parlor behind. There he indicated a deep chair on one side of the fender which encloses the hearth, reached for a worn meerschaum pipe and began to settle himself.

"I forgot about Mike," he said suddenly, rising. "I'll be back in a minute."

After a brief time he returned, explaining that he had to look after the one-year-old thoroughbred red Irish setter a friend had shipped him from New York. "I'm afraid he's going to be a turkey dog," he sighed, stretching his stocky legs to the fire, his round solid face worried. "I took him out for a walk on the farm this afternoon. He stopped by a ditch and froze just as pretty as a picture. 'Sst! At 'em boy,' I told him. He jumped in the ditch and there was a squawking and beating and out flew—two hens. Then he made a false point. To top it all he walked right through a covey with the wind blowing to him. Nine flew up. He turned around and looked up at 'em like he was wondering what in the world they were. Then the damn fool turned right around and walked back, scaring up eight more birds." He paused, tapping the tobacco into his pipe with a stubby forefinger. "Well, one thing about him: he didn't bark at the birds so maybe he won't be a turkey dog after all."

A short young man about Marsh's height, well-built and almost handsome, came through the dining room door. He is twenty-four but his curly brown hair and ingenuous brown eyes make him look younger. He was dressed in riding breeches and leather lumber-jacket.

"I want to go to the show, Marsh. Lend me a quarter." Jim Taylor spoke in a soft voice and his words were slurred into an almost Negro dialect.

When the boy was gone, Marsh commented about him. "He's no good. Won't work, won't do anything but play around. Father left him $18,000. Know how long it took him to spend it? Just about eighteen months. He is good at that. He can spend more money foolishly and more quickly than anybody I've seen. Well, he was the baby so I reckon he was spoiled. Father made me work. I plowed out in the fields with the hands. I know what the work of farming is like.

"My father was a shipbuilder and farm owner. Captain John Taylor was the first of the tribe to come to this country—in 1639 with a magistrate's commission signed by George II. I was in Massachusetts a few summers ago and went to the old Taylor home there. That commission is framed and hanging on the wall, the first thing you see when you enter the door.

"My great-grandfather landed in North Carolina off a New England vessel, his intentions unknown. All I know about him is that he worked on the Dismal Swamp Canal and married a propertied widow. Grandfather was a merchant and married a Marshall of Kentucky, kin of the Marshalls of Massachusetts—which accounts for my name.

"There were four of us boys, and I'm the oldest. I went to State College in Raleigh and majored in chemistry. Those were the days when they had one way to take a bath, a shower of cold water against the back wall of Culver Hall. Many's the freezing morning I bathed in that icy water."

Marsh talked slowly and deliberately. There was something almost stolid about him, a decided reserve— when he is not among friends. He reached down to feed the fire and the light glowed on his sparse sandy hair. Slate gray eyes complete the picture. Here is a man who will not speak hurriedly nor reveal anything of himself but what he chooses to reveal.

Within six months after graduation from State

College, Marsh was working for Bethlehem Steel at $150 a month. He was with them less than a year when the World War broke out. Dupont offered him a job at $200 a month plus $50 war bonus. When the United States entered the war, Marsh, along with many Dupont men, tried to enlist but found himself placed in the lowest qualification, the one least likely to see action. Dupont was keeping its skilled men at home.

Marsh was working with representatives of the English, French, Rumanian and Russian governments, testing war materials. "A bottle of wine and a woman —the Rumanian representatives would forget anything. So would the French; but then they knew nothing. The British were about the most solid scientists of the lot, but I found the Russians most cultured and highly educated."

Dupont was turning out millions of pounds of gun cotton a day, selling it at $1 a pound. There was an excess profits tax so salaries were high partly to avoid that tax. Marsh was drawing $400 a month and $200 war bonus when the Armistice came. The company dismissed many of their men with two months' pay for every year of service, and transportation home. Marsh was offered a supervisory position in one of the big textile plants but declined.

He had met and was courting Old Man Ben Williams' daughter, Nancy, a pretty young thing just out of St. Mary's College. Mr. Williams sent for him. "What are you making, Marsh? . . . Well, you can support Nancy on that. But she's the only daughter I have. Tell you what I'll do. If you'll settle here with Nancy, I'll give you the Humphrey Farm—750 acres, build you a home here, turn over part interest in the Williams Company and allow you a salary of $100 a month."

Marsh decided it was the thing to do; he loved Nancy, he liked Old Man Ben and the town. Besides, it was a good offer—and Marsh is shrewd.

He likes to talk about the Williamses almost as much as about his own people. Old Man Ben's father owned a farm along the Roanoke River during the Civil War. He didn't like the Civil War; he was willing to free his slaves, and the South couldn't win anyhow. He did send off two sons to battle but there he drew the line; he would not give up his cotton either to the Southern supply division or to the raiding Yankees. There was a mill pond on his place with cypress stumps in the middle of it. Between these stumps he had his slaves erect a platform and place on it more than a hundred bales of cotton, then cover the cotton with brush. The cotton survived the war and laid the foundation for the Williams fortune: Northern buyers paid Old Man Ben's father $50,000 for the precious bales—in gold. Then the first Williams began making loans to less fortunate neighbors and taking mortgages. Soon he was the biggest landowner in the county.

One of those neighbors was Charles Humphrey, owner of rich acres along the river. The Humphreys were a cultured, hospitable people, accustomed to entertaining lavishly. Mr. Williams' loan was never repaid. At Charles' death the mortgage was foreclosed. It was typical of the Williams founder that he sent his surveyor son out to measure off homesteads for the Humphrey heirs so that Charles' children would not be wholly destitute. The third generation of Humphreys still lives on those homesteads, heavily covered by mortgages; they are a disgruntled people with little education and less ambition. It seems that one of their ancestors got a raw deal.

It was this Humphrey Farm that Old Man Ben gave to Marsh Taylor when he married Nancy and came to this town to settle. And the fire before which Marsh is so comfortably settled is in the house which the old man built for him.

"This house cost $17,500," he said solidly, puffing at his huge pipe with a glance around the room. "It's a good house."

Marsh's father died, leaving an estate of $200,000 to be divided among five heirs. Marsh was executor and with typical shrewdness bought in much of his father's property which he considered was selling at too low a price in the settlement. He purchased several of the lots for $9,000. The other heirs thought he was gobbling up the property so he offered them all shares with the exception of the youngest son Jim, a minor, and one brother-in-law of whom he wasn't fond. When the lots were sold shortly afterwards they cleared $5,500.

This money with a few thousand more he deposited in one of the town's two banks, at that time run almost as a family institution by the Martins. Now Marsh has a strict business code. One day in Peter Martin's store a group of men were discussing the owners of great wealth in the county. One they estimated to be worth $2,000,000; another, $1,000,000; and still another, $500,000. Then they got around to Mr. Bob Morgan. They started him off at $500,000 but finally decided that he was worth $250,000. Frank Martin, the bank cashier, who was in the crowd, didn't like Old Man Bob and couldn't stand to see him valued at such a sum. He got up and said, "Well, if Old Man Bob Morgan is worth so damn much I don't see why he don't pay that $5,000 note over at the bank."

Next day Marsh went down to the bank, stopped at the cashier's window.

"How much I got in here, Frank?"

"About $6,000."

"How much exactly?"

"Six thousand four hundred and fifty dollars and sixty cents."

"Well, I want to draw it out."

"Why?"

"Don't see that it's any of your affair. I just want it."

Marsh wouldn't do business with a bank whose officials discussed its depositors' affairs outside. It is such incidents as that which have secured for him the reputation of being a good business man.

During the depression he saw Harry Lawrence, cashier of a Wentworth Town bank, park before the remaining town bank, get out and go in. Now Harry was a good friend of a certain woman who owned lands in the county and had money in that bank. Banks were shaky and Marsh figured that Harry was over checking on the condition of this bank. He waited for the man to come out.

"Harry," he asked, "how did you find it?"

"How in the world did you know what I was doing here? . . . Just guessed, eh? Well, it's in pretty good shape, got a lot more reserve than the law requires. Nope, I don't know the condition of its collateral. Our bank in Wentworth Town is sound as a dollar."

Two days later Marsh opened his paper. There on the front page was a picture of Harry Lawrence, resigning his position for a better one. Marsh got in his car and went to Wentworth Town.

"Got plenty of money, Harry?"

"Sure, why?"

"Well, I'll be needing some, about all I've got."

Harry got red in the face. "Would you just as soon have North Carolina bonds?"

Two months later the bank went broke: Marsh knew that Harry could have no better position than staying in Wentworth Town looking after his family's interests, which totaled over a million dollars.

There was a story circulated around town that Marsh Taylor broke the Bank of Willsport, that he went down the day before it went under and withdrew a whole lard can full of money. Marsh only had $600 in that bank. He was planning a trip to Norfolk and on his way to the store stopped by the bank to withdraw that. He had a lard can in his hand. As it was only a few steps from the bank to the store, he walked a quarter of a block with the lard can in one hand and the $600 in the other. When the bank went under the next day, the rumor spread.

"But when they saw the report on the bank's condition, that rumor died quickly. Moses Martin had let several men in the town borrow thousands of dollars with scarcely any sort of security. Three men had borrowed as much as $13,000 each. One morning I was short of funds and needed about $500. I stopped by the bank with a government bond for $1,000 which expired in two months. 'Moses,' I said, 'I want $500 for a month. Here's the security for it,' and I shoved the bond through the window. He knew that I would clip several thousand in dividends at the first of the year. And besides I had a note up for clearance that came to $4,000. 'Sorry, Mr. Taylor,' he said, 'I simply haven't got it.' That same day John Martin, a Methodist, came in and wanted the same amount. His daughter, Sarah, owned a farm and he told Moses that she would endorse the note. Moses let him have the money. He signed and said that Sarah would come down that afternoon and sign. In the evening Moses saw Sarah passing by. He called her in. 'Here, Sarah, sign this note. Your father said that you'd endorse for him.' 'I'll do no such thing,' she told him. And there Moses was with a note for $500 backed with only John Martin's signature—and he owned no property. That was the sort of business that put that bank under.

"You want to know about the supply business, how I handle my tenants and some personal questions. Suppose we take them in that order.

"First, the Williams Company isn't operated primarily for profit but mostly as a matter of convenience to the tenants and to us. The company is a corporation and is handled apart from the farms. Each of the three of us has a separate account with the store, that is, our tenants do. I am responsible for my tenants' accounts, J. B. for his and Ben for his. Prior to the depression of 1929 we sometimes did a $50,000 business, but since then it has dwindled to half that. We have followed every possible policy of retrenchment. Under present conditions we do not feel that it is good business to try to do a larger amount of business. To be frank, the idea of making money in the farming and farm supply business under present conditions seems vague. The only thing most of us can do is play safe and hold what we already have. And that in itself is a problem.

"As I said, the Williams Company is not run primarily for profit. In good years we each of us draw about $100 a month out of the store. In years like this we aren't entitled to draw over $50. Most of the supply businesses charge the ten percent rate of interest on time accounts allowed by the law. They issue books of coupons and the first thing they do is tear out ten percent of them. It really comes to about eleven and a half percent because those tickets represent trade and so include profit. We do have, along with other such stores, a markup of about ten percent for time price over cash price, making a total profit of over twenty percent. This seems fair to me because whereas the cash merchant can reinvest his money and turn over his stock several times a year our money is invested in that original article all year and there is the risk that we may not get it at all if a bad year strikes.

"Time was when we did some business outside of our tenants under the old two-price system. The time price was marked on the goods in figures. Below it was the cash price in code and above it the cost price, also in code. That proved unsatisfactory however because one of our tenants would come in the store and pay $2.50 for a pair of shoes. Then some Negro paying cash would come in and get the shoes for $2.25. It caused dissatisfaction and we abandoned it. That two-price system was generally abandoned during the early twenties.

"Our company, when it handled outside accounts, never followed the ordinary practice of giving a farm owner a ten percent rebate on his tenants' accounts to get the trade. There was also a practice over which the storekeeper had no control but in which he often cooperated—of selling fertilizer to the owner at such price that he could resell to his tenants at a profit. This practice was broken up by the fertilizer companies themselves, unintentionally. They had two

prices, cash and time. Government loans for seed and
fertilizer make it possible for tenants to receive the
cash price. However, the government checks sometimes are permitted by the tenant to go altogether to
the landlord, who can, if he wishes, continue the practice.

"We think that the less we furnish our tenants, the
less we allow them to run into debt to us, the better off
we are. They would come in the day after settlement
and cart off the whole store if we would let them.
'Boys,' I tell them, 'you just got paid off. Take that
money and live on it until plowing time.' They can
take that cash and buy things they need for their
personal use cheaper at the cash stores than we can
supply it. We don't mind that at all.

"Of course, the store has this advantage for the
landlord: it strengthens his control over the tenants.
When they know they 'gotta see the Boss' for their
needs, they are much more easily handled. The good
landlord can use this to his tenants' advantage and keep
them from going so deeply in debt. Of course, when the
landlord is bad he abuses this power and takes advantage of the tenants. Remember this, though, the
tenants catch on surprisingly quick when they're being
abused.

"I don't mind giving them a little cash every now and
then. But they know they won't get a cent from me
to buy whiskey and gasoline. That leads to stealing.
I can take my dogs and gun and go out hunting right
now and I'd run upon piles of corncobs under the scrub
at the edge of the fields. Some of the Negro boys have
gone into the field and stripped several bushels of
ears, taken them to the woods' edge and shelled them.
There is generally a little filling station along the road

that buys stuff from tenants—corn, peanuts, cotton. The owner pays them about half price and gives them gasoline, whiskey or some cash. Sometimes a merchant in town buys the stuff. Old Man Bob Morgan made thousands on what he bought from tenants when they came into town on Saturdays.

"Sometimes the tenant himself does the stealing. More often it's the boys. They want to go into town and raise hell and the old man won't, and can't, give them money to do it with. They wait until he has gone off and then they go into the shed and take a couple of sacks of peanuts, or down to the hen house for a few fat hens. The mother usually sides with the boys. In good cotton years those devilish boys will get together on moonlight nights and pick out some good field and strip a couple of hundred pounds, bag it and sell it to the 'agricultural fence.' In years like this we aren't bothered with it because it would take all night to pick that much cotton.

"We're not bothered with stealing much anyway, but you always have to discount some loss on account of it. It's men like Peter Martin who really lose from it, men who try to crook their tenants out of every cent they can. Peter Martin is one of those men who jerk out ten percent of his tenants' credit coupons first thing they are issued.

"Take Peter now. He owns a good deal of land, and the next house down the street belongs to him. He's just gone out of the supply business and is on the rocks all way around. One of his girls is working in the bank, another had to quit college and come back here to work. In 1932 conditions were pretty bad. A lot of folks went hungry. The tenants were in a bad way and the landlords hadn't made anything. Martin sold his tenants up the river. An old Negro man came into the store and wanted some stuff for Christmas, a little food, a little cash. 'Hell no,' Peter said. 'I won't give you a goddamn cent. I need what I have for my own family. Now get the hell out of here.' 'Yassuh, Mr. Martin, if that's the way it is I reckin that's all they is to it.' Do you think that Negro was resigned to it? No, sir, that Negro wasn't going to let it lay at that. All he did was to go home to the shed where he had some bags of peanuts stored and take them and sell them, and cotton and corn. There is a law against a tenant transporting cotton at night—but try to catch them when they're 'bagging off' cotton. Well, every one of Peter Martin's tenants followed suit.

"That year a fellow running a service station near Martin's place came in to see me one day. In the office he asked a favor: he wanted me to keep some money for him. I told him to put it in the bank, it was open then to receive deposits as a matter of convenience to local business and was perfectly safe—it could make no loans. He said that there were some judgments against him and that he didn't want anybody to know he had the money. I thought he had a few hundred dollars, knew he had been buying stolen cotton. Well, I consented to keep the money for him and I'm damned if he didn't count out $2,200. When I saw how much it was I told him I would take it only on the condition that I'd be given a week's notice before having to produce it, because if I took it I intended to use it. He said that was all right, all he wanted was a receipt. It was four years before he called for that money. I invested it in town bonds, county bonds and a few North Carolina bonds. They were down pretty low and as a result I now have $4,000 worth of bonds after paying back the original $2,200. Most of that money came from Peter Martin's tenants.

"Now the man who does business like Martin is going to end up on the rocks sooner or later. In 1932 my tenants owed me $16,000. One Negro owed $2,000, many $500 and $1,000. I had no security for this. I called together my thirty-eight tenants, and told them: 'Well, boys, you all owe me a sight of money. I want to tell you one thing: I've got some money—you boys helped me to make it. As long as you stay here and work you're going to get part of it, not all of it but plenty of clothes and enough to keep you going.' I got back all but $1,000 although I did lose about $4,-000 rent along those years. Some of the Negroes on my farms have been there all their lives; some of them are seventy-five and eighty years old. I haven't had a man to leave me in nineteen years.

"Speaking of the store, the only year we charged that ten percent carrying charge was in 1919. Old Mr. Williams did it then because everybody had so much money they didn't know what to do with it. The old man was afraid currency was going down the way it did after the Civil War and took $54,000 and bought a barrel of gold. When things showed signs of clearing up we paid the tenants with that gold. I actually heard a blind Negro talking with one of his poorer colored brothers outside the bank: 'I wants to show you that mah heart is in the right place. I'se going to give you $125.' And he did. Peanuts were selling for five cents a pound. I told old Mr. Williams that things were looking pretty good. 'No, they're not,' he said, 'peanuts aren't worth that much. It's going to make trouble. Niggers won't work when they have money.' But they did and the next year peanuts went up to eleven cents a pound, and trouble did break. The tenants had too much money to want to work. I know now the old man was right: it's just as bad for prices to be too high as it is for them to be too low. An article ought to bring what it's worth. Incidentally the Negroes who started farming in those high price times are much harder to handle than the older farmers.

"Tenants have a craving for luxuries they can't afford. In 1923 all the tenants made money. A one-horse crop would clear $800. Some of my tenants I paid from $400 to $1,300—all clear. Peanuts were selling at seven cents a pound and cotton at forty-five cents. There was not one automobile on the Humphrey Farm. I paid off on a Saturday and went to Norfolk for a few days. When I came back, out of the nine tenants on the Humphrey Farm, seven of them had automobiles sitting under the shed, most of them new. One of the two men who didn't buy was the old Negro who had cleared $1,300.

"That craving for luxuries is a God's blessing—for a select few of us. If they worked and saved their money they'd be landowners. Now I admit that the system which a comparatively few men like myself run doesn't make for a healthy condition, nor is it economically sound. But if the tenants did become landowners it certainly would upset my playhouse and that of others like me. Of course it wouldn't bother me. I'd simply start supplying them. With energy and good sense I simply wouldn't stay poor. Then they wouldn't keep their property long, certainly no longer than the third generation. Particularly the Negroes who inherit property lose it rapidly, which reminds me of this government ownership plan. I believe it is going to fail; the government is giving them too long to pay it off.

I don't believe one piece of land out of a hundred will stay in the hands of the original long-term buyer.

"As for the way I handle my farms, it's generally on halves although I rent some land. When land is rented a crop mortgage is taken. Land rents for around $5 an acre in this section although some people get $8, but that's too much.

"On halves, sharecropping, the landlord usually furnishes half the cost of peanut bags, ginning, picking and fertilizer costs. He furnishes the tenant with house, tools, team, a store account and medical attention. When the tenant owns his own team, the landlord supplies all the fertilizer and leaves the tenant to supply half the harvesting cost and labor.

"Sharecropping on thirds the landlord furnishes land, one-third the fertilizer under money crop, one-third cost of picking peanuts and ginning cotton. He receives one-third the income from the money crops. The tenants supply labor, team and tools, two-thirds of the fertilizer under the money crop, all the fertilizer under the corn, pays two-thirds cost of picking and bagging peanuts and two-thirds cost of ginning cotton. He receives two-thirds and income from money crops and all the corn. This method of farming isn't practiced in this section.

"Methods of working with tenants differ in each locality, due to local peculiarities. The relations between landlord and cotton farmer are somewhat different from those between landlord and tobacco farmer. In this section the tenant is expected to keep up the land, ditching and that sort of thing. But in Currituck and some of the other counties in the northeastern-most part of the state where ditches cut the fields at every fifty feet for drainage purposes, the tenant receives several hundred dollars a year to keep up ditches. There is so much work involved in keeping the land in usable condition that it would be unfair to ask him to do it as part of his regular upkeep duties.

"The tenant secures all his firewood from the woodland that goes with the farm and in addition has as much land as necessary for a garden and usually has a pasture for his stock, pigs, chickens and team.

"In most cases the landlord requires the tenant to put the peanut vines back in the land. That is done because peanut farming takes everything out of the soil and unless the vines are put back the soil will soon be depleted. The tenant is allowed to use as many pea vines as necessary for hay. In that event the vines go back to the land in the form of manure. No, in no event are the peanut vines to be considered as a crop to be sold or taken away from the farm. When growing cotton, corn and tobacco the stalks and some leaves and fodder are left on the land, thus providing some vegetable matter to be put back into the soil.

"Of course the landlord has to keep the buildings on the farm in good repair, because the type of tenant he can secure depends quite a bit on the condition of his farm and buildings. Besides, it would be poor economy for me to let my houses run down. I can't get them to come and tell me when a window light is out. They don't seem to feel at home unless they've got some rags stuffed in the window. It only takes a year to rot out sap timber, and water getting into the mortise of a window sash may start rot which would spread to the sill and from there to the beam beneath the sill: eventually the whole side of that house has to be repaired. I'm not playing the Good Samaritan. I've got common sense enough to keep sound roofs on my houses to keep the water from leaking in on my property.

"I provide medical attention for my tenants whenever they need it and generally the bill runs into several hundreds of dollars each year. It's a strange thing but it seems that the sorriest tenants are always the ones who ail the most. Usually a landlord has a chronic family of ailers, and usually it's the most shiftless family on his place. The Negroes along the river plantations are fairly healthy. Right after the Civil War all the white folks along there moved out because of hemorrhagic fever but the disease never seemed to affect the Negroes. In the last nine years I have had at least 150 children born on my farms. In only six cases was a doctor used; midwives were used in the rest. I never lost a woman."

Marsh rises to his feet and stretches. His pipe is out, having long ago outlasted its hour's capacity of tobacco. "Well, that's the set-up. The thing to do next is to interview some of my tenants. I have two white tenants and only have them because Negroes are no good at raising tobacco. One of them, J. T. White, is leaving me the first of the year; the government's going to help him get a farm. He'd be a good man to see. As for the Negroes, I suppose Clement Humphrey's about the best of the lot. For an average Negro tenant, see Lulu Caldwell, a Negro woman. She wanted to work in the fields suckering tobacco last year. I wouldn't let her but she swore she could stay in there when the last man was toted off."

There were footsteps on the stairs and Mrs. Taylor came in. "If you men are through talking, perhaps I can come in."

"Sure, Nancy, I reckon we're about through," Marsh

told her. "Except you could tell what it feels like to be a farmer's wife!"

"Law, Marsh Taylor, you know I don't know anything about farming," Miss Nancy exclaims. She leaves business entirely to her husband. The last time she was on a farm was "heaven knows when." She has little interest in farming, tenants or business of any kind. "I know it doesn't pay to tell women about business. They can't keep a secret. Marsh is fairly safe with me though because what he says goes in one ear and out the other." In reference to her attitude toward farming and supplying, she says: "They talk about women being so soft-hearted. Let me tell you women are a lot harder-hearted than men."

Miss Nancy doesn't vote; Mr. Marsh is a conservative Democrat and votes a straight Democratic ticket because he believes firmly in the two tenets of old-line Democracy: white supremacy, low tariffs. He does vote liberal in the primaries because he feels that to do otherwise would be throwing away his vote; the socialistic trend is necessary and coming. The best thing is to make it sound and peaceful. He doesn't object to the government's spending relief money because he thinks that in addition to providing needed work for people idle through no fault of their own, he is, as a taxpayer and property owner, paying for security. His property is safe as long as people are housed and fed.

There are two things, among others, of which Marsh is proud: the position he holds as a member of the state's committee on agricultural development, in the service of which he makes frequent trips to Raleigh and Washington, and his membership on the board of trustees of a university.

In the field of secondary education Marsh believes

that vocational training should be much more stressed than it is at the present. Every student ought to have every opportunity to make out of himself what he can. But too many students are going to college who ought to be mechanics, farmers and in other such occupations. He is opposing a grant of $10,000 to the local high school to build a gymnasium because of the debt the county and every town in it has to carry: if one high school had a gymnasium then every other high school would expect the same thing and the expenditure wouldn't be in keeping with the financial status of the local government.

"Nancy is the one to talk to about religion," Marsh is like a boy teasing. "Personally, I don't belong to the church. It's all right for those who want it, I guess. But I'm this way: I know what I think is right and I do it. I don't have to be bribed or bullied to follow my convictions. Then, too, I don't believe in a lot of the things the church teaches. When a man dies, he's dead —and that's the end of him."

"Marsh, you ought to be ashamed of yourself," Miss Nancy attacked. "You know a lot of the women in this town think they'd like to be in my place. They say they wouldn't let Henry chain them down, that they'd put him in the hospital or hire a nurse if they had as much money as we have. If I didn't believe in life after death, I'd take Henry and drown both of us in the river."

Marsh became serious. "You want to know my idea of a good life," he says. "My tenants think that if they were in my shoes they'd be content. I suppose that ordinarily I'd say so too, and work for more money—and power. Now when I come in at night I never know when I'm going to have to stay up until morning. Henry has convulsions without any warn-ings. He goes crazy and I'm the only one who can hold him. I'd swap every stick and stone I own—I'd be more than willing to start all over with nothing if I could wake up in the morning and find Henry a normal boy."

"I would," Miss Nancy said sadly. "Don't talk to me about money: the most important thing in the world is health." She looked steadily at her husband for a moment, then quietly: "It has made Marsh more con-siderate of others—but then he always was that—I can't understand it—"

Miss Nancy brightened up after a few moments. "Marsh," she said gayly, "I want to go to Norfolk tomorrow and do some shopping."

Marsh's expression is one of playful exasperation. "Ever so often I go out to a club we men here in town have about fifteen miles out," he said. "We have a pretty nice place there—rugs, radio, beds and a cellar. We play poker. Somehow Nancy always finds out when I've been and the next day—sure as shooting— she wants to go to Norfolk. Isn't that just like a woman?"

W. S. HARRISON

In Mill Village And Factory

A Day at Kate Brumby's House

THEY STILL CALL HER KATE BRUMBY. SHE SAYS THAT
she was already twenty-four when she married Jim
Sampson, and her neighbors so long accustomed to
addressing her as Kate Brumby kept it up even after
she was married.

Above her mantel there hangs a framed family
record. It is a picture containing garlands of roses,
an open book, and two centrally placed ovals bearing
the words Father, Mother. On the leaf of the open
book the following recordings have been made: Kate
Brumby born Oct. 10, 1878; Jim Sampson born May 9,
1876; Charlie Sampson born Oct. 1, 1902; Jessie
Sampson born June 3, 1905; Ira Sampson born Sept. 5,
1910; Jim Sampson died April 23, 1926; Charlie
Sampson died Aug. 11, 1930.

I went to see Kate the other morning, a brisk October
morning it was, and Kate was dropping a piece of
coal on the fire when I opened the door in response to
her "Come in." When she saw that I was not a neighbor, she got up and came toward me apologetically.
"I thought you was one of Stella Roberson's children,"
she explained. "Set down in that chair. Spot, git
down and let the lady have a seat. When Iry or company ain't here the kitten restes in that chair while I
set in this one. Me and him both is pretty lazy, I
reckin."

It was nine o'clock in the morning and Kate's house had already been put in order for the day. The room in which we sat had not been difficult to straighten. It contained an iron bed, an old Singer sewing machine, a small walnut table and the two rocking chairs before the fire. Sweeping must have been the most difficult job she had to perform because the floor was old and splintery. Many bright colored pictures, most of them calendars, were nailed to the dingy gray walls, but, firmly fixed against the walls as they were, they added nothing to the burden of housekeeping. After finishing with her room there was only Ira's room and the kitchen to put in order.

Kate had arisen at six-thirty in order to have Ira's breakfast ready when he got in from the mill. Breakfast over, house-cleaning finished, and pinto beans in the pot ready to boil for dinner, she had begun at 9 o'clock to sit the morning away. "I'm glad you come by," she said as I rocked slowly in my chair. "I like compny, fer the days is long since I got disabled to work in the mill." She gave a quick, throaty chuckle which was a spontaneous expression of her pleasure at having someone to talk to, and then lapsed into silence.

Her little, grayish brown eyes caught up the firelight and shone with a brightness like eyes belonging to some woods animal. Though not actually very small, they looked somehow like tiny bright openings in her narrow face. All of Kate's teeth were gone, and because there had been no false ones to replace them her chin had turned upward with an apparent determination to meet her nose. Her thin and graying red hair was combed tightly up and twisted into a flat knot on the top of her head. She wore a print dress of beet-red with a tiny white figure, and bedroom slippers of sky-blue felt.

"Have you lived very long at the Spring Road Mill?" I asked.

"Since it were first started," Kate said. "The Brumbys was up there on opening day to help break in the machinery. Old Mr. Hall owned the Alberta Mill where we worked and he got us to move here. He wanted families that he knowed was good workers to start his new mill.

"Ma moved to the cotton mill when I were nine year old. There w'an't nobody to work then but me and her and Alice. Pa, he was deformed, and he couldn't do no work like that, though he had as clever a turn as you ever seen at some things. He walked on his knees —born that way, you know. The rest of his leg dragged on the ground and his foot turned out. Ma had six children by him and not a one of us was deformed.

"Pa had a good education and he teached some sort of school once up in Rockridge County where he was born. They was eleven in his family and granpa owned his own farm. Pa had books too, but he got shet of all of 'em but one. Hit's old, awful old, and somebody told me once that if I'd write off to the American Book Mart I'd find out I could git a right smart fer it. I told 'em maybe so, but not as much as that book was wuth to me. I'll git it and show it to you. I keep it in the drawer of my wa'nut table that Pa made.

"Uh, uh, I liked to fell. I ain't got good used to them bedroom slippers yet. Iry jest got 'em Saturday and they've got a little more heel than them others I had. Here 'tis, right in the drawer where I put it. Hit's so old it's turned yellow. You can see fer yourself when it was printed."

I took the small book from Kate's hand, opened it and read:

Christian Psalms and Hymns:
To Aid In
Public and Private Devotion
selected and arranged
By Jasper Hazen
Albany, N. Y.
Published for the Association
1849

On the fly leaf written in brown ink were the words:

Joshua Brumby
his book
October the 19 day 1850

I turned a leaf and read the Foreword in which Isaac Watts, Wesley, Doddridge, Newton, and Montgomery were listed as contributors.

"It's a nice book," I said, looking up at Kate. "I guess you've read in it many times."

"Not nary time," Kate said solemnly as she looked at me with her small, bright eyes. "I've got no education atall.

"I woulder had if Pa hader lived," she continued presently. I had given her back the book and she sat there holding it with both her hands. "He learnt me some spellin', and how to write my name, but hit were sech a little bit I knowed that in time I fergot it all.

"As I told you, I w'an't but nine when I went to work in the mill, and when I'd come home of a night I never felt much like learnin'. Sometimes Pa'd make me do a little spellin' but I never done so well at it. Then Pa died when I was twelve, and after that they weren't nobody to try to learn me. Ma never had a day's schoolin' in her life but she worked as hard fer her family as any woman I ever knowed.

"Ma was a Rivers, born in Catawba County. Her Pa owned a little farm there before the Rebel War. His two sons was killed in that war and it seems plumb funny to me they had to go. Grandpa Rivers never owned no slaves nor Grandpa Brumby neither. Truth to tell none of my folks never did. Like I asked my brother one day, have you ever knowed of any niggers in this part of the State taking the name Brumby or Rivers? Just the same them uncles had to go and they both got killed. Grandpa Rivers sold his farm or lost it one— I don't know which—and moved to Rockridge County. He died soon after; that left granny and Ma to git a livin' the best way they could. It wasn't long until Ma met Pa and they was married.

"Pa's old maid aunt—Nora was her name—died and willed him a house and a little land at Grantland Depot. That's how Ma and Pa happened to come to this county. Pa made might nigh all the furniture they had in the house and it was pretty too. Beds outa white maple, and not a one of 'em in the family now. Ma sold 'em durin' hard times.

"Pa provided us a decent livin' even if he was deformed. He made furniture, horse collars, and shoes. I've set up many a day all day long placin' pegs fer him to drive in the holes he'd made with a awl. He fastened the soles and the uppers together with wooden pegs, you know.

"Ma, she worked in the field and raised a good part of what we eat. She could plough as good as any man and she was never one fer shirkin' work—no kind of work. Of course when she married she brought granny along, her not havin' nowhere else to go.

"Granny had turned blind by the time I come along, had big cataracts on both eyes. A quare sort of thing happened to her and she got to where she could see fer awhile. She were comin' outa the kitchen and she dropped her knittin'. When she reached down to pick it up she hit one eye on the end of a chair post. In a few days, when it quit hurtin' her so, she was gettin' a little glimmer of light through that eye. Not long after that, granny went out with me and my sister to gather some peaches. Alice, she were up in the tree ready to shake it when she hollered to granny not to look up. For some reason though, granny done jest what Alice had told her not to, and a big, hard peach come down and hit her ka-plop right in the other eye. And I want you to know that fer a while granny could see well enough to know when a person was before her vision though she couldn't recognize who it was. What had happened, them cataracts had busted. Once they growed back she were in plumb darkness and she never had sight agin.

"I done a awful mean thing to the poor old woman and her helpless blind too. I've thought about it many a time since and wondered what ever made me do sech a thing. Granny smoked a pipe, a clay pipe with a long reed handle. It were my job always to fill that pipe and I got mighty tired of it. One day when Ma was out in the field, and the little children was outa doors playin'—I was about eight then myself—time come to fill the pipe. I knowed it was comin' and I'd set there and thought this meanness out. I tuk that pipe and cleaned it out real good. In the bottom I put a little tobacco and then I went over to the powder horn hangin'

on the wall. I put a little pinch of powder in on top
of the tobacco, thinkin' all the time I mustn't put
enough to hurt granny. I put tobacco on top of that
and handed it to her.

"Granny started puffin'. I remember jest as well
how she looked, a old woman her eyes closed up with
them cataracts and her hunched over puffin' at that
long-handled pipe. 'Pu, pu, pu, pew,' she was sayin'
between each draw. And I was settin' there as still as
a mouse, waitin' and gettin' a little bit scared. 'Pu,
pu,—pew,' granny kept sayin' with her pipe. But
even that puffin' didn't seem to make a real sound in the
room. Hit were quiet, awful quiet. Then of a sudden
they was a loud pop and the bowl of that pipe went in
one direction and the stem in t'other. When granny got
settled good enough to speak she said, 'All right, young
lady, when your mammy comes you'll pay fer that.'
Mama come in at dinner time and granny told her what
I'd done. She looked at me and she said, 'What made
you do sech a thing, Kate?' And all I could answer
was, 'To have some fun, Ma.' 'I'll learn you how to
have fun,' Ma said. She jerked me up and give me sech
a floggin' I ain't forgot it till yet. Worst part of it
all, though, granny never would let me light her pipe
fer her as long as she lived.

"Granny died just before we moved to the mill—
the Carona Cotton Mill down on the river. Ma had
already got jobs fer me and her and Alice. She drawed
25¢ a day and we drawed 10¢ apiece a day. Pa stayed
at home with the children. It was winter time when
we first went there and we started to work by lantern
light and quit by lantern light, the kerosene lanterns
swinging down from the ceiling. I never seen no electric
lights until we moved to Hopsonville two year later.

The first mornin' I went in the mill I kept alookin' up wonderin' what on earth them things was. I walked over to the woman I was to work with and I asked her, 'What sort of bugs is them up there on the ceilin'?' That sure tickled her and she never let me forget it long as I stayed there.

"Pa died the first year we was at Hopsonville. His death was jest the beginnin' of a long, hard time. Clarence had growed big enough to go in the mill, makin' four of us to draw money. Come summer, Alice tuk the typhoid. Then Clarence. Ma had to stay outa the mill to wait on 'em. That left lone me makin' 10¢ a day fer the family to live on. But the neighbors was awful good to us and they brought in rashins. If they hadner we woulder starved, I reckin. Alice was still awful puny when she went back to the mill. And the very day she went to work I tuk down with the fever. It was hard times fer us and hard on poor Ma.

"I must've been around fourteen when we left Hopsonville fer Alberta. But before we left Hopsonville I'd learnt that a little grit'll help a body along. I hadn't been back to work long after the typhoid when I went to my boss and done straight talkin'. 'I think I'm wuth more than 10¢ a day,' I said to him. And he raised me to 20¢. Ma had got up to 50¢ and he raised Alice same as he did me. I was around 15 when Mr. Hall got us to move here to Spring Road to help open up. I've been here off and on ever since. I've been in this one house nigh on to 20 year. Hit oughter be mine by now.

"Hit ain't been long ago I said to Robert Hall—him and his brother Albert runs the mill now—'You oughter make me a deed to my house.' He answered right quick and said, 'Well, I'll send you the bill for the paint when we paint it.' As you can see it ain't been painted yet—and I disremember jest the last time it did git paint. Hit's a awful dingy little shanty but hit's been home to me fer a right smart while.

"Come on out on the back porch and I'll show you my flowers. I've got three peach trees out there, too, that I planted when they was nothin' but seedlings. They bore right good peaches this year."

Kate got up to put her book in the table drawer. "Wish Pa hader kept more of 'em," she said as she turned away from the table and led the way through the kitchen to her back porch. Out there around the edge of the floor were ten or twelve cans and buckets containing flowers, some of which had never grown since they were set out as cuttings. But there was one bright coleus, luxuriant with life, and when I looked at it, Kate said, "That's my prize. Hit's growed from the first and ain't slacked since. Some of these others ain't done so well but I like tendin' to 'em, coaxin' 'em along sorta. And I planted them flowers you see out there in the yard too. Digging's hard on me but I do love flowers, I shore do. I had my womb tuk out about 15 year ago and I ain't been much fit for heavy work since. But I'd dig a while and rest a while. You can see bunched over there together them October pinks and marygolds and bachelor buttons. They are about gone now but I've had a sight of blooms from 'em. I had petunias scattered all over the place and they was colorful all through the summer. A neighbor give us them three burning bushes the past spring. I set that poplar out myself about fifteen year ago. They call it a London poplar."

"I see you have a vegetable garden," I remarked.

"Yes, a piece of one. Iry ain't no good atall fer workin' in a garden. Truth to tell, he jest won't do it. I dug up a little patch and planted a few hills of okry and corn and tomatoes. Right over there I had beans planted, but a neighbor ploughed that patch fer me. Hit made pretty good beans too."

We stood there for awhile in silence while the warm October sunshine beamed down on us and dispelled to some extent the chilliness of the accompanying breeze. "Haint the sunshine good?" Kate said presently. "And the fresh air too. Most days even through the winter I put on my old bonnet and sweater and come out here and set awhile. I caint get along like some folks without fresh air.

"That's half of what's wrong with Jessie's baby. Livin' like they do up there above the old bus station with jest one window in the whole place. I went up there the other day and told Hugh—that's Jessie's husband—he jest had to git them younguns out from there and move 'em to a place where they could play around on the ground sometimes. Poor little things, cooped up there with no place atall to play. I forget what the doctor calls what the baby's got, but he says the white cells is eatin' up the red cells. I think half of what's wrong with it is she's needin' fresh air and sunshine.

"The baby was puny when Jessie first brought it down here from New York. Hugh had got work up there somewhere in a cotton mill and was makin' a good wage but the mill shet down. That's why they come back home. While they was up there Jessie's second baby were born. Hit were jest three month old when she brought it down here and the puniest lookin' thing you ever seen, and it born in a hospital up there too.

Well, when she come in the door I looked at it and said, 'Jessie, what on earth's ailin' your baby?' And she said, 'I don't know, Ma, it never has done no good.' 'Hit's starvin' to death,' I said. 'I'll put it on Borden's milk and you'll see a change in no time.' And sure enough, the little thing growed off real healthy. But since they started livin' above that old bus station it's got as puny as it were to start with. Hugh'll shore have to rent a place where them children can git outa doors. Course, he don't make much, workin' fer the PWA but they can do without somethin' else and git a house to live in.

"I've got a picture of Jessie's oldest, and she's shore a pretty youngun. Come on in and I'll show it to you."

Back in Kate's room I looked at the picture of a bright-faced, curly haired child dressed in a fluffy white dress, slippers, and socks. "She is very pretty indeed," I said as Kate stood waiting.

"It was tuk when she were two year old," she said. "She's four now and jest as pretty as ever. Stella Roberson says she's the prettiest youngun she ever seen. Stella'll more'n likely come over this evenin'. She gen'ly comes to see me fer a little while every day."

While I sat there listening to Kate talk of other things which made up her daily life Ira came from his room where he had been sleeping since breakfast.

"What's wrong? Caint you sleep?" Kate asked. "Taint twelve yet. That's my youngest," she continued, turning toward me.

Ira looked at me and nodded in a solemn sort of way, and then went into the kitchen to get himself a chair.

Ira was about six feet two inches in height, measuring straight and not around the slouchy stoop of his shoulders. His eyes of indefinite blue were not so small nor bright as his mother's. There was nothing of brightness in his long, expressionless face except the occasional suggestion of a smile which invariably faded away before reaching its full-grown proportions.

"You never put on your brown suit," Kate said to Ira. "I bet you're waitin' to put on your new one to wear up town," she finished, giving her characteristic throaty chuckle with its underlying metallic tones.

"Naw I ain't," Ira replied, annoyed. "I may not even go to town today."

"Thought you'd have to go to make the paymint on your suit." Then turning to me Kate continued. "Mr. Howard sent Iry a letter not long ago sayin' he had some awful good suits for twenty-seven dollars and a half, and he was throwin' in a pair of shoes with every suit. When Iry read the letter he said, 'Mama, I believe I'll git me a suit. Hit's just two dollars down plus tax, and a dollar a week.' I said 'Well Iry, think twice before you act because they's a sight of things has to be paid fer already outa them twelve dollars a week you make.' Hit ended with him gittin' a plumb pretty suit—oxford gray, 'tis. I try to git him to wear the brown one he got last winter, and hold off that new one till Christmas."

Ira rammed his hands deeper into his overall pockets, pushed his chair back on its hind legs, and said nothing.

"I threatens him every now and agin with gettin' me a job," Kate continued as she looked at me. "I am a old rat at the barn, but I believe I could still do mill work if they'd let me."

"If I hear of you goin' out askin' fer a job I'll quit work and you'll have to take care of me," Ira said, coming very close to a smile.

"They wouldn't have me nohow," Kate replied dryly.

"Once a person breaks down in health and goes back fer his job, they always say they ain't got one fer him. I broke down at fifty and I've never got back in the mill. I missed it too fer a long time because it was all I really knowed how to do.

"But I'm here to tell you I learned mill work from a to izm. I could do anything they was to do but run the cards and the lappers. In them days machinery weren't speeded up and a body could catch up with his work and go over to see what his neighbor was doing. When I went avisitin' I went alearnin'. That's why they could put me in pretty near any part of the mill and I could hold down the work."

"There's sure no chance now to learn anything but the job they put you on," Ira said. "You don't never catch up with your work enough to go see what the other fellow is doin'. Weaving's the job I first learnt in the mill but I don't get to do that. They use me fer a handy man because I don't grumble when they tell me to do odd jobs of cleanin' and such. They keep promisin' me some looms but I don't never get 'em. A man can make a decent livin' weavin'."

"I could weave, I could shore weave," Kate declared. "Ma and all her children was good hands in the mill. Old man Terry Dugan would tell you that if he was livin'."

"Well, Ma, I got to go on down to the mill to get my check," Ira interrupted. "I'll be back by dinner time."

"Lordy me, I'd better see if them pintos is boiled dry," Kate said as she got up from her chair. "I put a heap of water in 'em but they've been cookin' a long time. Come on in the kitchen and you can talk while I make bread," she continued. "As fer that, I can talk and make bread too. I hope you'll stay fer dinner."

"I really should be going," I said, following Kate into the kitchen. "It's nice of you to ask me though."

"I don't blame you fer not stayin' fer we don't have no fine rashins. You maybe couldn't eat what we'll have noway."

"Oh, I'm sure I'd enjoy eating with you," I said, "but I really ought to be going in a few minutes."

"If you don't think the rashins is too sorry fer you. I'll be disappointed if you don't stay. I'm gonna lay a plate fer you anyhow."

With the matter of whether or not I should stay to dinner still unsettled between us, I settled myself in a chair and watched Kate as she moved about the kitchen. After adding water to the pinto beans she began to sift flour for biscuit.

"Yessir, Terry Dugan was sure one to know whether or not us Brumbys was good workers or not," Kate said as she knocked the sifter with the edge of her hand. "Back in 1917 we had already worked fer him 25 year. Tell you how come I remember that so well.

"Jim Sampson was workin' over at Oak River that year and he wasn't at home much of the time. I'd tuk boarders off and on fer years, and one day Clara Brown come to me and said she wanted to board at my house. She was stayin' with Thelma Branson and she said Thelma were mean to her. I told her I'd make room fer her, and I never thought no more about it until I seen Thelma comin' to my alley not so long before dinner time. She walked up to me and said, 'So you've tuk my boarder.' I answered right quick, 'I've done no sech a thing. Clara come to me and asked to be tuk in.' 'Well, I'll whup you at dinner time,' Thelma said and frisked away.

"I knowed they was liable to be trouble so I went to

Terry Dugan. He was a big, red-faced Irishman, who'd been superintendent fer the Halls at Alberta and then Spring Road. He never spoke like we do, and it was funny to hear him roll my name around on his tongue.

"I said to Terry Dugan, 'The Brumbys have worked fer you a right smart while, ain't they?'

" 'For to be sure Ka-ty,' he said. 'It's all of 25 year you've worked for me.'

" 'I'd like to know if you think we've been good hands,' I said to him.

" 'The Brumbys have been fine workers and givin' me no trouble atall,' he said.

" 'Thelma Branson is threatenin' to whup me because her boarder is comin' to my house,' I told him then.

"Old man Terry Dugan looked at me right hard before he spoke. Then he said, 'You ain't bein' afraid of her, are you Ka-ty?'

" 'No, I'm not,' I said to him right quick.

"Terry Dugan straightened up in his chair and he said, 'Stay out of trouble if you can, Ka-ty, but if Thelma comes botherin' you, give her all you've got in your shop.'

"Well, dinnertime come. I was goin' home to dinner, botherin' nobody atall. Thelma, she come along and kept runnin' up against me like a rooster. At first I paid her no attention. But Thelma was itching fer a fight and she wouldn't leave me alone. All of a sudden I decided not to take it no longer. And when she come sidin' up to me agin I were ready fer her. I hauled away and slapped her and it never tuk but that one blow to knock her down.

"That day at quittin' time, Terry Dugan called all the Bransons in and give 'em their time. It was two or

three year before they ever got on at this mill agin.
When they did come back me and Thelma was jest as
friendly as anything. I don't know where Thelma's
livin' now.

"Yessir, I've been at Spring Road fer a long time.
Of course, I were off with Jim Sampson a year or so
every now and then, and they was one year I spent in
South Carolina when I were 17 year old."

Kate's reference to her stay in South Carolina seemed
to draw her against her will into silence. The kitchen
was full of quietness except for the occasional thump
against the cook table of the bowl in which Kate kneaded
her dough. I looked around the kitchen at the cleanly-
scrubbed pans hung against the wall. There was a
gourd too, and a string of dried red peppers. There
was a squatty brass kettle with a cover over its spout
which looked like a chicken's head. The old-fashioned
tin safe in the corner had sometime in its past acquired
two upper glass doors. From the shelves inside hung
lace paper doilies, held in place by blue flowered bowls.
Over in another corner a big wooden box, raised from
the floor by iron legs, served as a place for storing quilts
and old clothes not in use. Kate's cook table was large
enough to hold a small tub of water, and to give her
working space too. A shelf across from the table held a
bucket of water for drinking purposes.

"Where do you get your water from?" I asked Kate,
suddenly realizing that there were no water pipes in the
kitchen.

"From a well out there by the side of the house. It's
awful convenient fer me, havin' the well close by. Some
of 'em livin' on this hill has to tote water fer a long
way."

Kate talked on while she pinched off big wads of

dough placing them in the long black pan and patting them down with the back of her hand. "No rollin' pin and fancy cut-out biscuit fer me," she said. "I cook 'em thick too, so's they'll be a heap of crumb. Little thin biscuits wa'n't meant fer gummin'," she continued, laughing at herself as she spoke.

Just as Kate started toward the stove with her pan now filled and ready for baking, she looked up at me and gave a quick, loud chuckle. "Lordy me, I don't know where in the world my manners has been all mornin'. Rest your hat."

Laughing with Kate I removed my hat and put it on a near-by chair post.

"Dinner'll be ready in a little while," Kate said. "Iry oughter be gittin' in soon."

I had when I removed my hat unconsciously accepted Kate's invitation to dinner. Before long the odor of baking biscuit began to mingle with that of the boiling pinto beans. I made up my mind they'd go very nicely together.

When Kate had got the fly swatter down off the safe, and killed to her complete satisfaction the only fly in the kitchen, she drew up a chair in front of the stove, and resumed her conversation.

"I've got a bowl of stewed apples too," she said. "Nearly every day I cook Irish potatoes and pintos, and I'm glad when I have a change. We don't care much fer meat and I reckin it's a good thing we don't. On the little bit Iry makes we couldn't buy steak and roast, and sech like. Iry gits him a little mess of liver puddin' near bout every pay day and that's all the meat we buy. I don't like it myself and it gen'ly lasts him fer two meals. The doctor tells me to eat chicken and fish. I get my chicken when I go to a supper at the church—and fish too if you count oysters. The members of my class know I ain't makin' nothin' now and they don't expect me to pay. I go over and stay all day to help with the work and that pays fer my meal.

"What we have we uses and what we don't have we do without. I don't believe in makin' no big debts. Hit's jest been fer the past three months that Iry has had regular work. Fer five or six month he'd been gettin' one, two, or three days a week. We done what we could during work times to prepare fer short times. We'd buy up flour, lard, and coffee knowin' we could make out if we had bread and coffee. But one time when things was so bad and the mill wa'n't runnin' atall we never had even bread in the house. I went up to Robert's office and I said, 'Robert, I'm hungry.' He looked at me jest like he never knowed what to say fer a minute, and then he spoke, 'Miss Kate, haven't you got anything to eat at your house?' I said, 'Not a bite.' He run his hand down in his pocket and pulled out a ten-dollar bill. He said, 'Miss Kate, go buy yourself somethin' to eat.' Robert Hall's a good-hearted man. I've knowed him ever since he was a child.

"Last year I was sick with the bloody flux, been in bed from Tuesday to Saturday. I hadn't had no doctor, and I kept hopin' I could pull through without one. Then Saturday morning in come Dr. Brown and asked me how I were gettin' along. Said he'd heard I were a little sick and he thought he'd come to see about me. It turned out Robert had heard about me bein' sick and he sent the doctor. That evenin' Robert hisself come by. When he left here he went by the store and ordered chicken soup and fruit juices and told 'em to bring it up here to me. I hadn't been able to stand the thoughts of eatin', but when Stella fixed that chicken

soup up it looked good. I eat a few spoonfuls and from
that I got to where I could take other rashins. Hit were
jest the thing I needed.

"There's Iry comin' and jest in time. The biscuits
is done and I'm hongry, ain't you?"

"I believe I can eat all right," I said. I watched
Kate pour the steaming beans, the color of dried locusts,
into a big yellow bowl. She went over to the safe and
got the bowl of stewed apples, left there from yesterday's dinner. She took from the oven the big crumby
biscuits browned to dark gold on top, and put them on
a thick, big-flowered plate. She opened a pint jar of
relish, stuck a spoon in it and placed it close to the
beans. While Ira was washing his hands in the tin
pan beside the waterbucket, she filled three enormous
cups with coffee and placed them in deep saucers at the
three places she had set when we first came in.

"Pull up to the table," Kate said to me, and I did.
Ira came presently and took his place just as his mother
sat down. Kate placed her hands together, held them
close against the edge of the table, and bowed her head.
"Dear Lord, make us thankful fer what we are about to
receive, and fer all the blessings we receive at Thy hand.
In Jesus name we ask it, amen." Her blessing finished,
Kate began to dip up the pinto beans into blue flowered
bowls, passing one to me and then one to Ira. "Here's
a spoon," she said to me. "I forgot to put one at your
place."

"Try some of my ketch-up in them beans," she continued, passing the pickle relish to me. "Hit helps 'em
out a whole lot."

I mixed the pickle into the beans as Kate directed
me, reached for one of the big biscuits; I bit into it and
found it good in spite of its size. We sat there, the

three of us, without much talk for awhile and ate our pinto beans and biscuits.

"A man workin' as hard as I do oughter make $15 a week," Ira said after conversation had been dead for three or four minutes.

"We could make out pretty well with that much," Kate said. "Buy meat now and then, though neither one of us is much of a hand fer it."

"They could pay me that much too," Ira continued as he scooped up a spoonful of beans. "The mill's makin' money and I know it. They sell enough cloth."

"Them Halls has always made money," Kate said presently. "They've sure got fine houses. Robert's and Albert's two old-maid sisters got the brick that had been used in the old Allendale Mill to build their house. The brick must've been all of a hundred year old, and I was sure tickled at Rosa Smith when me and her went by to see the house while they was still building on it. Rosa looked at it fer a few minutes and then she said, 'Why, it looks old before they finish it.' I said, 'Well, Rosa, that's jest the way they want it to look. It's a an-tick house.' Rosa said, maybe so, but she never wanted no new house lookin' old. It was sure fine on the inside too, all fixed up with wa'nut panelling."

"I seen Rosa when I went after my check," Ira said to Kate. "She's gettin' up a Larkin order and she said she'd be by this evenin' to see if you wouldn't give her one."

"I do need a pair of scissors like they sell to cut my fingernails with," Kate said.

We finished our beans and Ira excused himself, saying he wasn't very hungry today.

I could not drink Kate's coffee. It tasted like the odor of molding cornstalks, and while the odor was not particularly offensive to my nostrils it was definitely so to my palate. "Don't you drink coffee?" Kate asked me, observing that I had not drunk any after the first sip.

"Too much coffee is not good for me," I answered.

"Hit don't hurt me," Kate replied, and reached for my cup of coffee. She poured it into her deep saucer and began to drink.

When we had finished with dinner I offered to help Kate with the dishes but she insisted that she'd rather do them by herself, and suggested that I go into her room where I could have a more comfortable chair. While Kate washed the dishes I sat and looked at the smiling picture of Dick Powell which hung by its frame from a nail placed directly in the corner and above the walnut table.

It was not long until Kate joined me, and by the time she had seated herself and had her mouth comfortably filled with snuff Ira came from his room to say he was ready to write down the grocery list. He sat down, paper and pencil in hand, and waited for Kate to speak.

"Flour's got to come this week," she said. "Put down pinto beans and dried butterbeans too. I've got enough potatoes to carry me through. Three cans of Pet milk, and two pounds of lard."

"Anything else?"

"My snuff."

"I'll get some liver puddin' too."

"I reckin so, but jest enough fer yourself. I don't want none."

"Is that all?"

"I'd like to have a dozen eggs but they are awful high and hard to git. You might git some turnip greens too, if he's got any."

Just as Ira folded the list and put it into his pocket someone knocked on the door, opened it, and came in.

"Let me make you acquainted with Stella Roberson," Kate said to me. "She lives right across the road."

Stella was a pale-faced woman of perhaps twenty-five. She had supplied herself with a generous dip of snuff which gave a slight fullness to one side of her face. Presently her four-year-old daughter came in and leaned against her mother's knee.

"I sent her up to the Baptist Sunday School Sunday, but she never liked it," Stella said as she brushed the child's hair back from her forehead.

"You ought to send her to the Methodist," Kate said, chuckling. "I bet she'd like our Sunday School."

"Law, the Baptist have been carryin' on a real revival," Stella stated. "Rains is sure a strict one. He don't believe in folks goin' to no picture shows atall."

"And I don't neither," Kate spoke decisively. "Hit's wrong."

"Why do you think so?" I asked.

"Because it's the devil's territory," Kate replied promptly. "If eternity should come and you'd be caught on the devil's territory what hope could you have? Do you go to shows?" she questioned me.

"Yes," I admitted. "I don't feel that it's wrong."

"Have you ever got down on your knees and asked God if it was wrong?" she wanted to know.

"No, I really haven't," I answered.

"Well, when you do he'll let you know it's wrong."

"Some folks says the Bible speaks against snuff-dippin'," Stella Roberson said as she spat into the tin can close to her chair.

Kate waited a full half minute before she spoke.

"Well, I've never heard it were a sin, and the Lord's never told me it was."

"Have you ever asked the Lord if it was wrong?" Stella wanted to know.

"No I ain't," Kate admitted, "but good as I love it I could quit snuff if I knowed it was sinnin's to use it."

"The Bible says it's a sin to eat anything that parts the hoof and don't chew the cud," Ira said. "And most folks sure do that."

"We ain't tempted none with breakin' that part of the scripture," Kate said. "They's very little meat comes into this house and no hog meat atall."

I sat there thinking of the fat meat with which Kate had seasoned her beans, and decided that hog meat to her must mean pork chops, ham, or bacon.

"Rains's against Christmas trees in churches," Stella said.

"We have one every year at our church," Kate said. "You've got to do somethin' to entice little children to Sunday School, and they shore oughter be there."

Kate and Stella and Ira sat very quiet for awhile, each one seemingly trying to bring out of memory some miraculous portion of scripture which condemned the habits of mankind. Kate spoke first.

"If you go to Deuteronomy you'll see it's wrong fer a woman to bob her hair," she said. Then looking at me she asked, "Have you always wore your hair long?"

"Since I was a child," I replied, quite pleased to gain back some of the prestige I had lost in admitting that I attended picture shows.

"Well, Deuteronomy says that your hair is your glory and you are the glory of man. If a woman cut her hair let her also shave."

Stella toyed nervously with the bobbed ends of her

permanent and could think of no defense to offer for them.

"Sometimes I'm afraid to do almost anything," she said after awhile.

"You'll have to try to get over some of your fears," I said hoping to be both helpful and unoffending. "Fear can keep us from enjoying life."

"But how you goin' to do it?" Stella inquired.

"Fight against it," Kate said quickly. "Jest keep sayin' to yourself, 'I won't be afraid, I won't be afraid.' Hit helps."

"I'm honestly afraid to be in the house a minute after dark when Paul ain't at home, and he has to work at night."

"I stay here by my lone self and don't mind it atall," Kate said.

"You know you don't like it, Ma," Ira said. "I'd get somebody to stay with you at night if I could."

"Well of course hit's a lonesome time to set here by myself, it bein' human nature to want company, but I sure ain't afraid, I sure ain't.

"Them's good rules to go by," Kate continued, pointing to the red felt square above her bed on which were written in white letters, "Rules for Today." "I caint read it but I know what it says."

Stella and I both turned our eyes toward the bed and read silently:

"Do nothing that you would not want to be doing when Jesus comes.

"Go to no place where you would not like to be found when Jesus comes.

"Say nothing that you would not like to be saying when Jesus comes."

And while we were reading Rosa Smith came into the room with her Larkin Plan Book. After Kate had introduced Rosa to me and she had greeted the remainder of the group, Stella got up to leave. "You needn't be runnin' from me, Stella, because I've already got your order," Rosa said with a high, fluty laugh.

"Paul's got to eat before he goes on at three," Stella explained, "and it's past two now."

Rosa had heavy black hair, drawn back into a ponderous knot on the back of her head. Her face was lean and narrow, and taken with the rest of her head reminded me of a picture too small for its frame. Before she opened her order book she talked lengthily of her bad health while she moved about in her chair with the alertness of a sparrow.

"I've had all my teeth pulled since I seen you, Kate. We was over at Grantland then, and my health got down to nothin'. The doctor said I was being slowly poisoned to death with pyorrhea. Then on top of that I took the old pellagra and I got so nervous I thought for sure I'd lose my mind. I actually got so weak I'd give out before I walked from my house to the mill, and Frank bought a old trap of a car to take me in. I worked when I couldn't hold up my head for long at a time. Every few minutes I'd go and lean over on the doff box till a little strength would come back to me, and I'd go at it agin. Frank tried his best to make me stay at home but it seemed like I just had to work.

"When I'd got down to eighty-five pounds I went and had all my teeth took out and some false ones made."

"How much did them cost you?" Kate asked.

"Fifty dollars."

"Hunh, I guess I'll keep on a-gummin', then. I'd

thought maybe I might git some in a few year but if they cost like that I ain't likely to."

"I thought I'd never get mine paid for, but I was sure glad to have them old diseased teeth outa my mouth. I felt sorta like the girl I heard about one time. Her teeth never looked to be in bad shape, but everytime she eat anything sweet they ached her pretty near to death. She went to the dentist and said, 'Clean 'em out, but put 'em aside somewhere and save 'em for me.' The dentist thought that was awful queer but he saved 'em for her, and she wrapped 'em up and took 'em home. She went in the kitchen, spread them teeth on a newspaper, and poured molasses all over 'em. She said to the teeth, 'Ache now, damn you, ache.' I felt like saying to mine, 'Make me puny now if you can, make me puny if you can.'"

All of us joined Rosa in her laughter.

When the laughter had died away Rosa got down to business. "I'm gettin' up a eleven dollar and a half order, Kate, so's I can get me a rug. I knew you'd want to take somethin' from me."

"I've been wantin' some scissors to cut my fingernails with and they've got some in the Larkin book that's good fer sech. Jessie used to have a pair when she worked in the weaveroom, and whenever she'd bring 'em home I'd get 'em and trim my nails. Give me the book, Rosa. I think I know jest where they are."

"I've got six dollars and a half on it already," Rosa said as Kate looked for the scissors. "I sure hope I can finish it because I'm needin' the rug bad and I ain't able to buy one. The mill at Grantland was shut down for so long and when it started up it curtailed for so long that we got in bad shape. We got clear outa clothes, pretty near naked the whole family was. It don't seem like we'll ever catch up.

"Maybe it'll be better since Frances has got to makin' pretty good at the hosiery mill. At least she can take care of herself. She drawed $17 last pay day—that was for two weeks. Back in the summer I tried to get her to go in the mill with me so I could learn her up. She said, no indeed, she didn't intend ever to work in a cotton mill. She was goin' to get herself a job in a full-fashioned hosiery mill. Well, the child walked herself nearly to death goin' backwards and forwards to the different mills. Finally she got on at the mill across over yonder where they make socks. She hated to take it because she said it looked like whatever kind of work you started in that's where you had to stay the rest of your life. She couldn't turn down this other job, though, while she waited for the full-fashioned mills to take her on. When she learns up good so she can turn off enough work I think she'll do all right where she is."

"Here they is," Kate said, pointing to the scissors she wanted. "That'll be a dollar, won't it. 'Twas when Jessie got hers."

"That's it," Rosa said as she painstakingly recorded the order on the orderblank in her lap. "Now Iry, what do you want?" she continued as she passed the book over to him.

While Ira was turning through the book to make his selection Rosa turned to Kate and asked, "Is the woman boardin' with you?"

"No, she's jest a friend come by to visit me," Kate explained. "I wouldn't mind havin' one or two girl boarders though. Maybe I could buy me a radio like I done when I kept Rhody and Sary. I had a single bed in here for myself and they slept on my bed. Them

girls stayed with me for nearly a year. That's how I
bought the radio I used to have."

"What become of it?" Rosa wanted to know.

"I sold it to Edgar Wynn fer $6. Hit cost me
$27.50—paid a dollar a week on it—and after I had
used it two year it wa'n't worth a thing."

"I'll take this hair tonic and this belt buckle," Ira
said, getting up to hand the book to Rosa. "Tonic's
30¢ and the belt 50¢, ain't it?"

"No, Iry, you ain't readin' it right," Rosa declared.
"The premium price is 60¢ for the hair tonic and a
dollar for the buckle."

"Oh, is it?" Ira said to Rosa who, busy recording the
order, had obviously never thought that the unexpected
price would cause Ira to change his mind. And Ira,
though his surprise had manifested itself in his quick
change of expression, stuck by his bargain.

"Why are there two prices listed?" I asked Rosa.

"Well, you see women all over the country form
Larkin clubs and order off after things, payin' cash
and not gettin' a premium. Like if you ordered the
hair tonic through a club it would be 30¢. But when
I'm gettin' a premium you have to pay the premium
price which is 60¢. Larkin stuff comes high but it's
awful good.

"I reckin I better be goin' on down to the glory hole,"
Rosa continued. "Why, it's twenty minutes to three,"
she said after consulting the big gold watch on her
wrist. "If I take about $2 worth myself I'll pretty
near have my order up, won't I?"

Rosa said good-bye, and in a moment she and her
plan book were gone. "Iry, I reckin you better go on
to the store and git your groceries," Kate said after
the door had closed behind Rosa.

"I guess so," he agreed, getting up and reaching for his hat. "Come to see us if you are ever over this way agin," he said to me as he walked toward the door.

I sat and rocked slowly in my chair while Kate took a tin box from her dress pocket and poured snuff into her mouth. Once the snuff had settled into position so that speech was easy, Kate said, "Rosa do look stringy but she's peart enough. Them teeth cost aplenty too. I reckin I won't git none. It costs when the body gits wrong. Back in 1912 I was in the hospital fer a operation and it cost me $75. I were there agin in 1922 and it cost me $230. Three year ago Iry had a operation fer rupture and it cost him $150. Hit looked like he'd never git that one paid fer. Robert Hall had made the arrangemints at the hospital and when Iry went back to work he took out so much a week. Taint been long neither since he stopped takin' out fer it."

I agreed with Kate that doctor's bills were always hard for most of us to pay, and from that we went to other things. Kate told me of Gloria Paradise, a French girl, and stepdaughter to the overseer, whom she had learnt up in the mill, and how the women would group around her to get her to talk in her queer language, they not knowing any more than a doodle in the woods what she was saying.

Finally Kate got around to talking about educatior. again. It was such a handy thing to have, she said, and a body didn't know how unconvenient it was not to know how to read. She'd told her children, "I want you all to get a education. I never got nary one, and I know how bad a person needs one. Hit'll be nice fer me too, havin' my children with learnin' enough to read to me.

"Jessie, she went to the seventh grade," Kate had

continued, "and Iry he quit in the sixth. Charlie—he's
the one that's dead—went as fer as the sixth too. Jessie
was good about readin' to me when she were at home.
I took the *Comfort* then, and she'd read me the little
stories and then turn over to the ads and read them
too. I miss her about helpin' me with my Sunday
School lesson more than anything, I reckin. Most times
I don't git to study it atall before I go to church."

"Would you like for me to read next Sunday's lesson
to you?" I asked.

"Why sure I'd like it if you don't mind doin' it," she
said, her face brightening.

"Get your book," I said, and Kate went over to the
little walnut table, got her quarterly, and handed it to
me. "You can explain it to me, too," she said.

I think I shall always remember how Kate looked as
she sat there in her chair, her hands folded in her lap
and her shoulders curved in their peculiar accent of
weariness. Her little bright eyes were fastened on me
with intense interest, and once or twice when I looked up
while reading the quarterly's interpretation of the
scripture to ascertain if Kate was following the trend
of thought presented, I saw only that she was following every movement of my lips as they read the words.
The process of one reading without faltering held a
singular fascination for her and the reading itself had
become inconsequential.

When I had finished reading all the story as it was
explained in the quarterly, I told it to Kate in simpler
words than the quarterly had used, but with the same
interpretation. The lesson based on scripture from
Ecclesiastes was, in brief, as follows: A man looking
for peace tried wisdom and found it not. Wisdom failing, he tried the things of the world, particularly the

constant use of wines, but peace did not come. Next, he tried the acquisition of material things, building for himself fine castles and filling them with the treasures of the world, but still there was no dawn of peace. Finally, he found the love of God and with it came peace.

"That's a good lesson and I thank you fer readin' it to me," Kate said when I had finished. "The love of God can keep you from bein' so awful lonesome sometimes too when you are settin' in a house by yourself thinkin' of the things that's tuk place in your life."

There followed a silence broken only by the ticking sound of the clock on the mantel. A full minute passed before Kate spoke again.

"Of course I could marry but it would sure seem foolish at my age."

"Yes," I agreed. "You'd rather stay on here and keep house for Ira."

"I wouldn't have to do much talkin' fer old man White to marry me and I know it. As I said, taint no sense in it though. I caint do family duty no more, and Mr. White is sure too old to make me a livin'. He ain't worked none in years.

"I know I'm too old to marry but I ain't too old to think about one I used to love. That were way back when I were seventeen year old."

Those last words had a reminiscent sound and suddenly I remembered the expression on Kate's face earlier in the day when she had told me of spending a year with her uncle's family when she was seventeen years old.

"Was that when you were in South Carolina?" I asked.

"Yes," she answered. "He lived in Columbia, South Carolina, and I met him the year I stayed with Uncle Zeke.

"Uncle Zeke had nine children of his own, but he'd tuk a likin' to me when he come up to see us one time. He kept after Ma to let me come down there and work in the mill with his family. He seemed to think a year away from home would do me good because I'd been so tied down ever since I was a child. They was three others at home to help Ma so she let me go.

"Not long after I got there a big revival started. One of the leaders in the choir was Ross Cole. He were twenty-two year old then and everybody said they'd never knowed him to keep compny with a girl. But the girls was crazy about him. I'd seed in the mill that they'd buy fruit and give it to him, and little flowers to wear on his coat too. He'd take them flowers and that fruit and give it to the doffer to bring to me. I'd take it of course, never thinkin' nothin' about it because nobody had made me acquainted with him and he'd never made a chance to speak to me. I was struck on him jest like the rest of the girls but not nary soul but me knowed it.

"When I went to the meetin' I set up there thinkin' what a pretty boy he was and wishin' he'd get struck on me. And that very night after church I seen him go over to his pa and speak a few words. Annie Belle, Uncle Zeke's daughter was right behind me and she whispered 'Ross Cole is goin' to take some girl home because he was askin' his pa to close up the church fer him.' I sorta slowed down then, waitin' to see who he was goin' to walk home with. And when I got even with the door he stepped up and asked me fer my company. I never had been so happy in all my life, and I felt awful bashful too, because I knowed everybody were lookin' at us.

"From that, me and Ross got to keepin' company

and we went together fer nine whole months. It was shore a strange thing how I took to doin' after I found out he loved me. Sometimes when he'd come of a Sunday evenin' I'd be gone out with a crowd of young folks, but Ross would set right there and talk to Uncle Zeke until I got back. There was times when I even wondered if I really loved him.

"Then one Sunday when he come he wanted to set the weddin' date. That pleased me and I knew in reason I loved him well enough to marry him. We decided to git married at the church the next Sunday, and I were goin' to ask off from the mill for a week so's I could make me up some clothes.

"About four o'clock Ross said his head was hurtin' so bad he thought he'd best go home and rest awhile before church time.

"That night all Uncle Zeke's girls had done gone on to church with their fellers and still Ross hadn't come. After while I heard steps but they never sounded like his. I went to the door and it was his brother John.

" 'Miss Kate,' he said, 'Ross asked me to come and take you to church tonight. He's right bad off. We've just had the doctor and he says its typhoid fever.'

"I never wanted to go to church and I told him so. Then after thinkin' a minute I changed my mind because I knowed Ross were such a Christian he'd be disappointed in me if I missed a single Sunday night. I'd gone regular since me and him started keepin' compny.

"Of course I never went to no town to buy a weddin' dress on Monday. I went to the mill every day durin' the week and of a evenin' when I'd get home Aunt Minnie would ask me if I didn't think I oughter go see Ross. Well sir, I were so afraid in them days of somebody talking about me that nothin' she said could git me to go see that boy. Then too, I've always thought they must of been something in the way Aunt Minnie talked to me that kept me away from Ross. They was two of her girls that had tried to strike his fancy even before he started keepin' compny with me.

"On the next Monday evening when I were checkin' up and gettin' ready to go home I seen Mr. Cole comin' toward me. He walked up to me and he said, 'Kate, Ross wants you.' I thought to my soul I couldn't speak, but finally the words come to me. 'I'll be there after supper,' I told him. 'Don't put it off, Kate,' he said, 'or it might be too late.' They was tears in his eyes when he turned away and they was plenty standin' by to see it. I knowed the house wouldn't be empty when I went that night.

"But I hadn't dreampt it would be as full as it was. Hit seemed to me that everybody on Factory Hill was there. They crowded on the porch and they was in the room next to where Ross lay and then a good many was crowded in his room. Some stood out in the yard near the windows. Somehow, when I got there, I picked up courage and marched right through them people straight to Ross's bed. I bent over and tuk his hand and then kissed him on the lips, never carin' who saw it. 'I'm glad you've come, Kate,' he said.

"They was somebody in that crowd that had feelin' enough to get up and leave the room. In a little while they was all gone.

"I set there by Ross's bed and he told me he knew he didn't have long to live. He said he was goin' home to his Maker and they was no fear of death in his heart. 'And I don't want you to grieve after me,' he said. 'And if ever you meet another man you love, marry him. All I ask of you is, don't never go with any but nice decent boys.' Then after awhile he asked me if I'd promise to stay there in the house until the end come, and I said, 'I won't leave you, Ross.' And I never.

"I slept durin' the day and of a night I set up with Ross. Over and over he asked me not to grieve, and more than once he said he hoped to take my hand in heaven as his wife. Hit seemed strange to me as I set there by his bed that I never knowed until I were losin' him how much I loved him.

"He died Thursday night while I held his hand and looked down at him, my eyes as dry as dry sand.

"I never shed a tear at the funeral and folks said I was the hard-hardedest girl they ever seen. Of course none of 'em knowed how much I were grievin' in my heart.

"I didn't stay in South Carolina long after Ross died. I wanted to come home to Ma. They was weeks and weeks that I could see Ross before me, and of a night I always dreampt he was livin'. I never had no picture of him because he thought it was sinful to have 'em made. 'Thou shalt have no graven images,' the Bible says, and Ross lived more accordin' to the teachin' of the scripture than any person I've ever knowed. Many a time I've thought the Lord tuk him away from me because he was sech a Christian and I were a sinner. He thought it was best to take him while he had him saved, and not take no chances on me makin' a backslider out of him. Yes, Ross were one good Christian, and I'm goin' to meet him in heaven one day too, and there'll be no parting."

There was conviction in Kate's voice as she expressed her intention of meeting Ross Cole. I looked up at her as she stopped speaking and then at the glowing coals in the grate. What mental disposition Kate had made of Jim Sampson was a question so active in my mind that I almost asked it. Kate looked at me and as if she had literally picked up the current of my thoughts she said. "As fer Jim Sampson, I'm sorry to say he died a unsaved man. He won't be in heaven I'm pretty certain. I never knowed him to say his prayers and he didn't go to church. Jim Sampson was never a godly man and I know in reason he were lost. Jest how much sin they were in his life I don't know, but I do know he'd stay away from home of a night and never say where he'd been. No, I'm sorry to say, but Jim Sampson never went to heaven."

Kate stooped over and put three lumps of coal on the fire with the small tongs which leaned against the wooden coal box. She stirred in the glowing coals and brought them into blaze. Then she straightened herself in her chair, folded her arms across her withered breasts, and gave her quick, throaty chuckle with its metallic undertones.

"Well I declare," she said, "hit do seem I've talked all day."

"It has been a good day," I said, getting up to leave.

"Wish you didn't have to go," Kate said.

"It's beginning to get dark and I must hurry," I replied.

"I've sure enjoyed your visit," Kate declared, "and if you ever come to Spring Road agin, please stop by to see me."

"I certainly shall," I promised, "and thank you so much for the dinner."

"Hit wa'n't much, but I'm· glad you enjoyed it. They's one thing I'd like to ask you before you go. Do you think I'll git the old age pension if I live to be sixty-five? Even if Iry ain't married by then? They say you don't git it if you've got somebody able to take care of you.   Married or not, Iry ain't able to take care of me on what he makes.   A little money of my own would help out a sight.   Do you think I'll git it?"

"I don't know all the provisions of the law," I answered, "but I believe you'll be eligible for a pension when you reach 65."

"I worked as long as I could and I'd work agin if they'd give me a job.   That is if I could hold out.   Hit may be, like they've got things speeded up in the mill now, I wouldn't fit in atall.   But I shore did once; I run everything but the cards and the lappers."

Kate followed me out on the porch, and called my attention to a plant of green moss which hung in long streamers over the sides of the bucket in which it grew. "Stays green all winter," she said.   "I'd better bring it in tonight too, because the air is blowing up chilly. I do love to tend my flowers."

IDA MOORE

Grease Monkey to Knitter

E D SMALLEY, A WELL-DRESSED, BESPECTACLED YOUNG fellow, was standing on a street corner when I asked him for a history of his life.

"History of my life?" he asked in a puzzled tone. "What do you mean?   What is this?   What right have

you got to ask me for a story of my life?" His voice
and manner were resentful.

After I explained the purpose of my request he
became more friendly.

"I don't know if I could tell the story of my life so
it would be interesting to anybody," he said, "but I'll
give it a try anyway. Let's go sit in my car while
we're talking. It's right near here."

He led the way around the corner into a side street
where his automobile was parked.

"I am a knitter," he said, after we made ourselves
comfortable in the car, "a full-fashioned knitter. I
was born on a little cotton farm, near Fort Worth,
Texas, August 18th, 1912. I am twenty-six years old,
been married three years, and have one baby, a little
girl, two years old. Here's her picture, just taken last
week."

He pulled a wallet from his pocket and showed me
the picture of a beautiful little child. She had a doll
in her arms. The doll seemed to be staring straight
into the camera, but the little girl was looking down at
the doll.

"Go ahead," I encouraged. "I got all that down.
What was the most interesting experience of your boy-
hood?"

"I guess the most interesting experience of my boy-
hood was a trip into Mexico. When I was about ten
years old my father and mother went on a visit to
Mexico. One of my uncles lived there, in Vera Cruz.
He was a cotton broker or something of the kind. Anyway, he was connected with the cotton business and I
guess he made money because he lived in a big house.
It was a stone house, built around a little court. The
windows were covered with iron grill work.

"My uncle had been in Mexico a long time. Both he and his wife spoke the language. They had Mexican servants. I remember how astonished I was the first day we were there. We were at breakfast and my uncle was talking to my father. Suddenly he turned his head and gave an order in Spanish to one of the servants. I don't know why it startled me so, but it did. I must have been staring with my mouth open, because he and my father laughed.

"That visit made a great impression on me because everything was so strange. The people dressed different, and spoke a different language. Even the signs on the business buildings meant nothing to me. They were in Spanish, and I remember how strange they seemed.

"One time my uncle and aunt dressed in Spanish costumes and took us to a fandango. My mother and father could not dance the fandango, but my uncle and aunt could. They danced with the others. My uncle wore a long red and yellow sash and I thought he cut quite a figure. No one would have suspected that he was not a Mexican himself. My aunt was dancing with a man and when the dance was over she led him to where we were sitting and introduced him to my mother and father. As they came up he spoke to me and said, 'Hello, Sonny,' and I was astonished, for I had thought him to be a Mexican. But as it turned out he was an American, and was connected with the same firm as my uncle. I guess we stayed about two weeks, and I'll always remember that trip to Mexico.

"My mother was raised 'way out in west Texas, near the New Mexico state line. When I was about twelve years old her health began to fail. That was in 1924. I remember that it was just after Christmas because I had been given an air rifle for a Christmas present.

"My father urged my mother to make a visit to one of her brothers who still lived out there. My mother decided to go and see if her health would improve. She took me with her, and of course I carried my air rifle.

"My uncle lived on a ranch, and he had a twenty-two rifle. That is what I recall most about that trip. First, shooting at prairie dogs with a real rifle; and second, my mother's death. Her health did not improve, and while we were there she got sick in bed. She was too sick to make the trip back home. My father came out there, and we stayed until her death. She died March 21st, and she's buried there on the same place where she was born.

"My mother's death was a great blow to my father and me, but it drew us closer together. I was the only child. We returned home and continued to live on the farm. It was just a small place, but my father owned it and it was home.

"My father made a little crop each year. I didn't help him much because I was in school. I had lost a lot of time and my father urged me to study hard and try to make up for lost time. I did study hard, and I passed my grade that year and graduated from grammar school.

"I remember how we missed Mother. Father did not say much. He was a quiet man and a great reader. In the evenings I would study and my father would sit with a book open on his lap, a far away look in his eyes. I knew that he was thinking of Mother.

"The next year I went to high school. My father continued to farm the place. I know that he didn't make any money, but we had a good living. I helped him when I won't in school, and we got along all right.

We did all the work ourselves, both the farm and house-work.

"In 1927 my father had a sick spell. He managed to 'tend the place but his health was none too good. I wanted to quit school so I could help him but he wouldn't agree. By the spring of 1928 my father was hardly able to be about, so he hired a man to help out. After I finished school I helped with the farm work and we had a fair crop that year. But expenses had been high due to my father's illness and to the fact that we had to have a hired hand. My father borrowed some money that year. He died in February, 1929.

"After things were settled up and my father buried, there was little left, so I rented the place for two bales of cotton. Then I got a job as waiter in a café in Fort Worth. I was paid $6 a week, room and meals. I was hoping to earn and save enough money to pay off the mortgage on the place.

"I had saved a little money, and I sold the two bales of cotton that I had been paid for rent. I was planning to pay the interest on the loan, and what I could on the principal, but in December, 1929, the house caught fire and burned. The place now had no house on it, so I decided to let it go for the debt.

"It's a good thing I did, for in January, 1930, the café where I worked went busted. I was out of a job and I couldn't find a single thing to work at. I was young and had no training, and lots of people were out of work. I had nothing to do all the balance of that winter, and when spring came I was down to $30.

"There was another young fellow there in Fort Worth, Sam Haines. He had an old Ford car and we decided to hit the road in search of a job. Sam was a waiter, too, and we got three other fellows to go along with us. Sam was to furnish the car and we were to furnish gas and oil.

"We set out in April, 1930. We traveled around over Texas—Dallas, Waco, San Antonio, Houston— but we didn't find any jobs. We left Houston heading for New Orleans. In Monroe, Louisiana, 'old Lizzie' gave out. Something went wrong with her 'innards.' She knocked a few loud whacks, then threw off a connecting rod and busted the block. It's a good thing that happened in a town instead of out on the road. Sam sold her to a junk dealer for $5. That was a good thing, too, because we needed that $5 before we found a job.

"We all caught a freight train in Monroe and rode it to New Orleans. There the gang split up. One of the boys got a job on a banana boat bound for South America. The other two struck out for Florida.

"Me and Sam stuck together. We made it to Mobile but there was nothing doing there. We rambled on up to Birmingham and there Sam found a job as waiter. We had just sixty cents between us when we got there.

"Sam got his room and meals and $5 a week. The proprietor agreed for me to occupy the room with Sam for awhile until I could find something to do. I stayed around Birmingham for a week, but couldn't find any kind of job. Sam wanted me to stay on but I wouldn't. He was only making $5 a week, and was giving me a part of that to eat on.

"We had both kept our clothes nice. I had two good suits and plenty of shirts. I left all my clothes with Sam and hit the road light. I only had fifty cents that Sam had give me. I made it to Atlanta in one night on a freight train, but things seemed duller there than they were in Birmingham.

"I bummed around in Georgia and South Carolina for three or four weeks. Everywhere I went it was the same old story—'No help wanted.' My clothes got pretty dirty and soiled from sleeping out. I could wash my shirt and underwear, but I had no money to have my suit cleaned and pressed.

"But there were lots of people on the road worse off than me. I was young, in good health, and had only myself to look out for. That summer I met whole families wandering around homeless and broke, even women with babies in their arms.

"Between Augusta and Charlotte I met a man, his wife and seven children. The oldest child was only eleven and the youngest was a nursing baby. I guess the baby was the luckiest in the lot because he had something to eat. The other children were all hungry. Some of the little ones were crying for food.

"The family was stranded on the highway. It was late in the evening, and neither the mother or father seemed to know what to do. They just stood there on the outskirts of a little town, hoping. I had nothing to give them so I walked on ahead, trying to catch a ride. Nobody stopped to pick me up and at dusk I walked back to where they were still standing. I suggested that we walk along the road until we come to a patch of corn. They agreed, and we didn't have to go far before we come to a cornfield. Across the highway from the cornfield was a little patch of woods. I told the man to build a fire while I gathered corn. We roasted corn around the fire and we all ate it except the baby. We spent the night there in the woods. The next morning a big truck picked us up and carried us to Chester, South Carolina. There I caught a freight to Charlotte. I never did learn what became of those people; I've often wondered.

"I stayed around Charlotte two days looking for work. I slept in the depot at night and hunted for work in the daytime. I found nothing there, so I caught a freight for Greensboro. I got off at Pomona Yards and walked on toward town. I left the tracks and went over to the highway. I come to a big service station. A lot of cars were parked in and around the place. Something caused me to ask for a job, and sure enough I got one. It was on July 3rd, 1930, and a lot of people were having their cars washed for the Fourth.

"The manager put me to helping a colored boy wash cars. It was about ten o'clock in the morning when I went to work, and we washed and greased cars until midnight. The boss gave me $2 and told me to come back in the morning as he might have something else for me to do. I hunted up a little all-night café. They still had a plate lunch on. I bought one for a quarter and I still think that was the best meal I ever ate. I was mighty black and greasy but I was hungry, too. I hadn't had anything to eat for about thirty hours. I sure enjoyed that plate lunch.

"After eating I went back to the service station. An old truck was parked on the street nearby and I slept in it until morning. Then I went over to the service station and the boss gave me a job as grease monkey. I don't know why unless it was because I looked the part. My pay was to be $12 a week; my hours from seven to seven, seven days a week. I was to grease and wash cars, clean up around the place, wipe windshields and do other odd jobs. It looked like a hard job but I was glad to get it.

"I had no clothes except the ones I had on, and they were so dirty that I wouldn't have gone to a rooming house to rent a room. I slept around the service station for the first week; just any old place. I wrote Sam to send my clothes and he did. I had them addressed in care of the service station, and the expressman brought them in about a week. That evening when my work was finished, I took a bath and put on clean clothes. Boy, I felt like a gentleman! I hunted up a room where I could sleep for $2 a week. It was not much of a room but good enough for a grease monkey. That was the first night I had slept in a bed in about two months. The next morning I was sore all over from sleeping in that soft bed.

"I didn't like my job much but it was better than being on the road. I decided to make the best of what I had because jobs were hard to find. Lots of people were out of work, but lots of other people had money. That was a big filling station, on a main highway, and in the course of a week I would serve big cars from nearly every state in the Union. Those folks had money—I'd often see a flashy roll as they paid their bill. They were rich folks, I guess. Business people, tourists, and all kinds stopped there.

"A guy had a nice little café just up the street from where I worked. It was a small place, kept by him and his wife, but she was a good cook, and the place was new and clean. They were just getting by, serving twenty-five-cent plate lunches to workingmen in the neighborhood. I ate there regular, but I only ate two meals a day. I was saving my money because I wanted to get out of the grease monkey business.

"One day they had a chicken for dinner, and they gave me a piece on my plate lunch, as well as some cream gravy. It was a fine piece of chicken; tender, tasty, and well-cooked. The gravy was good, too, and I got an idea from that piece of chicken. I suggested that they serve a special fried chicken and gravy meal all through the day for tourists. They didn't think much of my idea, but finally decided to try it. The price of the meal was to be fifty cents, and I, the grease monkey, was to send the tourists along to the café. If the plan succeeded I was to get three free lunches a day.

"As I think this over now I can see the absurdity of the scheme. Imagine a grease monkey, all black and smeary, wiping your windshield and at the same time trying to sell you a chicken dinner. Now that I think of it I can't think of anything more unappetizing.

"But despite its absurdity, or possibly because of it, the scheme went over big. I well remember our first customer. He was a big fat fellow, driving a Lincoln with Florida plates.

" 'Cap,' I said to him as I wiped his windshield, 'how would you like to wrap yourself around some of the finest fried chicken in all this great land?' "

" 'Sounds interesting,' he returned, smacking his lips.

" 'I'll tell you,' I went on confidentially. 'It's some country people moved to town, real southern folks, and they opened a small place just to have something to do. The woman does the cooking herself, and she can fry a chicken like nobody's business. The funny part is they don't even know enough to charge. They serve a half fried chicken, a big bowl of cream gravy, and fresh hot biscuits, all for fifty cents.' "

" 'Where is this place?' he demanded abruptly.

" 'Just up this street, half a block.' I pointed and he

touched his starter and whirred away. I watched him park in front of the café, then I got busy and forgot him. About an hour later a Lincoln drove into the place and honked loudly. The pump attendant ran to his pump, and I grabbed my smear rag. 'Here,' said a voice from the car, and I looked in to see the fat man. He had a big blob of gravy on his shirt front, and a contented look in his eye. He handed me a quarter and said, 'You told me right. Best fried chicken I ever ate, and the gravy, Yum, Yum! I'll be coming back,' he added as he drove off, and the very next week he was back, driving a Packard with Illinois license plates. I've often wondered if he drove all the way from Illinois just to get another mess of that fried chicken.

"Well, our plan succeeded. It was a poor day when the little café did not serve fifteen or twenty chickens, and the folks were well pleased with the arrangement. I got my three plate lunches a day and an occasional piece of chicken.

"I didn't like my job as grease monkey a little bit, but I reckon the boss liked my work all right. The third week he raised my pay to $14. I was only paying $2 for my room and getting my meals free, so I decided to save $11 a week. I guess I did save about that much, for I had $80 in September.

"Along in September, 1930, a guy drove in one day to have a flat fixed. I cleaned his windshield, and as it was a slack time we got to talking. He told me that he seldom had a puncture because he traded cars every year, and that he was a knitter.

" 'Must be a pretty good job,' I ventured.

" 'Oh, it's not so hot,' he replied. 'About forty a week.'

" 'Wish I had a job that good,' I said.

" 'They're taking on some learners over in Merlton this week. Takes about three months to learn, and you don't get any pay while learning.'

"He got his flat fixed and drove away. I kept thinking about what he'd said. I had about $80 saved. I could count on having ninety when I got my back pay. But I decided not to quit. I played cagey. I sort of moped around for the balance of the day, and in the evening I told the boss that I was sick, and asked him to get somebody to work in my place the next day.

"The boss let me off for the next day and I took the first bus for Merlton. I got a job learning to knit at the first mill I come to. They told me that if they didn't have a machine for me when I learned they'd give me something at which I could earn expenses. It was understood that I was to learn three months without pay.

"I hustled back to Greensboro and got my pay. I had $89.89 when I got back to Merlton. I found a boarding place for $5 a week. As I was going to go three months without a pay day I resolved to stretch my money pretty far, and it held out all right. After a learner has worked a couple of weeks he can be of much help to the knitter. My knitter made good money, and he gave me a dollar or two every week. Knitters ain't bad guys. I've learned a couple of fellows myself and I always give them a little something every week.

"I worked the rest of that year for nothing. I got a machine on the night shift the first of January, 1931. I'm still on that same machine, but I'm now on the first shift, from seven in the morning to three in the afternoon. I saved enough money the first year to buy a car. In 1935 I married. My wife is a looper. She worked on for awhile after we married and we bought a lot and had a house built on it. But we've never lived in the house. When it was finished a fellow wanted to rent it. He offered a good price, so we rented the house to him and we lived on at the boarding house.

"Before the baby was born we bought some furniture and rented a little place in the country. Maybe I am just a farmer at heart. Anyhow, I love to putter around in the garden, and my wife does, too. We keep some chickens scratching around. It's only three miles from town and I can be home in five minutes after I get out of the mill.

"Knitting may look like an easy job, but it's not so easy as it looks. For one thing, it is hard on the eyes; for another it's exacting. The full-fashioned knitting machine is a delicate and highly complicated machine. A knitter must keep his wits about him constantly. It's very easy to smash a machine, doing hundreds of dollars' worth of damage and maybe putting that machine out of commission for a couple of months.

"A knitting machine has twenty-four heads and knits twenty-four stockings at a time. Every head has hundreds of needles, and while they only cost one cent there are several thousand to each machine. The needles are fine and easy to bend or break. Moreover, they have a little barb, or beard, finer than a human hair. Every needle must be straight and in exact line, and every barb must be set correctly or they won't work.

"A stocking is knit flat, spread out, and is then seamed, or sewed up. If you want to understand why knitting is such a particular job, and puts such strain on the eyes, spread out a silk stocking and examine the weave, or mesh. Then try to stick a fine needle through one of the spaces in the weave. There are 420 spaces in the stockings knit on my machine. That means that every head has 420 needles, and when a knitter tops a stocking on he spreads it out and slips those 420 spaces down over 420 needles. When a thread or needle breaks it spoils that stocking at the break. The knitter tops it back on and ravels it down to the break. Fortunately, he may knit several dozen without having a break.

"When a stocking is being knit a wide line of needles, 420 on my machine, come up through the mesh at every stitch. The beard on the needles catches a silk thread and draws it down through the mesh, and that is the way a silk stocking is knit. This is a poor description, and you would have to see a machine in operation to understand how it's done. Even then it would be hard to see into because the needles work very fast. But you can see from this that it's hard on the eyes, and that every needle and barb must be in line.

"The silk threads are fine, and the needles are small and slender. Unless a man has very good eyes he will have to wear magnifying glasses soon after beginning to knit. Knitting is a young man's job. You'll see ten times as many knitters under thirty as you will over thirty. A man's eyes were not made for such fine work. The eyes of some knitters go bad after five or six years, sometimes sooner than that. In fact, unless a man has good eyes he can't learn to knit. Some learners fall down the first week on account of their eyes.

"The mills around here teach their own knitters. Some of them have an age limit of twenty years for learners. They prefer young fellows under twenty, just out of high school. I imagine a knitter would have to have very good eyes to last ten years. But knitting pays well, comparatively speaking, and there's no lack of applicants. A full-fashioned knitter is considered to have a good trade hereabouts. The wage is much higher than common. A good knitter can average $40 a week the year round. The work is not hard except on the eyes. The light isn't always good. If a man had daylight to work under it wouldn't be so bad, but that can't always be. Most of the mills around here run three shifts, and some are naturally dark and require artificial light even at midday.

"There's a boom on in the silk hosiery trade. All the mills around here are running full blast, and those that don't have third shifts are starting them. Many new mills are being built close to Burlington. I've heard that the mills up around Philadelphia are not doing any good. Silk hosiery is a new industry in the South, but it's growing fast."

JOHN H. ABNER
GEORGE L. ANDREWS

I'd Take the Mill Anytime

IN 1886 CAMDEN WAS A VILLAGE WITH A RED MUD
main street, a few stores clustered about a square,
and one cotton mill, the McDonald.   However, at that
time young H. J. Filmer, a partner in Filmer-Holmes
Dry Goods Store, was building another cotton mill.
Among the workmen on this job, as bricklayer and
carpenter, was a stolid "Dutch" farmer from the Hick-
ory Hill section of Culpepper County.   His name was
Coon.

Today two of this man's sons have been with Filmer
Mills longer than any other employees.   I talked with
Smith, the younger son, who has worked in the mill for
forty-nine years.   At fifty-nine he is wiry, healthy,
young looking.   He owns his own home, a comfortable
two-story bungalow on Ashboro Street.   The house is
spacious and furnished in better taste than many so-
called middle class houses in town.

"I don't know what good hit'll do you to talk to me,"
Smith said modestly, "for I ain't done nothing much."
But he was really pleased that he had been sought out
and once he started talking he forgot his shyness.

"When Mr. H. J. got ready to open up his mill back
in '86, he didn't have but thirteen houses for his hands.
That don't sound like many nowadays when many a
house jest has one hand in it, but Mr. H. J. figured if

180

he hired big families, he could get enough hands in them thirteen houses to work his mill.

"I reckon that's howcome he wanted us. Anyway he wrote my father a letter asking him to move his force to the mill—hit was ready to start work. My sister had that letter, but when she was a-cleaning up some-time back, she burnt it up. I sure hated that; I'd a-give most anything for that letter.

"I won't never forgit that day in the fall of '86 when we moved in to Camden. We started out before daylight and hit was way after dark when we got here. Hit don't look like it could take that long to come sixteen miles, but back then there jest wasn't anything you'd call a road; why two teams always went together so if one got stuck the other could pull it out. I was six year old whenever we moved and what I mainly remember about that trip is hanging my head over the side of the wagon so that I got my chin bumped underneath when we hit the pine log road.

"Soon as the mill opened, my father and all the younguns that was old enough commenced to work. There was nine of us younguns, five girls and four boys and everyone of us 'ceptin' one got their start in that same mill—hit's the one they call plant number one now. I was too little to go to work right away, but whenever I was nine or ten I began. At first I doffed. I got ten cents a day for working from six o'clock in the morning to five minutes until seven o'clock in the evening. Course you keep a-goin' up, so I went to the spinning room and on to the weaving room. Then they put me to fixing looms. I've always been a good hand to fix any kind of machinery and after while they made me the overseer of the shop. Well, I stayed at that till fifteen year ago when they give me the job

I've got now—the overseer of the yard. And believe me hit *is* a job too! I have to weigh ever bit of cotton goin' in and out and see to the loadin' and unloadin' of it. Why jest today we handled close to 500 bales— that's somethin', let me tell you, and the worst part of it is bossing the niggers that handle it. You have to talk to 'em like you're a-goin' to kill 'em or they'll lay down on you and not do a lick of work. I've got so I can talk jest as mean and hateful as anything—oh I don't mean it, but I have to git the work out of 'em.

"Since the cut I'm not a-makin' but 56¢ a hour. That sounds like a lot more than what I started out at, but money don't go nowheres any more. Back when I was a-gettin' ten and twenty-five cent a day you could take your money to the store and have something to show fer it. Why my father, before he died, had a pile of gold pieces he had saved from way back yonder when we used to git paid off in gold money. A body could save then, but it takes everything you make now to live.

"Education? Don't ask me about that 'cause I never did have none to amount to anything. They didn't have no city schools then like they has now. Mr. H. J. had a school that run in the daytime for the young'uns too little to go to the mill and at night for them that worked. Well I went to his school some before I commenced to work and at night for a while too, but it didn't amount to so much.

"My wife, she come from Blacksburg. You know'd old M. J. Black who used to be sheriff, didn't you? Well, he was her father. She looks stout enough to pull a freight car, but she ain't been so well here lately. My youngest girl, Katie, just finished high school last year so I'm having her to stay here at home and

help with the work.   No sir, I don't want no nigger
girl around the house, I can't stand to have 'em about.
There never was but one nigger whose cooking I could
eat, and she's dead now.   She was all right.   When she
fixed something, all you had to do was set right down
and eat it.

"We've got four children in all, two of 'em is boys
and two is girls.   My boy that's married and lives down
near Matthews with his wife's folks, he works in the
hosiery mill.   My other boy works down here at the State
Theatre.   Janet, that's my oldest girl, is a cashier at
McLellan's Store, but she's anxious to go to work in
the mill.   Well, you know, there's lots of 'em in stores
now that feels that-a-way about it because they can
git better pay in the mill and don't have to work sech
long hours.   If you was to ast me, I'd take the mill any
time, and if my children wants to go into the mill, I'm
glad fer 'em to.   Hit's jest as good work as anything
they can get to do and won't hurt their good name none.
Course mill people are jest like anybody else, there's
some that's no 'count and shiftless and it's no wonder
they're looked down on.

"I'll tell you hit's a pleasure to work for a company
that treats you like the Filmers does.   I've know'd all
of 'em well.   Many's the time back yonder that I
hitched up Mr. H. J.'s buggy for him, drove him up
town or down to the mill, and went to the postoffice to
get his mail.   Jack and Reeves is the boys I know the
best and they've turned out the best.   Why I consider
Reeves Filmer jest as good a friend as I've got in this
world.

"I've got a picture of Mr. H. J. in with my insurance
policy—I'll show it to you if you'd like to see it.
Yessir, he was a fine looking man and a good man too.

See this insurance policy? He give every hand down at
Culpepper then one of these, and if I was to die tomorrow, my wife would git $500. There ain't but
four or five of us has these any more because they took
the policies away from all the hands that walked out
during that big strike some years back.

"Yes, me and a few others kept right on going to
the mill all the time they was having the strike. It took
nerve too to walk in that gate with all the crowd standin'
there hollerin' at you. They'd call us all kinds of
names, but I didn't say a word back to 'em—that was
the best way to do. The mill wasn't running, but we
got our pay fer going there.

"Plenty of 'em that walked out was sorry they had,
some of 'em didn't want to go out in the first place but
they was threatened. You couldn't begin to git me
to join one of them unions. All they want is the dues
they can git from you, and you don't never know what
they do with the money because they won't give a report on it. I read in the paper not long ago where they
wanted some union to show its books and it wouldn't
do it.

"In this last strike every mill here and up at Filmerton kept a-running all the time and no hands quit. I
jest wisht you could've seen Filmerton. Law it looked
like a war, guns and soldiers all about. The mill had a
airplane flying around to watch all the main highways
and when it seen a band of cars (flying squadron)
starting out from some town, it would fly right low
and drop a note down to let us know what was coming.
At our mill we never was bothered by anybody. The
funniest thing happened up at Filmerton when one of
them squadrons went there. You know the mill owns
the whole town. Well, the sheriff was on the lookout

for these folks from out of town and every time they started off the main street—hit's a State highway—the sheriff would say, 'This is private property, you can't come on it.' So that squadron couldn't do a thing but go up and down main street till they got so wore out they jest give up and went back home.

"What party do I belong to? Well I served two terms on the city Board of Aldermen so you know I'm not no Republican. I think what the government's been a-doing is all right. I tell you what's a fact, I believe we'd a had a rebellion back when Roosevelt come in if the government hadn't done like it did. A man jest couldn't hardly keep going when Hoover was in; you can't live on no dollar a day like he said to do. You know, there's a sight of folks down at the mill has changed over to being Democrats in the last couple years.

"You take when they had that NRA, Mr. Filmer made us keep all the rules to the letter. If a man worked overtime one day, I had to allow him that much time off the next. Mr. Filmer is mighty particular about all sich rules.

"I like to read the paper and listen to the radio right well, but I don't care a thing about the moving picture show. Why I reckon I ain't been to see one—let's see, hit's been five year or more now. The State Theatre give me three annual passes for fixing some machines for them and I could a'gone to the show, without paying a cent, any time I took a notion to for three years, but I never did use them passes a single time; I wore 'em out jist carrying 'em around in my pocket. Nobody else couldn't use them, because they had my name written across the front.

"When I git off from work I like to piddle around

the house. There's most always something or other to
be fixed or some kind of work to do about the yard.
I wisht it was light now so you could see my back
yard for hit's a lot bigger and prettier than the front.
This summer I run lights out there, fixed a pulpit and
benches that I keep down under the back part of my
house, and every Sunday evening hit was pretty we had
preaching down in my backyard. It's mighty nice.

"I'm the sexton up at the church. I git $10 a month
for cleaning up, running the furnace, fixing the organ
if it gits out of order, opening the church and ringing
the bell whenever they're a-going to have a meeting,
but I declare hit's more trouble to me than what I git
out of it. If they could git anybody else who could run
the furnace right, I don't reckon I'd keep the job, but
them young boys they had been getting to fire it just
nearly 'bout ruint it.

"Yes ma'm, this here house is mine; I saved up to
build it and I planned it myself. Well now, I like
these big rooms too—I was determined that when I
built me a house I was going to have plenty of space
about me, so when I planned this one, I made it like I
wanted hit to be. If there's anything I despise it's to
be scrouged into little bitty rooms. My wife and the
girls see to keeping the rooms fixed up this a-way—that
there music box (piano) is a real old timey one my
sister bought somewhere.

"I've got an electric refrigerator that cost me $200
—that's a lot of money and I hated to put it out at the
time, but law, now I wouldn't begin to take what I
paid fer it. I jest wouldn't be without it since I've got
used to it. Something else I like mighty well is my
automatic hot water heater. Hit keeps the water hot

all the time, all you have to do is jest open any tap and you've got hot water right now, day or night.

"I would sure hate to go back to living like folks used to. Didn't nobody have things then the way we do now, living wasn't as good. There's a lot of people feel they can't git along without a automobile and some of 'em can't so well. I don't have one fer I ain't got no use fer it; I walk down to the mill, to the church, or uptown when I'm obliged to go.

"Well I've sure enjoyed talking to you and I hope you'll come back agin when my wife's here fer I know she'd like to talk to you.

"I'll just walk across the street with you. I told Sam Heilig I would come over sometime tonight and work on his stove fer him. Cold weather'll catch us soon."

MURIEL WOLFF

Old Man Dobbin and His Crowd

IT WAS PAYDAY AT THE MILL AND OLD MAN DOBBIN HAD drawn his last check. He held the little blue slip in his hand and not paying any attention to me or to his wife or to his two grandchildren he read the figures again and spoke aloud. "Five dollars and ninety-three cent and a dollar and sixty-three cent of it took out for rent. Never got in but two days last week. It ain't so much but it's goin' to push us to get along any sort of way without it."

"It'll shore be hard but then its near 'bout always been hard," his wife said in a slow, twanging voice.

Her statement was one beyond which none of us could for the moment pass. We sat there in a semi-circle around the little laundry stove which furnished heat for the small room, and my mind reviewed the conversation I had had not more than fifteen minutes before with the man who was passing the Dobbin home. "That house there? That's where old man Dobbin and his crowd lives," he'd said. "They's twelve or thirteen of 'em, I forget which, livin' there now. More'n likely you'll find the old man hisself at home. I heard tell they laid him off the other day. George Dobbin's his name. Yessum, he's got children aworkin' but I wouldn't be surprised if the old man don't need his job too to get along on."

George Dobbin shifted his chair a little further from the stove. "Yessir, it's goin' to be hard to get along and me not aworkin'," he said.

"How did you lose your job?" I asked.

"Well, as you can see, I'm agettin' old. Be sixty-eight comin' June. But I coulder held out if my age hader been all was against me. Seven year ago a automobile struck me when I was crossin' the street down yonder in front of the comp'ny store and I was right bad injured. It laid me up for three months and left me with a game leg once I did get about again. They give me a elevator job when I went back to the mill but awhile back when they took a spell of stretchin' the stretchout they cut out my job and divided the elevator runnin' amongst the four ropin' haulers. And they put me on a job of sweepin' and haulin' and cleanin' that would just about finish up airy forty-five year old man I know. I stuck to it for a day and when I come home that night my whole entire body hurt me so I couldn't lay in bed atall. The next mornin' I went to my bossman and asked him if they wasn't some lighter job he could put me on for maybe lower pay. And he answered me, 'You've got as light a job as they are in the mill. The New Deal's made all mill jobs heavy.' He never explained what he meant and I've been awonderin' since what he had in his mind. Then he told me if I wanted a job I'd have to keep the one I was on, and I says to him, 'If I tried to keep it up it'd most likely kill me and if by a miracle it happened not to kill me it'd lay me up in bed for six months with big doctor bills for my children to pay. Since I see trouble abrewin' if I stay on,' I says to him, 'I'll nip it in the bud before it matures by quittin' right now.' When you get disabled to do hard work they want to get rid of you and they know how. And so, I reckin this here is the last mill check I'll ever draw."

George Dobbin slipped the piece of paper into the pocket of his old brown coat. He removed his battered brown hat and sat hunched over with his big-knuckled hands pushing fingertip to fingertip and then quickly pulling them apart. Obviously he had never been a very large man, but as I looked at him I had the feeling that for a number of years he must have been dwindling away with pernicious regularity to have reached his present emaciated state. His energetic voice and his equally live gestures did not seem to belong to the puny-looking body from which they came.

"Have you lived here many years?" I asked George.

"I moved to Rimmerton eighteen year ago and every one of my crowd learnt up in the mill down yonder.

Up till then it'd been me and the old lady to make a livin' for all and we had plenty strugglin' adoin' it.

"We started off farmin' and stuck to it up to the fall of 1913 and '14. That year we planted cotton on a fourteen cent basis and got six cent for some and four and a half for the rest. Europe had got started in the war and the countries that had put in orders for cotton countermanded 'em and flooded our home market. Me and Sally made fourteen bales of cotton, thirty-one barrels of corn and three hundred bushels of potatoes besides a sight of peas. It was one of the best crop years I ever knowed in Johnson County and we come out about the porest we ever done. We worked let me tell you, we worked to make that crop."

"Law, I reckin we did. I hoed seventeen acres of cotton by myself without one lick of help except for the little grass pickin' done by the geese, done my house-work, and looked after three children. Many a night after supper I'd scour my floors or do my washin' and have it ready so's I could put it on the line before I went to the field at sun-up next mornin'. In gatherin' time I'd take my little baby to the field and put him in a wooden box at the end of a cotton row of a early mornin' when the frost lay thick as snow on the ground. Me and George picked every boll that went into eight bales of that cotton and I never got so much as two yards of ten-cent apron gingham."

"We didn't pick the last bale," George said, "and I never seen prettier cotton in a field. I'd hauled thirteen bales to the gin and hadn't brought back a cent. Mr. Wilson, my landlord, got half of it because the land was his'n and he took the other half to pay for what rashins he'd furnished. Me and the old woman was busy tryin' to get the peas picked and the potatoes

dug so's to have somethin' to live on and I had no notion
of stoppin' to pick that last bale of cotton. I said to
Mr. Wilson, 'Now, they's some pretty cotton down there
in the field, and it's all yourn and on yore land. I've
wore out and I've not got time to pick it neither and
pickin's sixty cent a hundred. They's not enough
money at my house to pay for the pickin' of one hundred
pound. If you want your cotton you better see to
gettin' it out.' Mr. Wilson said, 'I'll get some hands
in there and get that cotton ready for ginnin', but if I
don't come out on it, I'll charge up half the loss against
you.' And I answered him like this, 'Mr. Wilson, you
charge it if you want to but it'll be what's called a dead
debt. I ain't gonna work like a mule raisin' fourteen
bales of cotton off of which I've got nare cent and then
pay somebody extry money because I was fool enough
to raise it.'

"He come back to me a few days later and he said,
'We come out four dollars in the hole on that bale and
yore part is two dollars. I thought maybe you'd just
let the shoulder of meat I borrowed from you when you
killed that hog the other day go to settle up with me.'

"I felt right sorry I was a human then. I looked at
him and I said, 'Mr. Wilson, I loaned you that meat
thinkin' of course you'd pay it back. But if you want
it that bad keep it.' He kept it.

"And it's hard to believe, but a few days later he
come to my house and said half of my four hogs was his
because I'd fed 'em out of the crop."

"Yessir, he done that thing, he did for sure, and me
and George had cut weeds to feed them hogs and we
give 'em corn we'd made the year before. He'd got
everything we'd growed on the land but a few potatoes
and peas and then wanted half the hogs."

"I'd rented corn land," George said, "on the terms of one dollar for every barrel I made and me furnishin' the fertilizer. We come out even on the corn.

"I said to Wilson when he asked me for the hogs, 'Do your mortgage call for hogs'—he'd took a mortgage against my half of the crop before he'd furnish me you know. 'No, the mortgage don't call for 'em but if you think about it honest you know they're mine.' I answered him with, 'Take everything your papers calls for but I'd advise you to leave the rest alone.' He never got my hogs.

"We had them peas and potatoes and hogs and no clothes atall to face the rest of the winter with. Good luck come to me though, and in February I left the farm and went to public work. The Nursery Company at Turnersville give me the job of stable-boss and paid me $30 a month and furnished a house to live in too. That wage did seem powerful good after the long hard year of work that hadn't cleared us a nickel. I reckin it must've been about July when I got a chance at a better job."

"It was August, George. I remember it was three weeks after the twins was born we moved to Henderson."

"Mills was beginnin' to pay good," George continued. "It wa'n't long till I was makin' $20 a week."

"We done some good livin' then," Sally remarked. "It seemed like we never had to study and contrive so hard. I could buy all the milk my children needed."

"Groceries kept agoin' up," George began again, "and they took up most of the wages, but then we did have enough to eat.

"In 1919 we moved to Durham and first thing I knowed I was makin' from 25 to 35 dollars a week. Times stayed good with us up to '21. When I say

times was good I don't mean we done no fancy livin'
atall but we set down to the table three times a day and
always found somethin' on it.

"Then one day I went in the mill and seen a notice
tellin' of a twenty-five percent cut and a shortenin' of
time to three days a week. Hard times really set in
like always groceries never come down accordin' to the
cut."

"Them was miserable days for us," Sally declared,
"and many a time my little ones cried for milk."

"And when it begin to look like the livin' wa'n't
worth the worry of gettin' along I lost my job complete
—left without ary little piece of a job.

"It was human kindness that caused me to lose it
too. A body is hard put to it to understand how kindness can work against him sometimes but it sure happens. Word got out amongst the neighbors that we was
havin' a struggle gettin' along with me one workin'
and seven children lookin' to me for a livin'. First
thing we knowed a woman come out and set to talk
awhile with my wife. She asked her how we managed
to live on what I made and the old lady answered we done
the best we could. At different times three women
come out and done just about such talk as the first one
and Sally, she answered 'em all alike, but not ary time
did she ever ask help of 'em. But it wasn't long till
baskets of groceries started comin' to us and it seemed
just like manna from heaven. That'd been goin' on a
few weeks when my boss told me Mr. Wilder, the superintendent, wanted to see me.

"Soon as I could I went to Mr. Wilder's office and
told him Mr. Henry said he wanted to see me. He
answered right quick, 'Yes, Dobbin, I did. The
comp'ny's decided all who can't live sumptuous on what

they make at this mill is to be given ten-day notice. I'm givin' you yores now.'

" 'But Mr. Wilder,' I says, 'I don't understand what's causin' this. I have never raised one word of complaint against this mill.'

" 'Mr. Dobbin, it's awful knockin' on the mill,' he says, 'to have folks workin' for this company that calls on the welfare and the Salvation Army for help. We don't like to have the Salvation Army callin' up this office and tellin' us they'd like a contribution from us to help them take care of our hands.'

"I looked at Mr. Wilder settin' there behind his desk and I knowed he couldn't help feelin' I was tellin' the truth when I spoke. 'Before God, Mr. Wilder,' I said, 'to my ricollection I've never spoke to a Salvation Army man or woman in my life and I've never been to no organization to ask for help.'

" 'But you've been agettin' help, ain't you?' he asked.

" 'I've got help and I highly appreciate it,' I said. 'It's kept my children from goin' hungry.'

" 'You've got your notice,' he answered me.

"I took some of the money I drawed that week and bought me a ticket to New Falls. Had a brother livin' here then and he took me to his bossman and helped me get the promise of a house and job. But I knowed it cost money to move and I thought to myself it won't hurt none to go to Mr. Richards, the general manager, and see if he won't be more reasonable in his ways than Mr. Wilder.

"On a Wednesday I went. And I says to him, 'Mr. Richards, I want to ask you, do you find fault with my work and my way and manner of livin'?'

" 'None whatever, Mr. Dobbin,' he answered me.

" 'Then why is my job bein' took away from me?'
I asked him.

" 'We may be doin' you a favor, Mr. Dobbin,' he
said. 'It'll be for your own good if you can go somewhere else and get more time and better pay. The
picture for this mill looks mighty gloomy. Have you
got any notion where you're goin'?'

"'I've got a house and a job waitin' for me,' I said,
'but I've not got a copper to pay for movin'.'

" 'Go out and hire you a truck,' he says, 'and charge
it to the mill.'

"Well I couldn't get nothin' but a delivery truck and
it wouldn't bring all of our furniture. When I went
back to Mr. Richards he told me to have the balance
crated, take it to the depot, and he'd pay the freight.

"You know them neighbors of mine crated every-
thing I had and wouldn't let me raise my hand to help.
They's never been no better people than them at that
Durham mill."

"They's another thing they done always comes to my
mind when I think of Durham," Sally said reflectively
and her eyes looked beyond the two of us who listened.

"Two year before we left, when George was out one
time with a sore foot, they'd come by our house after
quittin' time of a evenin', them that worked in his de-
partmint, and they'd drop coins in his hands till he
had more'n he woulder made workin' that day. It's
always stayed in my ricollection as a powerful sweet
thing to've done." Her chair was rocking steadily now
that she had ceased talking and her eyes were still
gazing toward the hall.

"The welfare bought us train tickets and the neighbors fixed up dinner for us to eat on the train," George
reminisced.

"They was cake and salmin balls and ham biscuits," Sally said. "Yes, they was a custard too."

"A old bachelor that boarded and never had no way of fixin' things bought the children some peppermint candy," George said. "I remember how the old lady worried with them twins tryin' to keep 'em from messin' up their clothes with the red off of that candy. That little Mary smeared it all over her face and Sally was washin' her when the train pulled into New Falls."

"We've been here at the Rimmerton Mill since," Sally said. "Twan't but a few months till Dan, our oldest, was fourteen and went in the mill with his pa. Now there's one good religious boy; anybody around'll tell you that. He never misses a Sunday goin' to church mornin' and night and of a evenin' too if they's preachin' goin' on. Pays no attention atall to the girls and uses his money to help out at home. He never got no education much on account of havin' to stay at home and help me with the other children, but he sure puts a heap of study on his Bible."

The last lingering tone of her monotonous voice trailed away into a silence, broken only by occasional sounds created by two small children who played in the rear of the room. Presently I became conscious of the movement of persons in the room overhead, listened as the sound became that of slow-moving feet descending stairs, and caught the jumbled noise of two girls talking as they moved through the hall outside. One suddenly ran ahead of the other and opened the front door. Her voice was loud as she said, 'Come on in Mrs. McBane.' A moment later three persons came into the room where Sally and George and I sat.

"Them's my two girls that stays at home," Sally said, "and that there is my friend neighbor, Mrs. Mc-

Bane." Mrs. McBane, a massive woman wearing a sky blue coat, shoved herself across the room and sat down with measured gradualness in a chair near the ramshackle dresser. As the concluding move toward settling herself she brushed her bobbed hair away from her ruddy face and laid her hands comfortably at rest in her bulging lap.

"Hannah nor Venie neither can't seem to get on at the mill," Sally said referring to her two daughters who sat on the bed. " 'Course, Hannah there has always had a bad head trouble and I don't know as she'd ever be able to work if she could get work to do. Her ears just takes spells of bleedin', and little pieces of what looks like bones comes out too."

Sally's words produced in Hannah such an acute embarrassment that she could not for the moment speak though her lips moved. Finally when she did speak it was in a cracked, nervous voice which except for the restraint forced upon it would have cried out rather than spoken out its words. "Mama, I wish you wouldn't be talkin' about my head," she declared. "Just cause my ears used to bleed you tell it like I still have head trouble. I can hear good as anybody now."

"Well, honey, you can't help it about your head and it ain't nothin' to be ashamed of," Sally said. "The doctors says your head ain't just like anybody else's but you shore ain't to blame for that. Her head treatmints and tonsils cost us $91 three year ago. She's not had the doctor in a right smart while now."

Hannah, unable to think of any further defense of her health, made a few final gestures of retreat. She brushed nervously at her frizzled yellow hair, shrugged her shoulders and stared out of the window.

"Hannah quit school when she was fourteen year old

because it made her awful nervous," Sally was saying presently.

"I quit when I was fourteen too," Venie said, "but it was because I wanted a job. I've been waitin' five years for it and I guess I'll set here waitin' five more."

The suggestion of prolonged waiting instantly drew George out of his silence. "We'll all about perish before five year unless work picks up," he said. Venie giggled, but George, unmindful of interruption continued, "After I found out the mill was through with me I went up to the welfare and put in for a old age pension. The lady at the desk told me she'd have to wait to see what the legislature done about the appropriations for pensions before she could give me a answer. And when I asked her how long that'd be she said the first of July and I says to her, 'I'll be perished by then.' She laughed at that but t'wan't meant for no joke. Times is gettin hard for us."

"Taint like if they could make the full time the mill runs," Sally explained. "Now Dan, he'd make $10.08 if he worked four days but every week he's sent out to rest a day. Same with Mary and Louise. Mary's married now but her husband works in the chair factory at Jones Forks and she boards here like the rest that's workin'. She draws on the average of $9 a week and Louise draws about $7. Ruth, the mother of these two children you see here and one more that ain't come home from school, she makes the same as Mary. The four workin' pays me $5 a week apiece and I feed thirteen out of it and keep up best as I can with the rest of the debts housekeepin' makes. George's always went for wood and coal and rent and some for clothes. Now this week I can't get much board out of Mary and Louise because they both near 'bout had flu last week and never put in but a day apiece. They say it's all they can do to keep up with their work when they're well and to go down there sick would sure enough finish 'em up."

"I bet Ruth never missed nare day they'd let her work," Mrs. McBane said.

"No sirree," Sally answered. "I believe she'd go till she dropped in her tracks. She's at work today and her with a cold that ain't fur from pneumony but I couldn't keep her at home. She says a woman with three children to raise ain't got time to be sick. It's the same answer she makes when I try to get her to go to the sanitorium and be pleuriscoped. Beins her husband died with the tbs the doctor said her and the children both oughter be pleuriscoped ever six months, but she won't go. She says if she's got it she don't want to know it because with no money to take care of herself she'd die any way and knowin' it would make her worry and bring death on that much quicker. But she do cough awful of a night.

"Bud, he had the gallopin' kind, you know. Seemed like the more we done for him the faster it worked. Old Mrs. Smith over on 12th St. fixed him up a remedy that's guaranteed to cuore it but we couldn't see as it done Bud one bit of good. Some says they's nothin' you can do for the gallopin' kind nohow and I reckin they're right.

"These babies here, though, I do all I can to give 'em milk so's to build 'em up enough to keep 'em from havin' it. I worry more about Ruth than I do the children naturally since the work she has to do ain't none too good for her health nohow. Ruth never was no strong person but I always said she had more grit than anybody I knowed. I believe that's the children comin' now, ain't it George? It's past three o'clock."

"That there little Sarah'll let you know in a minute," George said, grinning. "First sound she ketches of Ruth atalkin' she'll make a beeline for the front door." And no sooner had he spoken than Sarah, the older of the two grandchildren, who had been trading doll chairs with her baby-sister, poised her head for listening, and the next moment scrambled to her feet and rushed out of the room.

"Of a pay day Ruth always brings her somethin'," Sally explained.

There was laughter in the hall and a child's grunt of pleasure, and the next instant, Sarah, leading the crowd, pranced into the room licking an ice-cream cone with great delight. The baby emitted a little squeal and stepped her feet high over the obstructing doll chair to reach her mother. Ruth bent down to pat the child on the head and to put into her outstretched hands the other cone she'd brought.

"This here is Ruth and that one's Mary and the other Louise though I doubt if you'll remember long which twin is which. George says they's times when he can't. That there is Dan." When Sally had finished introducing her daughters they looked about the room and fitted themselves in wherever they could. The twins, hardly more than five feet two and weighing not over ninety pounds, sat side by side on the further end of the bed. They had pert-looking narrow faces with pug noses, smooth skin, and eyes which must have been bright when less fatigued. Ruth, smaller than the twins, seeming so weary that she did not want to talk, slid into a chair in the corner partly shielded from view by Mrs. McBane. Dan went into the kitchen, came back occasionally to stand in the doorway listening to the conversation but never contributing to it.

And before the crowd had fully adjusted itself a small boy bearing two books and a tablet under his arm dashed into the room. Still panting, he stopped before Ruth and asked in great eagerness, "What'd you bring me, Mama?"

"I wasn't lookin' for you so soon," Ruth said. The Dobbins laughed and with greater abandon laughed Mrs. McBane.

The laughter was like a stinging blow to the child. Instantly he was sobbing and in his embarrassment he flung out his fists, pounding his mother and demanding a nickel. Before Ruth could calm him sufficiently to reach into her pocket, Mary came forth with a nickel and said, "Now be a little man, Johnny, and hush your cryin'. Your mama's got to save her money to pay her insurance with." The child took the nickel and his sniffles gradually died away to leave only the sound of an occasional shuffle of feet within the room.

"Talk like you ain't got no insurance to pay," Louise said to Mary.

"Well I never made enough this time to pay mine nohow," Mary answered.

"They's not a one of 'em," George began with a sweep of his arm which included Dan in the kitchen, "that draws much more'n half what they oughter." He batted his eyes and straightened himself in his chair. He looked about the room with a I-will-speak expression and began again to speak. "What labor's got to do is organize. I'd rather see it get its rights through laws but the laws they've got now is easy to get around. Seems like the union's the only chance."

"We joined the union durin' the strike," both twins spoke simultaneously. "All of us did."

George prepared himself for further speech. The presence of his children seemed to bolster his spirits and give impetus to his thoughts. He raised his right arm to elbow-angle and swung it to and fro like the pendulum of a clock as he spoke.

"Yessir, all mine joined," he declared. "I had that one there that's never worked a day in the mill to sign a card. I think it's the thing to do. If I was arunnin' the union I'd try to sign up all the new crop out there waitin' for jobs in the mill. Then, when the companies got ready to turn off union members workin' for 'em they couldn't find no non-union ones to take their places.

"They work—the comp'ny, I'm speakin' of—to keep a extry supply of help on hand out here in the village, folks that's been settin' around waitin' for a job like a dog waits for a bone. That away they can hold a threat always over yore head so's to drive you to the last breath and then if you can't do quite as well as they want you to, they can say, 'Git out, you can't keep up, we're done with you, and we've got a dozen that ain't wore out atall out there waitin' and abawlin' for yore job.' That's the reason they take in folks for miles around that's livin' out on farms and glad to get what extry money they can make in the mill. Yessir, they invite 'em in from far and near and they've got folks livin' next door to the mill in comp'ny houses that'd might nigh give part of their life for a job. They's young folks that's never had a job been awaitin' and abeggin' for years to get on down there. And it takes all able-bodied hands in a family aworkin' on the wages they pay to give theirselves a decent livin'. Boys

and girls aloafin'—time on their hands to do nothin'
with but get in trouble—and no money except what
they have to take from them that's not able to give it.

"A farmer out raisin' his stuff and ownin' his land
can afford to work twenty-five cent on the dollar cheaper
than reg'lar mill people. And the best part for the
comp'ny too, he don't need to mutter and grumble and
he goes around givin' 'em a good name because so
much extry is just so much extry. And families that's
helped the comp'ny make what they've got set here in
the village with half of 'em waitin' for the word to
come to work. Yessir, have 'em so glad to get a job
they'll take anything for pay."

The pause was transitory. George's hand was poised
in mid-air. Hannah leaned over from her space on the
side of the bed, caught her father's hand, and in a
sing-song voice declared, "Pa's a preacher, Pa's a
preacher."

All of the family laughed with unrestrained glee.
The little boy who had cried clapped his hands to give
expression to his great good feeling. Hannah beamed
over the success of her joke.

"Like back in '32," George was saying, his arm
beating in clock-like rhythm, "I come home and found
five jobless men settin' on my porch. Five that couldn't
to save their lives find a lick of work to do. One of 'em
was Clem Martin and I'd knowed Clem ever since I'd
been in New Falls. He says to me when I stepped up on
the porch, 'Well, George, I wish I was lucky as you, had
a good job to go to of a mornin'.' I says, 'Well Clem,
I'm thankful I've got a job to go to but it ain't what
you'd call a real good job, I don't suppose. I don't
draw but two dollars and five cent for a pretty worri-
some piece of work.' He says, 'George, if I knowed that

you'd quit the job and wasn't goin' to have it back noway nor nohow I'd go right straight down there and ask for it and if the boss said, 'You can have it if you'll work for a dollar a day,' I'd be so thankful at gettin' it atall I ain't certain I wouldn't cry right there and I've never cried but once since I've been a man.'

"Yessir, I think when a comp'ny like this owns a village they ought to be made by law to give a job to every able-bodied man and woman living in it and wantin' to work before they'd be allowed to bring in help from the outside. And I wish I could live to see the union sign up all the workin'-age boys and girls as well as the ones in the mill and I believe the workin' man would get a fairer deal."

"Did many of the people here join the union during the strike?" I asked.

"Lots of 'em joined but most is scared to tell it," George replied.

The girls laughed and exchanged glances among themselves. Mary said, "Maybe we oughtn't to be tellin'. But, law, I've showed my card to more'n one."

"They can't turn you off," Louise declared. "The new law gives a person the right to join the union. Taint like it was after the tater patch meetins."

"Now them was pitiful times for some," George said. "They come a man here back in '31 to hold union meetins and wouldn't none let him have a buildin' to hold 'em in. You see, the man that owns these mills near 'bout controls the whole city and he coulder ruint any man that rented his buildin'. But they went out yonder on the edge of town in a open field and a good many attended. Some joined. Now one way or another the company got word of ever one that joined and they give 'em ten-day notice. Some wouldn't move. The law come out and moved they things to the street.

"The next Sunday evenin' me and old man Tunney rode around Rimmerton where the worst was goin' on, and on two streets we counted eleven families settin' out on the sidewalk beside their things. To see them little children settin' out there with no manner of shelter over their heads, to see the women wore out with tryin' to live, sure put you to thinkin' and made you sorry you had to stop at thinkin'. What you thought about the ones that would do it wouldn't make no pleasant talk. It ain't no wonder folks here is still scared of the union.

"It looked for a while like them folks wasn't goin' to move off the streets. Up town they couldn't seem to figger out the law on it, but finally they got the health doctor to come out and declare the right sanitation wan't bein' carried out. He called their way of livin' a menace to public health and they moved 'em som'ers, I never did know where."

Ruth's eyes were like a flame as she spoke. "I'll stick by the union if it'll try to get me a decent wage for my work so's I can raise my children. I work like a dog in the spinnin' room and when I'm lucky enough to get four days I do as much or more as used to be done in five and a half but I'm paid about like what I ought to make in three.

"When they first put in that new Long Draft machinery women down there fainted and fell out. I fainted once myself. When I come to, my bossman was standin' over me and I was so scared of him I fainted again."

The picture of the second fainting drew laughter from the crowd. Its spirit still lingered in the room when the door was opened after a light rap upon it and a man walked in. He nodded at the crowd, leaned against the wall, and looked at the twins. "I've come to collect," he said. "We've got nothin' for you this week," Mary replied. "We can't even pay Mama our reg'lar board. We'll pay next week." "Don't pay to get behind with your insurance," the young man said. "I know but we can't help it," Louise said.

The young man turned and looked at me. "Selling insurance too?" he asked.

"No, but I feel very much at home with insurance people," I replied. "I usually meet one or two in most mill village homes I visit if it happens to be pay day."

"They're the hanginest round folks you ever seen," Mrs. McBane declared. "Before you can get a bite of bread in your mouth," she continued, raising her fat arm toward her mouth and stopping just short of reaching it, "they're at your door knock, knock." She concluded with imaginary raps in the air.

The insurance man grinned sheepishly and pushed his hat to the back of his head. "Well, insurance is a pretty good thing to have, Mrs. McBane," he said finally.

"I'll never be without it long as I can drag and make a dollar," Ruth declared. "I seen what it meant to have somebody you loved dead and waitin' to be buried and not a penny to your name to bury 'em with. If I can help it the welfare won't have to bury me and the children. I may have to do without things I need to eat but I'll have money laid back in insurance for my folks to buy a coffin to bury me in when I'm dead."

Mrs. McBane broke the silence. "I reckin that there insurance man has seen as many little new-born babies

as air doctor in New Falls. He's there to write 'em up
before they've let out their first yell."

A roar of laughter went around the room and was
sustained by a belated cackle from George who seemingly had thought upon the words before he allowed
them to provoke him to laughter.

Presently the young man made his departure but
first he warned the twins to have his money ready the
next pay day. He tempered the caustic tone of his
demand by smiling as he went out of the door.

A restlessness invaded the room which could not
immediately resolve itself into conversation. Bodies
shifted, feet shuffled. Presently Mary as if moved by a
sudden inspiration jumped to her feet, went into the
kitchen and came back with a pan of water and a cake
of soap. She placed the water on the stove, reached up
on the closet door, secured the big wash cloth hanging
there, and dipped it into the small pan. She soaped the
rag with a great display of energy, and began to give
her face a vigorous scrubbing.

"You talk about bein' strict," Louise said after
awhile, "if you had to inspect in the clothroom under
our supervisor you'd think you was in school with the
meanest teacher in the United States standin' over you.
She has a fit if we so much as open our mouths. For
eight hours we go as hard as we can pedalling the
machine while the cloth runs through, strainin' our eyes
to find a little bad place in it, and if we have three cuts
out of the two or three hundred we do a day to come
back on us she sends us out to rest the next day. It's
her way of punishin' us. The other day two girls had
went over to the fountain to get a drink of water—most
of us run there and back so's not to be fussed at for
leavin' our work—and a man they knowed passed by

and spoke to 'em. They wasn't gone no time but a little longer'n usual, so the supervisor sent 'em home and told 'em they'd better rest a day and then maybe they could stay at their work. They know how bad we hate to miss time when don't none of us make enough to get along on anyhow."

Mary emerged shortly from behind the folds of the big wash cloth, her face a glowing red. She went into the kitchen to empty the pan and returned with fresh water for Louise. "I think your face needs washin' too," she said to her, and instantly the other twin was engaged in soaping the rag for a face scrubbing. Her face was well covered in lather when someone tapped on the door and Mary tripped across the room to open it. A woman past middle age who carried a big black satchel in her hands came in. "Have this here seat, Mrs. Flack," George said, rising and placing his chair near the center of the room. Mrs. Flack seated herself and lost no time in opening up her satchel and drawing forth brightly colored dish towels. "These," she said to Sally, "are to be give away to everyone taking a $1.00 order this week. It's a very attractive offer. Wouldn't you like a little flavoring set this time, Mrs. Dobbin?"

"I'm afraid I can't take nothin' this time, Mrs. Flack," Sally replied. "The twins lost time last week and I'm shorter'n usual on money."

"And I've no longer got a job," George said, but Mrs. Flack did not seem to hear him.

"You don't have to pay me today," she said to Sally.

"I don't believe I'll take it," Sally said. "I don't won't to get no further in debt. 'Twon't be nothin' for me this week, Mrs. Flack. Ruth has took all that cough medicine she got from you but that little bit up there in the bottle, but it ain't seemed to do her no good atall."

Mrs. Flack raised her eyes to the mantel to look at the almost empty bottle. "It is nearly gone," she said. "Better let me leave you another bottle."

"No, I reckin not this time," Sally responded.

After unsuccessful efforts to supply the twins with vanishing cream Mrs. Flack closed her bag and departed, promising as she did so to return at an early date.

"That Garbo-Christian line's right good," Sally said when the door had closed, "but it comes pretty high."

George grabbed his chair, restored it to its former place, and speaking as a man who has discovered a truth he must express, he said, "Now cuttin' the hours ain't cut down on the joblessness atall. I believe it has actually increased it.

"What the manufacturer done was to stretch the stretchout a little more and speed up the machinery so's to get the same production with less help and shorter time. The mills is makin' the same amount of goods in three and four days as they used to make in a full week. Anybody'll tell you that.

"Twenty-four looms is aplenty for any person to run. Most runs thirty-two. Thirty-six batteries is enough for any young boy or girl to fill—takes 'em young on that job, old ones couldn't keep up—and they've got forty-eight apiece. The cardroom man used to run two slubbers and now they've give him three. When I come here it took seventeen men to keep up with the quill job; now the same work is bein' done by nine. They used to be a tangle man but now if you was to catch up five minutes with your own job the bossman says, 'Get over there and start to untanglin'.' First one and then another works at it till it gets done.

"What they really need is a committee of men that knows mill work from beginnin' to end—men hired by the governmint and not the comp'ny you understand—to go around and say, 'Now twenty-four looms is a fair job, so many batteries is enough for one person to fill,' and like that right on down to the sweeper. It's the work and not the hours that's needin' governmint regulation.

"I do think that Roosevelt is the biggest-hearted man we ever had in the White House. He undoubtedly is the most foresighted and can speak his thoughts the plainest of any man I ever heard speak. He's spoke very few words over the radio that I haven't listened to. It's the first time in my ricollection that a president ever got up and said, 'I'm interested in and aim to do somethin' for the workin' man.' Just knowin' that for once in the time of the country they was a man to stand up and speak for him, a man that could make what he felt so plain nobody could doubt he meant it, has made a lot of us feel a sight better even when they wasn't much to eat in our homes.

"Roosevelt picked us up out of the mud and stood us up but whenever he turns us loose I'm afraid we're goin' to fall and go deeper in the mud than we was before. That's because so many of his own party has turned against him and brought defeat to lots of his thinkin' and plannin'. The Bible says, 'A house divided against itself cannot stand, a kingdom divided against itself will end in desolation.' If they keep abuckin' against him and bigheads get in there that try to make too quick a turn back, desolation will follow in our country.

"Roosevelt is the only president we ever had that

thought the Constitution belonged to the pore man too. The way they've been areadin' it it seemed like they thought it said, 'Him that's got money shall have the rights to life, freedom and happiness.' Is they any freedom to bein' throwed out of yore home and have to watch yore children suffer just because you joined a organization you thought might better you? Does it make you think you've got liberty to be treated like that when the man you're workin' for has always had the right to join the association to multiply his own good livin'? Yessir, it took Roosevelt to read in the Constitution and find out them folks way back yonder that made it was talkin' about the pore man right along with the rich one. I am a Roosevelt man."

George Dobbin's children had listened absorbedly to his solemn pronouncements. They gave the impression once he had finished of persons who had had their own thoughts spoken for them. They were beyond the ties of family bound together now in the unity of common thought. There was no immediate need for continued speech or action and the silence which followed was restful and full of ease.

Presently a bright-faced boy of perhaps thirteen came into the room and Sally introduced him as her youngest child, Henry. "He's the only one I've got in school now," she added. "He's in the eighth grade. How come you so late, Henry?"

"I went by the Y awhile," the boy answered as he passed into the kitchen. There came into the room the sound of one plate being slipped from a stack of plates followed by the click of a stove door opening.

Mary in deep preoccupation cast a critical glance from first one member of her family to the other. "Why, Henry's already gone farther in school than any of us," she said finally. The thought amused her and she laughed. All the younger Dobbins joined her.

"None the rest of us ever got past the seventh grade, did we?" Louise said. "Dan, he was so busy totin' us younguns around he didn't get that far. Mama used to say she bet Dan had rolled me and Mary as far as from here to New York and back in that double baby carriage we had."

"They was a woman in Henderson," Sally began, "that had twins too but hers died. She heard about mine and sent word to me she'd sell their carriage to me for four dollars. Then I was considered one of the best hands in Henderson for doin' up bonnets. I done enough bonnets to buy the carriage and I don't see to save my life how I'der raised them twins without it.

"Mary, they's somebody else aknockin' on the door. It'll about be Mr. Hunter comin' for a paymint on my dress."

Mary came back presently followed by a fat, well-dressed man who after a general nod at the crowd directed his attention toward Sally. "How are you, Mrs. Dobbin," he said, and Sally, reaching into her pocket answered, "All right, I reckin, Mr. Hunter. Here's your fifty cent and I'll try to have the rest of it next week." "That's all right, Mrs. Dobbin," Mr. Hunter answered, and after a smile to all left the room.

"He's a dress peddler," Sally explained, "and a mighty nice man. Him and his brother runs a store up town and he puts part of the goods in his car and comes around peddlin' 'em out. Some times the children fusses at me for buyin' from him because they say his wash dresses is always about fifty cent higher than they are up town but he's so nice about waitin' for his money. Sometimes a body may be able to save fifty cent a week to pay on a dress when they can't save a dollar and a half at a time to buy one. I appreciate how nice Mr. Hunter is about waitin'."

I looked out of the window and already the foggy day was losing the little of its light that remained. I arose to leave and after I had said good-bye to the crowd Sally got up and accompanied me to the door. I was going down the porch steps when someone called my name. I turned around and George Dobbin stood there just outside of the door, and by the light from the near-by street light I could see the solemn expression on his face.

"If ever you get to talk to any that it'll do any good to talk to," he said, "they's one law you might tell 'em oughter be passed. It is a sin and a shame for air comp'ny in the world to run a elevator without a reg'lar operator. It's my ricollection I've never heard tell of a accident on a elevator where they was a reg'lar operator. But many a time I've read where folks has gone to a horrible death when they've got on one and never knowed how to run it.

"Course if this comp'ny was to get a reg'lar man for the job it'd more'n likely not be me. I'm old and they don't want me. But the law ought really to be passed.

"No, I don't know as I'll ever have another mill job," he muttered as he turned to go back into the house.

IDA MOORE

A Little Amusemint

THE MAN, CLAD IN FADED BLUE OVERALLS, RESTED a foot against the lower rail of the hogpen which was the last one on the left side of the long avenue of Spanish oaks. He propped his elbows on the top rail while he gazed speculatively at the two Duroc hogs in the pen. There was meat enough in those two hogs to carry him and the old woman through the winter. He watched while the hogs sniffed their way up and down the length of the trough greedy for the last drop of slop he had just poured out for them.

James was still preoccupied with his meat supply when a woman turned into the lane and stopped at the big Spanish oak whose branches shaded the hogpen in which James' hogs grunted contentedly. The woman might have been a bookkeeper, a teacher, a stenographer, a clerk, or perhaps a social worker. John looked up at her and made no speculation as to why she was standing there. He observed only that she was dressed in Sunday clothes and that she seemed friendly.

"Pretty hogs you have there," the woman said.

"Ain't they fine," James said and looked up at the woman.

"Does this land belong to the mill company?" the woman asked.

"Yessum, and this road leads up to the houses. It used to be called Hogpen Lane because then all hogpens had to be built down here. That rule ain't followed now and you'll find plenty up there amongst the houses. I like to have my hogs down here though. They's more space and it's easier to keep clean. That-a-way it don't make such a stink."

The woman looked up the avenue of old Spanish oaks green yet with the full ripeness of late summer. There were weeds all along, ragged and disorderly, and there were dilapidated hogpens up as far as the tenth big tree.

"Beautiful trees," she said.

"Ain't they for sure," James answered. "A tree's a pretty thing," he added. "I've been walking amongst these for nigh on to thirty year."

"You've lived here so long then?" the woman asked.

"Ever since me and the old woman's been married. Us two has 'bout wore out with the house we're in now and been in all the time."

"Any children?"

"Ain't never had none. Sometimes I wish I did. When I see the fine young girls of today I wisht I had a daughter of my own."

"I guess you've had a chance to save money then."

"Yessum I reckin I've had the chance but I never done it. I was thinkin' when you come up I'd give a good five years of my life for a little farm of my own to spend my last days on. I was born on a farm down in Cumberland County. Pa lost it, though, before I was full grown, and every year after that we moved from one man's farm to another, never satisfied nowhere and hardly havin' enough to barely live on. I got tired of that and when I got to be my own man I come to the mill."

"What things have kept you from saving money?"

"Corn liquor," James replied. "Back in good times I made as high as $30 a week. Livin' was awful high then, but I could've put by part of my wage if drinkin' hadn't got the upper hand of me. I don't touch a drop now but I quit too late for savin' money. I ain't makin' none."

"How much do you make now?"

"Well, I'm due to draw $11 a week but I don't because every Monday I'm sent out to rest. That's the hardest thing in the world for me to explain to old man Collins, the man I trade with. I'll say, 'I cain't pay you but five dollars this week because I never worked Monday.' And he'll say 'Well, I heared the whistle blow Monday; the mill muster been runnin'.' Then I try to explain to him how the mill's runnin' full time but most of the help don't git full time. Gen'ly I make between eight and nine dollars but I don't have much over six after the rent and insurance is took out."

"It takes the most of that to buy food for the two of you I guess," the woman said.

"Yessum, it does. And a little cornbread for the dogs. I've got five."

"Don't you find it expensive to keep five dogs?"

"Well, I reckin I could put that money I buy corn-meal with into somethin' else, but them dogs mean a sight to me. Huntin' is about the only amusemint I have, and the old woman don't object to me keepin' the dogs. I've kept dogs for thirteen year now, ever since I stopped drinkin'."

"How did you stop drinking?" the woman asked.

"I reckin to make it so you'll understand, I better tell you how I started. Bad company done it. When I got to makin' good money they was a free and easy crowd that got to askin' me to go round with them.

They was the kind of folks that never come home sober.
And it won't long till I was just as bad. It went on for
four or five year, and then one day I got hold of some
liquor that made me sicker than I had ever been in my
life. It looked like I was goin' to gag myself to death.
The old woman said she was gonna git somethin' to
settle my stomach and she did. She give me a big dose
of paregoric and it eased me right away. Fact is, I
hadn't never felt so good. The next day she didn't have
to give me none; I took it myself. After that liquor
never had no 'traction atall for me. But they wasn't
a day passed that I didn't dreen the last drop out of a
two or a four ounce bottle of paregoric. And lady, for
awhile them days was like heaven. No worry come in
my mind, and all the world seemed right. I felt as good
as anybody, and it never mattered that I wasn't a rich
man because I felt like one. But soon them good days
passed away.

"The time come when I was so nervous I hated myself.
I got to where I wasn't satisfied nowhere. Then come
along the narcotic laws and paregoric got hard to git.
By that time a half a pint a day wouldn't satisfy me.
I took to goin' around and gittin' the college students
to sign up for two ounces apiece.

"Finally my mind went bad on me. I reckin I got
what you might call plumb crazy. The cop, he got to
watchin' me, and one day he told me if I'd sign some
papers he could git me a bottle of paregoric. I signed
and went home. A few days later here come some folks
out from Dix Hill, and they told me they was takin' me
to Raleigh for a medical examination. I told 'em I
wasn't goin', but in the end I went. When I got there
they wrote down on a paper everything they noticed
about me, and all the time I was figgerin' on how I was

goin' to git away. They musta knowed what I was thinkin' because when they left the room they locked the door.

"Well, they kept me at Dix Hill for sixty days, and when I come back home the fight was pretty near over. They was a few weeks when I woulder took to dope agin if I coulder got it. As time passed on I got shet of the cravin'. But I don't never take no chances on what might happen agin. You couldn't git me to touch even a cocoa cola or a BC.

"Comin' back to the dogs. I knowed it would help me to have some sort of amusemint in my life. I took to keepin' dogs as I told you. I ain't able to have 'em, I know, but then I ain't hardly able to give 'em up. I jined up with the church too. Me and the old woman's been 'tendin' regular. I don't know whether we'll have clothes for wearin' to church this winter or not. While ago I was forced to put on my Sunday shoes and I reckin from now on I'll wear 'em for everyday. 'Bout all I've got left now is hope for another life. I've throwed away what chance I had in this one and I ain't faultin' nobody for it. I never could've been no rich man but I could've saved fur a little farm.

"Hear that whistle? My shift goes on in fifteen minutes. Come on and go to the house. The old woman would be glad to have somebody to talk to."

James and the woman started down the lane toward the house together. They were passing the third hog-pen when James stopped and, pointing at two scrubby yellowish-white pigs, said, "Look at 'em, will you. Ain't much bigger than rabbits. They'll shore have to take on growth if they mean to make hogmeat by Christmas." He chuckled to himself as they walked on up the lane. "Haven't growed off like mine," he said presently.

They had come to the beginning of houses before James spoke again. "After all it's better to be livin' than dead," he said. "Yonder is my house, that one with the porch ceiling ripped loose and swagging down. A peart little wind would blow the whole house down, I reckin.

"The old woman got a good laugh off me the other day. I was standin' on the hearth and of a sudden it give way. Who'd ever thought but what it was built solid, but t'wan't. Boards had been holdin' up that one layer of brick and they give way with rot. I went clean on through, up to my waist.

"Well, here we are. Lizzie's heared me talkin' and she's comin' to the door. Old woman, here's a young lady that's come to talk with you awhile. The whistle has blowed so I'll be gittin' to the mill. Jest go right on in."

The visitor opened the sagging gate and went in. Lizzie who stood on the porch said, "Come on in." The woman went into the room and sat down in the chair Lizzie offered her.

"They may be a breeze from where you are settin'," Lizzie said. "The day's turned off hot, ain't it? Hot for this late in September."

The woman looked at the bulging sack in the middle of the floor.

"Taters," Lizzie said. "He dug 'em this mornin'. We had a pretty good patch this year and they help out too. Them in that sack would cost a dollar at the store. Ain't things high?"

"Groceries do seem high when we don't have much to buy them with."

"I don't know where clothes is comin' from this winter," Lizzie said. "Last week I got some 10¢ a yard print and made me that dress over there on the bed. It's the first dress I've had in over a year. Week befo' last I bought me and him a pair of slippers apiece and made arrangemints to pay a dollar a week on 'em. Folks we trade with is awful kind. They don't never turn us down long as we keep payin' a little. C'ose we don't buy a whole lot of things."

Lizzie sat with her hands one on the other and palms turned upward. The woman listened to the dead, dragging tones of Lizzie's voice. Even while Lizzie talked and her lips moved slowly, her face remained expressionless. Her eyes far back under their heavy, thick lids gazed dimly out at the woman to whom she talked.

Presently three dogs came through the kitchen door and into the room where the two women sat. The big black one trotted over to where the stranger sat and rubbed against her. He was ready to place his front paws in her lap when Lizzie called him down.

"He's sort of a pet," Lizzie said. "We've raised him from a little puppy. James keeps five dogs and maybe we oughtn't, as po' as we are, but he's got to have some amusemint. You see he don't keep no bad company nor drink atall. I'd heap rather my husband would have dogs he wa'n't able to feed than to drink like some folks. He don't drink none atall, you see."

The woman thought of the things that James had told her. She looked up on the mantel and saw a picture of Shirley Temple. "Do you like to see Shirley Temple in movies?" she asked Lizzie.

"N'om, I've never saw her," the woman said. "I never did take up no time with picture shows and amusemints of that kind. 'Bout the only amusemint I git is 'tendin'

church. It all depends on what a person gits used to.
I used to enjoy readin' some but my eyes is got so bad
I cain't. Since I've had the kidney trouble they seems
to be a skim over 'em most of the time. Course me and
him neither never went to school much but we both have
some education. Enough for plain readin' and a little
writin'.

"In the wintertime he used to buy me a magazine now
and agin and I true enjoyed settin' by the fire and
readin'. I used to like the winter anyhow when we
could buy plenty of coal and wood but last winter was
sho a bad one. We never had a lump of coal and all
we had to burn was the sidins they give him down at
the sawmill for stackin' lumber in his spare time. They
wasn't enough to have a fire all the time so many a day
I went to bed to keep warm.

"I'm dreadin' this winter wusser because he ain't
makin' much and the house leaks wusser than it done
last year.

"Mrs. Lance right over there bought her a roll of
roofin' this last gone Satday and her old man tacked
it over the wust leaks. And jest today I seen the same
truck stop over there but I ain't had time yet to ask
her if she'd bought another roll of roofin'. I had to go
stir my peas 'bout the time they was unloadin' and I
never seen what they took out.

"They's a sick woman down the street that's got
married children and she said she's goin' to try to git
them to buy her a roll, enough to tack on the roof over
where her bed is anyhow. I wisht we was able to buy a
roll. It do leak so bad right over there.

"James said he wanted to buy a little heater this
winter but I don't see how we can. I don't even see how
we can buy coal."

The visitor did not know what to say so she looked into the kitchen at the semicircle of cooking utensils which hung on the wall. An old granite boiler hung in the middle and on its left two frying pans. On the right the biscuit pan hung. There was a table in the kitchen too, upon which the food left over from dinner was bunched close together and covered over with a bleached flour sack cover. Against the far wall an oilstove leaned.

Finally her eyes left the kitchen and came back into the room where she sat. She looked up at the only picture which hung on the walls. Its central feature was a garish green tree decorated with golden balls. At its foot an angel stood and pointed toward it while she looked down at a tiny boy and girl on the other side of the tree.

"What's the name of the picture?"

"It's called 'The Tree of Life'," Lizzie answered. "Them little yellow balls is got good words on 'em—like faith, hope, charity, and plenty. I think it's a pretty picture. I got a lot of comfort out of lookin' at it. The angel's so pretty."

"Do you like living at the mill?" the woman asked presently. "Or had you rather live in the country?"

"Well, if we had the fixmints I'd a heap rather live in the country," Lizzie answered. "But we've got no money for buyin' the fixmints. Sometimes he faults hisself for not savin' money when he had a good job, but I tell him tain't no sense in that. If he hader saved it and put it in the bank all of it wouler been gone anyhow. But they ain't nobody wants you on the farm now 'less you able to furnish youself.

"Two year ago when the mill wa'n't runnin' none atall for a spell, and most of us was sufferin' for food, folks said, 'What makes you stay on at the mill and starve while you waitin' for it to run agin?' But I said 'Well, where we goin' to go? Nobody wants you when you ain't got nothin'.'

"Like the old man that died here last winter. Some folks said, 'You ain't able to keep him.' And we wasn't. We got some help for him from the relief but still we wa'n't able to keep him. He used to bo'd with us, but he'd got disabled to work and had nowhere to go. I knowed he was goin' to die and I was worryin' 'bout how we'd get him buried.

"When he did die I went to see the county and after I'd been to a sight of trouble they said they'd make the arrangemints. I'll tell you it's a sad thing to see a person buried by the county. I thought of course they'd send out a awful cheap coffin but they never sent no coffin atall. They sent out a wooden box with a lid that screwed on. And to make it wusser they had painted it red. Sometimes yit when I'm here by myself it gits on my mind.

"Me and James's had out insurance for five or six year, and after I seen the way that old man had to be buried I said I'd rather go hungry than drop it. What we've got will be enough to bury us.

"It do seem like we've had a awful hard time for the past four or five year but I'm thankful to be amongst the livin' instead of the dead. He's got a heavy job at the mill that he wouldn't have took durin' good times. But they's plenty without jobs of any kind.

"What we'll do for clothes is botherin' me some. He had to take his Sunday shoes for everyday and I'm afeered he'll stop church when they git to lookin' bad."

The visitor got up and said that she must be going. Lizzie asked her to stay on a while longer. When the

woman said again that she must leave Lizzie followed
her to the door. As the two women stood on the porch
talking the dogs rushed around to the small front yard.

"Git away Blackie," Lizzie said as the dog nosed up
to the woman. "It do look like we've got too many dogs
for poor folks," she continued. "But he's got to have
a little amusemint. He don't drink like some folks,
and he don't have no other bad habits."

IDA MOORE

Solid Time

H UB'S HIRED SOLID TIME AND HAS BEEN FOR TWO
years. He works every day from six in the morning till six at night in Mr. Hunter's brick plant across
the tracks. Some day's more'n that—twenty-four
hours on a stretch. That's over-time, but it don't mean
no extra pay. It's forty dollars a month straight, no
matter what."

Rena Murray—small, stooped, hollow-chested—put
her whole ninety pounds behind the heavy flatiron.
Collar and cuffs came from under the heat, stiff and
slick. She lifted the shirt from the board for final
inspection.

"Hub fires the boiler most of the time. Then when
they're drying bricks, he has to run the fan for twenty-

four hours.   They couldn't make out in that kiln unless Hub was there.

"He ought to git more for the work he puts out. Forty dollars a month just ain't enough for us to live on.   Me and Hub and the three children.   We have to pay four dollars out every month for this shack.   Mr. Hunter makes the hands live close by the plant.   And he gits ahold of that four dollars for rent before we ever see a cent of Hub's wages.   This shack ain't worth four dollars a month, neither.   Mr. Hunter won't do nothing toward fixing it up.   If a window pane's broke, we do the putting in.   Leak done ruint the paper and it's up to us to see to new paper."

Rena stooped to the tub of sprinkled clothes.   She shook out a rolled-up bundle and slipped another shirt over the narrow end of the home-made ironing board. She settled the board again between the center table and the lard bucket set in a backless kitchen chair.

"I take in washing or do what I can to help out. Hub and Mabel has to pack all our water from over there at the plant.   When Mabel's to school and Hub's to work it's an awful lot of packing for me.   I got a weakness here in my chest.   The doctor says it ain't T. B., but he won't say what it is.

"I guess Louise taken after me.   She's thin as a stick and don't ever feel no ways well.   Mabel gits up of a morning pinching herself to see if she can't rake up some misery to keep her home from school.   Louise ain't going to miss a day, sick or no sick.   She ain't but eight.   They's both a big help to me . . . Mabel, tote yourself in here and spread out them dresses I've finished."

Mabel, fourteen, buxom, came into the front room from the kitchen.   She walked to the front door and emptied her lower lip's load of snuff into the yard. A cheap permanent wave tangled her blond hair. Her high-heel pumps flopped up and down at the heels as she walked. She carefully lifted an armload of freshly ironed dresses and headed toward the one bright spot in the drab room—the bed, gay with a cheap pink rayon spread.

"Mind the spread, Mabel. Turn it back and rest 'em apart on the quilt. I ain't had that spread but since morning. It's a premium for selling candy. I do a little bit of everything to help out. I could have got two dollars in cash. I knowed we need a lot of things worse'n we need a two dollar counterpane. But when I seen how pretty it was I just let myself go and take it.

"Mabel, mind Dot. That youngun's like as not to start across the tracks if she sees something she wants there. She ain't never budged out the yard, but you can't tell what a little un'll do. I never seen a baby play better by herself—just all day long messing in and out that old car of ourn alongside the house. That car's more help to me to keep her from under my feet than it's ever been for getting us places.

"Hub says little as he makes he's always going to have something to take him around besides his legs. I don't see why. There ain't no time a-tall he can go. We ain't been to church for years. I was taught working on Sunday was wrong. Folks that holds out against working on Sunday don't have to hire others to work for 'em if they don't show up. Hub had to pay a dollar and a quarter yesterday to git a man to turn the fan so's he could see after his sister. She's about to die. Dirty shame for a man to have to pay to go see his own die. I sure wish he could find hisself a better job."

Rena licked her finger and touched the iron. The sputter told her the iron was hot enough.

"They's been talking something about a new law on hours and wages. I've heard folks in town that knows say Mr. Hunter ought to be forced to pay us more. Twelve cents ain't no decent price to pay for a hour's hard work. But what you going to do? Mr. Hunter's got the jump on us. Hub ain't got nothing good in sight right now. Last year Mr. Hunter had every hand to sign a paper or quit. Hub he let 'em put his name down. He couldn't quit not knowing of a job nowheres else.

"Mr. Hunter made a big blow about a bonus he give the hands every January. Me and Hub ain't never got the straight of it. Here's how it is. Some money is set aside for bonus money. What's left after all the plant improvement goes to pay for broken tools and that ain't much. What little is left is divided. A hand gits his according to how much ain't been drawed from his share during the year. They fired a man last year in December. He'd worked steady all the year, solid time. But they fired him so's to make sure he didn't draw no bonus. He was a keerful worker and didn't have nothing to speak of drawed from his share."

Rena tilted the iron back on the handle. She found the wad of paraffin screwed up in a rag in her apron pocket and shined the face of the iron.

"The bonus ain't never very much. Last year it run from ninety cents to forty dollars. Hub was working solid time. They give him thirty dollars. He's going to hang on this year till after he gits his bonus. He can't quit then till he gits sight of something else. What he aims to do is to turn over every stone he can to git back on the WPA. We got along a lot better on the WPA. We had our check regular and had good warm clothes for the girls. And they give Hub clothes, too, because his work kept him in the open. I didn't git none but I could manage all right when the others was gitting all they did. Whenever one of us would git down, the WPA would send a doctor and medicine. They give us food, too. Things that are supposed to be healthy for eating such as prunes and raisins. We can't buy 'em now.

"It was three years back, in dead of winter, when a man in Paris talked Hub into taking this here job. He painted it up—how fine it would be to work inside and how it's the only kiln in Barnes County. Hub had been here for five years one time before. He was working here when the gov'ment shut the whole plant up. NRA done it. Mr. Hunter never would run the place noways like what the gov'ment said.

"I just can't figger it out how a man that's got money he ain't never seen, like Mr. Hunter, can be like he is. Won't share a thing with them that's needful. The doctor told Hub he'd have to git a cow since my health was porely. There Mr. Hunter had five big acres of good pasture and just one cow. But he wouldn't leave us put ourn there for love nor money. Hub offered him a dollar a month for the use of it. Didn't budge him. The second boss over to the plant told Hub to pick him up a roll of wire somewheres and take and fence the clay field for pasture. Hub done it. It's wild pasture, but better than nothing, and it's a good place to keep her in the winter up there in the powder factory. The gov'ment wouldn't let Mr. Hunter use it to make face powder like he'd planned. It was enough shame having the brick plant going like it was,

I reckon. That powder factory house is built better than this shack.

"Mabel, tote this iron out and git me a hot un."

Rena stacked the ironed flatwork on the wooden box covered with newspaper.

"A body ought to take good keer of a cow. Cows ain't cheap. Somebody shot ourn last year. We had to pay forty dollars for the one we got now. She's a good milker—gives six gallons a day when she's fresh. We aim to fatten one of them pigs out in the back yard off of extry milk. Then we can have a hog-killing. Nothing I'd like better."

She ran the paraffin wad over the fresh iron's face and lifted the three sprinkled bundles from the tub under the board.

"I was raised on the farm. I like it better than any way of living I know. Time and time again I says to Hub, 'Let's go to farming.' If he could just git a good shot at sharecropping, I know he'd do it right off. We was always poor—shifting from one farm to another. Pappy died when I was three. Mammy married two times after that. My last stepfather drapped dead right before us all one day when me and Hub come out to the farm to ask a setting of eggs. First thing I thought was, 'Ain't none of us got money enough to git him buried.' 'Fore we got him straightened out mammy says, 'Rena, git your pappy's Woodman's policy from under the dresser scarf. You can't tell who'll be drapping in on a time like this.'

"Hub took out a Woodman's policy soon after we were married. We're always so hard up he says every time dues comes, 'I've a mind to drap it.' But I ain't going to let him do it. Why, Mr. Hunter don't carry a penny insurance on none of his hands. If something happened to Hub, me and the children would plain suffer. Hub use to put on that Woodman's pin any time when he had clothes fit to be proud of. He says he ain't going to be shining a pin like that on overalls, and I don't blame him a bit."

Rena shook out the last rolled-up bundle. She smoothed the heavy roller towel the length of the board.

"Burial insurance is a good thing. I wish I had a policy on me and every one of the children. That's just wishing. It pinches us plumb to death to keep Hub's going. We was always behind in dues till he got put on solid time. I couldn't git no insurance noways on account of my bad health. I've had the pneumonia since we've been here. Down three months. There wasn't a Hunter had feeling enough to set foot in this shack. Mrs. Hunter has spoke to me times since, but Mr. Hunter don't trouble about speaking to them that slaves for him. My mammy taught me a dog was good enough to be nice to.

"It ain't nothing to be proud of going through life with a shut mouth. It don't help nobody. I done this ironing twice as quick having you here to talk to. Don't seem like I'm as wore-out as usual neither."

RUTH MONROE
JENNETTE EDWARDS

It's a Christian Factory

I LIKE MY WORK. I LIKE WORKING FOR CHRISTIAN people. Mr. Pugh owns the shoe plant here in Hancock and he sure is a Christian man. Do you know why he's made such a big success in life? It's the Christian way he lives. They tell me he gives a tenth of all he makes to the church and the Lord made him successful. It makes you feel good to work for a Christian man like that."

"My work is hard all right. It's hard on me because I ain't but only seventeen and ain't got my full growth yet. It's work down in the steam room which they call it that because it's always full of steam which sometimes when you go in it you can't hardly see. You steam leather down there and that steam soaks you clean to the skin. It makes me keep a cold most of the time because when I go out doors I'm sopping wet. Another thing that's hard about it is having so much standing up to do. My hours is from seven o'clock in the morning till four in the evening. And it's stand on my feet the whole time. When noon time comes and I'm off an hour, why I just find me somewheres to set and I sure set there. You couldn't pay me to stand up during lunch time.

"I'm on piecework now and I can't seem to get my production up to where I make just a whole lot. You get paid by the production hour and it takes fifty pair

231

of shoes to make that hour. You get forty-two cents
for the hour. Highest I ever made in one week was
eleven dollars and the lowest was seven dollars and
forty-two cents. I usually hit in between and make
eight or nine dollars.

"Now and then somebody will say, 'We ought to
have us a union here of some sort.' That kind of talk
just makes me mad all over. Mr. Pugh is a Christian
man. He brought his factory here to give us some
work which we didn't have any before. We do pretty
well, I think, to just stay away from that kind of talk.
All but the sore-heads and trouble-makers is satisfied
and glad to have work.

"I don't blame Mr. Pugh a bit the way he feels about
the unions. The plant manager knows Mr. Pugh
mighty well and he told my foreman what Mr. Pugh
said. Mr. Pugh said, 'If the union ever comes in here
and I have to operate my plant under a union, why I'll
just close the plant down and move it away from Hancock so quick it'll make your head swim.' That's his
word on it and I don't blame him none. I'd hate to
see a union try here. No plant and no jobs for anybody. They just operate these unions out of Wall
Street, anyhow, trying to ruin people like Mr. Pugh.
Man told me that and he knows. He worked in Detroit
during the War. Wall Street set some unions on
Henry Ford and tried to put his back to the wall. But
did they do it? Don't make me laugh!

"Next to the unions, this new wages and hours business of the government's is bad, too. Some people that
had been getting as high as thirty-five dollars a week
was cut to only twenty-five which is about ten dollars
a week less than they'd been getting before. They
didn't like it because it meant their salary wasn't as

much as it had been.   Then some that hadn't got but
five or six dollars got to getting as much as I get.
They liked that, but it don't seem fair to me.   Why
should a man that's not worth as much to the plant
as me get as much money as me?

"My money has to go a long way.   I've got to pay
eight dollars a month rent and I have to buy coal and
stove wood.   I got to buy clothes for the family and
something to eat for them.   Then twice a month there's
that five dollar ambulance bill which it's to take my
brother that's got the T.B. to the City Hospital in
Memphis where they take and drain his lungs.   Sure
charge you for an ambulance, don't they?   Now, some
people say if you just take one trip in an ambulance,
the undertaker won't ask a cent for it.   Figures he'll
get your custom if you pass on.   But they sure charge
me for my brother.

"Well, I'm always glad when it's quitting time.   I
like to work there, but you can't help getting tired.
I go on home.   I walk four blocks and I'm there.
Usually I have to wait a while for supper so I just set
at the window.   I like to watch and see if maybe something will come along the street and I can watch it.
Sometimes there's a new funny paper there and I will
look it over—specially if it's Tarzan.   That's the best
thing in a funny paper, the Tarzan part.   Nobody
ever gets it over old Tarzan, do they?   Most times,
though, I like to just set there and watch.

"That's one of the best things I liked about working
in the filling station that time—always something to
see.   Cars coming in and out.   I used to keep count
of the out-of-the-state license plates and how many
people wore straw hats.   It was the first job I ever had.
I waited on customers, such as selling gasoline and

patching tires. I got a dollar ninety-eight a week there, but sometimes there were tips, and anyhow it was fun. I'd have worked for nothing almost if they'd let me.

"Well, I got another job after that. My brother which he's my married brother is just about the best man to paper a house or give it a coat of paint in Hancock. They say around here that if you want a good job of painting or paper hanging, just call in the Sherrys. Lots of other men will work cheaper, but it's not a high-grade, A number-one, first-class job like my brother's. So I painted and papered a while. But I got to the place where the smell of paint didn't agree with me. I took painter's colic. I was afraid I'd get down sick like my other brother, so I quit and got a job in Pugh's shoe plant in the steam room which I'm still there in it after a year.

"I work steady but I'm most always financially in need of money. It takes a lot to keep a family going. My little sister needs glasses but they cost too much. All of my family has weak eyes but we can't afford to wear glasses.

"So I haven't the money for running around. I wouldn't if I had the money, either. The Bible is against running around and playing cards and seeing the moving pictures. People should study their Bible more and we'd have more Christian men like Mr. Pugh and more jobs. So me and a young lady I know of go to church and Sunday School instead of running around. My family belongs to the Baptist Church, but this certain young lady is a Nazarene and that's where we go.

"You know, when you're blue and down at the mouth and don't see any use anyhow, a good sermon just lifts you up. You haven't got a thing to lose by living a Christian life. Take Mr. Pugh. He lives it and look where he is now. And if you don't make out that way, if you're poor all your life, then you get a high place in the Kingdom. Just do the best you know how and the Lord will take care of you either here or hereafter. It sure is a comfort."

ROBERTA JOHNSON
JAMES R. ASWELL

I'd Rather Die

RAIN LASHED THE WINDOWS IN GUSTS AND SOMEWHERE immensely high and remote thunder muttered. Inside the pie wagon was bright hot light, the smell of greasy fryings, of dish water, beer, and stale cigarette smoke.

The young man with the dark broad face and heavy shoulders poured his beer. "Might as well go on talking," he said. "Looks like this rain's caught me here for some time. I live a mile from the end of the car line here and I'd be drenched before I could get home. Wet enough as it is." His curly hair dripped and the gray work shirt was mottled with rain.

From the cheap radio above the counter, where Gus the owner of the pie wagon leaned chewing on a match stick, the pant and grunt of a Negro singer came through a hammering beat of orchestration.

> "Flat-ah foot-ah floogie
> "With-ah floy-floy-
>   "Floy-doy, floy-doy, floy-doy."

The young man got up from the table, stepped across, and rolled his emptied bottle down the counter. "For God's sake, Gus, can't you turn that racket off?"

"Sure, Jeems." Gus nodded. He turned and clicked the switch. "These here popular songs gits crazier ever year. Nothing good on the radio no more but the Saturday night barn dance. I keep the doggone thing on all the time for the customers but it's got so I don't no more hear it than nothing. Gits to be a sort of silence, that noise does."

Gus took the bottle and dropped it in a case. Then he shuffled behind the beaver-board partition to wash the dishes left by the supper crowd. "Y'all need anything, just call me, just call me," he said.

Jimmy dribbled salt over the head of foam in his chill-beaded glass. "Well, as I started telling you, I went to work for Travis and Son a few weeks after Dad died. It's an overall factory—Everwear brand, you know. The name Travis and Son doesn't mean anything now. The Travises drank themselves to death a long time ago and the company's run now by Old Dave MacGonnigal and his four boys.

"I never in my life dreamed I'd ever have to work at that place. Of course, Dad was a pattern-maker there and worked for Old Dave over forty-five years. But if things hadn't gone the way they did, I'd never known what he went through to keep us alive all those years. Well, after Dad's death when the bottom dropped out from under the family I couldn't find a job anywhere. Finally I applied to Old Dave MacGonnigal.

"It was the first time I'd ever seen him. He's a tall man, kind of bent over, and with a long face and a long nose. He used to have a mop of hair, they tell me, but now his head's as bald as a brass door knob and just about as shiny. He looks glum and sour all the time and turns his head sideways and snaps at you when he talks.

" 'I'll give you something, boy,' he told me, 'but you've got to work.'

" 'I'll do my best,' I said, just like the boy in the books.

" 'Well,' he said to me, 'you needn't think that because you've got that high school diploma you can sit around on your tail here and talk Latin. We work here, boy. I put on overalls and work like the rest. You soldier on me and I'll fire you like a shot—understand?'

"I stood up straight and looked him in the eye. You're supposed to do that, you know, to show you've got character. I said, 'You can depend on me, sir!'

" 'All right,' he said. 'I'll expect you to report to the stock room at seven-thirty Monday morning. And I mean on the dot! I really don't need you, mind, but I'm putting you on because you're one of Bob's boys. Clear out now, boy. I'm busy.'

"Seemed to me at the time that the job was something handed down out of heaven. I was so happy and relieved I didn't even ask the old man how much he was going to pay me. Rushed on home as fast as I could go to tell Mama.

" 'Work hard,' she told me, 'and Mr. MacGonnigal will certainly advance you. Your father was a valuable man and they'll keep their eyes on you. Wait and see.'

"I promised I would. I guess I was about as happy as I'd ever been in my life.

"I can tell you I didn't feel that way when the end of the first week came around. I drew six dollars and fifty cents.

"But there's a lot before this that I'd better tell.

"I don't ever remember want or any feeling of insecurity when I was little. Dad made good money in those days—say, about fifty or sixty dollars a week. You know, a pattern maker has a pretty important job in an overall factory. If the patterns he lays out aren't right to the fraction of an inch the cutters will ruin a lot of goods. There's a good deal of figuring to it, complicated figuring, and he can't make mistakes. Dad never learned mathematics because he hadn't had a chance to go to high school. But he'd worked out a system of his own with all sorts of funny little signs and symbols. Nobody else understood it. He could take a problem of figuring up goods and have it done in a minute where some of the efficiency experts Old Dave had in from time to time would take an hour to work it. And Dad's would be nearer the right answer than the experts'. The boys in the cutting room told me all about it when I came there to work. So they paid Dad a pretty good salary, though not what he was worth.

"We had our own home in North Chattanooga and we had a car. My two older brothers and my sister finished high school. My oldest brother, after being a salesman for a few years with Radebaugh Shoe Company, worked his way through Columbia University. I don't guess he could have done it by work alone. But he won one scholarship after another and finally a traveling fellowship that gave him a year in Europe.

After that he came back and went into business in Chicago. My next oldest brother got a job on a newspaper after high school. Mother'd wanted him to be a lawyer but he wasn't interested. Sister married and moved away.

"The first hard times I remember came in 1933, when I was in the eighth grade. Travis and Son shut down and for six months Dad didn't draw a penny. Things must have been pinching for two or three years before that because by that time the house was mortgaged and the money spent. I don't know much about the details. Anyhow, my brother in Chicago couldn't help much. He was barely holding his job up there. My brother who worked for the newspaper was cut to practically nothing. He made enough to pay his expenses and that's about all. Then they cut the staff and let the youngest reporters off and he was one of them.

"Then we were really up against it. For a whole week one time we didn't have anything to eat but potatoes. Another time my brother went around to grocery stores and got them to give him meat for his dog—only he didn't have any dog. We ate that dog meat with the potatoes. I went to school hungry and came home to a house where there wasn't any fire. The lights were cut off. They came out and cut off the water. But each time, as soon as they left, my brother went out and cut it on again with a wrench.

"I remember lying in bed one night and thinking. All at once I realized something. We were poor. Lord! It was weeks before I could get over that. I was ashamed to look at anybody and to talk to them. I thought everybody was saying to themselves, 'This Douglas boy is poor.'

"I won't go into all the hard times we had. I hate

to think of them. I'll just tell a little. Well, we lost our car and our house and kept moving from one house to another. Bill collectors hunted us down and came in droves. Every now and then my brother or Dad would find some sort of odd job to do, or the other brother in Chicago would send us a little something. Then we'd go wild. I mean we'd go wild over food. We'd eat until we were sick. We'd eat four times a day and between meals. We shouldn't have done it. We ought to have gone easy on it, but we just couldn't help ourselves. The sight and smell of food sort of made us crazy, I guess.

"The winter of 1934 was the hardest time of all. Dad was working again at Travis and Son, but he wasn't making but around ten dollars a week. My brother was selling a little stuff free-lance, but it hardly amounted to enough to pay for postage and typewriter paper. And debts had piled up until we couldn't get credit anywhere.

"We were completely out of coal one time when we were living away out at the edge of town. The weather was freezing bitter then, so at night my brother and I would bundle up and go about a quarter of a mile away to a big estate on the Tennessee River. We made a hole in the fence and stole some of the wood that was piled a good distance from the house. We just walked in and got it. I don't remember that we tried to be quiet about it in particular.

"We hauled that wood through the fields in a coaster wagon and a wheel barrow. Lots of times we made nine or ten trips and worked almost until morning. We took two or three whole stacks of wood that winter, and it's all that kept us from freezing. Mama never did ask us where the wood came from. She always knew somehow when we were going to do it and those nights she went to bed early before we left. I was thirteen then and it was kind of exciting to me. Sometimes I was afraid we'd be caught, but we never were. I don't know why. My brother used to keep one heavy stick of wood in his overcoat pocket while we were taking the stuff. I asked him why he did it and he told me if anybody found us out and tried to stop us I'd see why.

"Another time when we were out of anything to eat and were getting pretty hungry, he went around looking queer. I saw him slip out late at night and he had a foot-long piece of iron pipe with him. I knew he was going to try to knock somebody in the head to get their money. I stayed awake, scared stiff until he came back. He mustn't have found anybody, because he didn't bring home any money. Maybe he got cold feet. I've never asked him about it.

"We sold everything we could except the piano.

"Mama wouldn't let that go. It was a Steinway upright and she said we'd never get another one if we sold it. All of us had taken our music lessons on it— especially my sister, the one who died when I was little. I guess that was the real reason Mama wouldn't let it go.

"After awhile things got some better. My brother in Chicago got so he could send money home and my other brother got another newspaper job. Dad went back to regular work at Travis and Son, though he only got about twenty dollars a week. We weren't over the hard time because of the debts from the bad years. Still, compared to those years we were just sailing.

"I went on through high school and made good marks. In my senior year I had an average of ninety-eight and was elected class president and was valedictorian at graduation. I expected to go to college the next fall. Now, I can't see how on earth I could have expected to. I knew that there was no money for it. But somehow or other it just seemed to me that a way would turn up.

"Mother felt the same about it. She'd say, 'If you want a college education badly enough you will get it. Any boy who is determined can work his way through. Brother worked his way through Columbia and you can work your way through U. T. All great men have had to struggle.'

"Well, I'd think of what I'd read about Lincoln and all those others and it seemed to me I could do it, too. You see, I thought I was going to be a great man."

Jimmy drained his glass. He set it down with a thump. The rain was drumming steadily on the roof. There was a dull clatter of Gus' thick crockery from behind the partition. Gus was whistling You're the One Rose.

Legs extended, hands in his pockets, Jimmy slouched down in his chair. "I was going to be great. I didn't know just what sort of great, but I was going to be a world-shaker." He gave a short dry laugh.

"The first of the summer after I graduated I stayed at home studying—reviewing my high school books. Mother wanted me to do that so I'd be ready for college. She had a notion that my brother in Chicago would be able to scare up the money for my first year in the University of Tennessee. After that, of course, I'd get along on scholarships. I kind of hoped football would help there, too. You see, I'd been a good linesman in high school. And since the football season and the good eating we'd begun to have, I'd been filling out. Gained twenty solid pounds and that brought me up to a hundred and ninety.

"That summer we had a scare. There was some sort of strike at Travis and Son. Seems that after the NRA blew up, Old Dave put the girls in the sewing room on piece work and some of them just couldn't make a living. They protested but it didn't do any good. They rocked along then for a long time, just talking. Then some organizer came and got them to go out on a strike. The men went out, too, and they ganged around the entrance blocking off part of the street.

"Dad didn't know what to do. He walked the floor at home. He said that the girls were right, but he didn't believe they could win out because the mayor had said he'd back Old Dave to the limit. I remember Mama telling Dad, 'Oh, Bob, please don't do anything foolish! We've been through such a hard time. What on earth would we do if we had to face it again? I couldn't bear it!'

"So Dad went to work the next morning. I had some errands to do for Mama so I went to town with him. Old Dave had called up and said he'd have policemen to carry Dad through the strikers. When we got there the policemen were ready all right. They told Dad they'd rush him through. He started out, with me tagging behind. Then he made me go back to the corner and started again. The strikers were bunched up at the door of the factory. They weren't saying a thing or making a move. Just men and women standing there watching.

"I saw Dad stop again. He had an argument with the police. I heard him say pretty loud, 'No, I'll go by myself or I won't go at all.' He said it two or three times.

"The policemen were mad. 'Okay, Cap,' I heard one of them say. 'It's your look-after, not mine.'

"Dad walked on without them, but they sort of edged along some way behind.

"All at once the strikers began yelling and meeowing. Dad walked on. When he was right at them, about a dozen men and women grabbed at him and started tearing his coat and shirt.

"I started running down there and so did the police.

"But right then the strikers got into a free-for-all fight among themselves. Dad had a lot of good friends among them and these friends jumped on the ones who'd grabbed him. They pulled them off and Dad walked on through and went into the factory. He never was bothered again. Old Dave and the others had to have the police to get in and out. Dad came and went without anybody trying to stop him.

"So the strike petered out and the strikers were out of jobs. Some of them came to Dad and he tried to get them back on. But Old Dave said he wouldn't touch a one of them with a ten-foot pole.

"One night late in July Dad didn't come home at his usual time. Hours passed and there wasn't any sign of him. Mother and I were worried to death. We didn't have a 'phone then and at first Mother was ashamed to ask the neighbors. Finally, around seven o'clock she did, though, and called Old Dave. He said Dad had left at the usual time.

"So Mama told me to walk to the car line and go to town and see if I could find Dad. 'I just know something terrible has happened,' she said. 'Bob has never been late. He wouldn't be if something hadn't happened.'

"I started out from home running. It was a mile to

the car line, so I took a short cut through the woods. When I came out at the end of Terry Road, still running, I saw a man coming down the last hill. He was sort of weaving as he walked, taking uneven steps, and stopping every third or fourth step. Then I recognized his brown suit and I knew it was Dad.

"My heart almost stopped. I'd seen men walk that way before and I knew what it meant. I kept on running.

"When I got to him, he just stared at me for a minute. His face was as white as a sheet: He looked awful.

"He said, 'Jimmy!' Then he caught my arm to keep from falling. And when he was that close to me I could tell that he hadn't been drinking. I knew he was a sick man.

"It took us more than an hour to get home, because we had to stop and rest so many times. A little at a time Dad told me what had happened. He'd been waiting for a street car up town when all at once he felt dizzy and had to sit down on the curbing. Every time he tried to get up things whirled and dipped so that he had to sit back down.

" 'People laughed at me,' he said. 'Must have thought I was drunk. I tried to say something but I couldn't get a word out. I sat there I don't know how long. A while ago I felt steady enough to catch a street car and come on. I've never felt like this before. Just don't know what it could be.'

"Well, it was death coming on. Dad knew it, I believe, but I just couldn't imagine such a thing and Mama couldn't either—even when he had to go to the hospital and any fool on earth could see he was sinking. Yet I just couldn't get it through my head until Dad

was gone. Then I felt like somebody had hit me with
a hammer. I wanted to run, not anywhere, but just
run till I dropped. I wanted to fight something and
beat it with my fists and tear it to bits with my fingers.
Never will be anything that can hurt me like that.

"The doctors never did know what was wrong with
Dad. He was sixty, but there wasn't anything like
cancer or tuberculosis. One of the doctors at the hospital told me that he was really just worn out completely. I guess he was right."

Jimmy Douglas called for his second bottle of beer.
He drummed on the table and stared at his fingers while
Gus was getting it. He didn't pour the beer in his glass
this time. He drank from the bottle and didn't set it
down until it was empty.

"Dad's insurance had lapsed during the hard time,"
Jimmy went on. "We had the funeral expenses and
doctors' and hospital bills to pay. Now I know that
the funeral ought to have been just as simple as possible. That's the way Dad would have wanted it. But
at the time I didn't have any sense. Mama wanted the
best and that damned undertaker was smooth. Every
time he'd point out a casket and say, 'Now this is a fine
piece of merchandise,' I felt like choking him. I was
glad when Mama picked out a casket that cost four
hundred dollars. She told them Dad had insurance so
she could get it.

"I'll skip a lot now. I've already told you how I
looked for work and couldn't find it and finally got put
on as stock boy at Travis and Son.

"The job was hard. Not on your mind but on your
back and legs. You see, the stock room is in the basement. I have to load lays of overall goods—I can tell
you that stuff's heavy, too—into a big wheeled push-

truck. Then I man-power that truck up a slope of concrete to the elevator door. The elevator takes me up to the cutting room where men cut the goods by pattern. In the cutting room I get the stacks of cut out goods and take it up to the sewing room and the girls sew the stuff into overalls. From the sewing room I haul the finished overalls down to the shipping room. Between times I unload lays of goods from trucks outside and haul it into the stock room or help load boxes of overalls to be shipped out. Never a minute of rest.

"The cutters and the girls are on piece work, so they are always crying for more goods. Jimmy! Jimmy! Jimmy! Until I feel like I'll go crazy. I didn't think I'd ever get through that first week. When I came on, Fred, the other stock boy, let up and shoved a lot of the work he should have been doing on me. But I didn't know enough about the work to see what he was doing right at the beginning.

"When I started to work I laid out a schedule of what I wanted to do. I was going to keep up my study at home so if my brother in Chicago could help me I'd be ready to go on to college. He was already sending money home to Mama and my other brother was helping as much as he could, but he'd got married about six months before Dad died and had his own family coming on. Well, I was going to study. But I was so dog-tired every night when I got home that I just dropped in bed after I'd eaten, and went to sleep. It wasn't sound sleep, either. I had nightmares of trying to buck a truck of goods up a steep slope, and the truck was as big as a house and the slope as high as a mountain, and Old Dave yelling and all of them yelling at me to hurry.

"So I said I'd study Saturday afternoons and

Sunday. Sunday, anyhow. We hadn't gone to church for years, so Sundays were open. But I didn't do it. I had to do work around the house on Saturday and on Sunday I just couldn't make myself get up until almost noon. I'd read the Sunday paper and go to sleep lying on the sofa in the afternoon. I found I couldn't get anything out of reading. I used to like to read, but now I was always so tired—tired down to my bones—that I couldn't get any sense out of a book and I'd go to sleep trying to read it.

"All that winter and next summer I was hard at it. Got to know all the people at the factory and liked some of them pretty well. But I'll tell you I never before knew that such people existed. Most of them had come in off of the mountains somewhere and they had such a funny way of talking that plenty of times I wouldn't know what they were saying.

"The girls were usually either sloppy fat or thin and dried up. Their hair all hung in strings and a good many of them dipped snuff and spit all the time. They wore the doggonedest clothes I ever saw, with their stockings wrapped around their legs in folds and full of holes and their heels run down. They told each other the slimiest jokes while they were working and they'd say things to you that would make you want to throw up. I've seen them have fights, pulling hair and scratching and biting.

"Some of them made as little as fifty cents a week. No, I mean it! Fifty cents a week! I've seen their pay checks. You see they were on piece work and hoped to get experience enough to make more. Others of them, the fast workers, made up to sixteen and eighteen dollars. They set the pace and everybody else had to measure up. The sewing room was right under the roof and in summer, too, and I was good and glad that I did some of my work in the basement. It reached a hundred and twenty degrees on hot days in that place and the girls would keel over on the floor. Got so hot in July that Old Dave shut the factory down during the day and had us work at night instead.

"I didn't have as much to do with the girls as with the men. They were funny people and there was only one thing that would make any impression on them. If they didn't think you were tough, they'd pick you to pieces. I got in my bluff as soon as I saw how they were. I'm big and I can make my voice sound like a big dog growling. So I told them I'd studied boxing and how I'd knocked a lot of fellows out. They believed me and sucked up to me then—even those that had been in jail and always carried knives. Anyway, most of them were awfully measly looking men. Not a beefy man among them.

"But they were tough. Always getting in knife fights on Saturday night out to Fount Dillon's joint and being thrown in jail. But my bluff worked and they left me alone. Some of them who hadn't gone on the strike had known Dad and they were always nice to me, too.

"All of them were afraid of Old Dave and hated him. They used to sit around at lunch eating their fried pies and egg sandwiches and talk about all the things they'd like to do to him. When he was around they just yes-sirred him like a bunch of niggers.

"He'd told me that he worked just like anybody else. Well, he does put on overalls and prowl all around. First he'll pop into the sewing room and then in the cutter's room. You can't tell when he'll be in a dark corner of the basement. He's always trying to find somebody loafing. It looks to me like it makes him happy when he can spot somebody and can bawl them out.

"Old Dave never has a pleasant word for anybody. When he's in the stock room it's 'Boy, get that truck moving! You look like the dead lice are falling off you!' And, 'Damn it, you lazy no 'count young-un, get those lays loaded—hear me?' Work your head off and he won't give you the least little praise. Stop to get your breath and he's all over you.

"They say he's worried about conditions and that's what makes him so mean. The way I look at it, that's no excuse. Dad had a hundred times more worry than Old Dave, but the more worried he got the politer he was to you. And another thing—Old Dave's a big man in the church. You see his picture in the paper every once and a while. But you'd never know it at the factory.

"The five MacGonnigal boys work in the office. I mean they're supposed to work there. I've never seen any of them but John do a tap. John's all right. I'll say this for him—he does keep pretty busy. The other four just sit around and read the paper or some magazine. They come in late and go out to lunch early. They stay out two hours and hang over the telephone talking to girls in the afternoon and leave before quitting time. Old Dave raises the roof but they don't pay much attention to him. One thing, though. They all draw good salaries.

"I was saying that Old Dave didn't exactly choke you with praise. He dingdonged at me so that one day I got good and mad. For a minute I didn't know whether I was going to jump on the old man and then go upstairs and clean up with his boys or whether I'd quit the job. But I didn't do either one. I said to my-self, 'All right. I'll show the old son-of-a-gun. I'll work so hard he'll have to say something.'

"I did it. I worked until I thought I'd kill myself with it. Fred, the other stock boy, told me I didn't have any sense. I worked a whole week that way.

"So when Saturday came Old Dave called me off and said he was going to raise my pay. There were two extra dollars in my envelope."

Jimmy laughed until his body shook.

"Yep—two extra dollars. And Fred got fired and I had all his work to do as well as mine. Boy! Was I the bright one, though!

"I was so mad I couldn't get to sleep for hours that night. I did everything imaginable to Old Dave—all the way from just knocking him down and stomping on him and burning the factory to cutting him up a little at a time.

"Well, I waited for a chance to get back on him. About a month later there was a big rush of orders and things were humming and they had me hopping trying to keep the cutters and the girls in enough goods. So I caught Old Dave in the hall. I said, 'I want a raise, Mr. MacGonnigal.'

"He looked like he was going to bite my head off. 'You get back to work or I'll fire you.'

" 'No you won't,' I said. 'I'll just quit right now.' I started off, untying my apron.

"He grabbed my arm—see, he knew they couldn't break a new boy in right in the middle of the rush, and he knew he wasn't likely to get another one that would work as hard as I did.

"So he grabbed my arm and said, 'Two dollars.'

"I said, 'I'm worth fourteen a week.' That was al-

most double what I was making, but no more than he'd
paid for both Fred and me. It looked like he was going
to try to hit me. I kept on walking off, dragging him
along because he still had my arm.

"Then all at once he turned loose. 'Twelve dollars.
Take it or leave it.'

"You could tell he meant it. So I took the twelve.
That's what I'm making now."

Jimmy got up and went to the window. The rain was
little more than a misty drizzle now. The tires of the
cars that flashed by on the highway sang against the
wet asphalt.

"I'd better get going now, while it's slacked up," he
said. "But first let me tell you the other surprise I've
got for Old Dave.

"I'm quitting next Saturday. My uncle in Florida
is sending for Mama to come and live with him. I've
got enough money to pay my fare down there and when
I get there he's got a job for me. Before I'd work in a
place like this again—why I'd rather die first.

"Boy, will I tell Old Dave what I think of him! No,
I don't really guess I will. What's the use in it? Anyhow, it's fun to keep on thinking that until the time
comes. I can go to sleep grinning like a 'possum."

JAMES R. ASWELL

Didn't Keep a Penny

"I WOULDN'T LIVE HERE FIVE MINUTES IF'N I HAD A family, but jest me, it don't make no difference." Clyde Fisher pushed his horn rimmed spectacles higher on his nose and laughed.

"I gits my mail at sixteen-hundred and seven Maynard Street. Uncle Sam don't deliver no mail in no alley. They's only two houses in this here alley. All the rest is coal houses with leaky roofs. Well, I got one of them houses!"

The place swam with a fog of coal smoke. There was a low ceiling and walls covered with badly soiled paper. In one corner stood a blue iron bed neatly covered with a white spread and a blue comfort folded across the foot. A Franklin heater, in which a fire was roaring filled the room with suffocating heat. Water in an iron kettle and coffee in a gray enamel pot boiled on top of the stove.

He laughed again and waved his hand about the cramped room. "Look 'er over!

"I'm a bachelor man now," he said. "I was jest settin' here patchin' my pants. If'n I had a wife I'd have to patch jest the same. Did when I had one. I know all about women. Mine ain't never loved patchin'. She sho' 'spised me to wear overalls, too. But Lord, I had to dress accordin' to the work I done. My work is the rough kind.

253

"Me and my wife warn't never together on nothin'. Not even raisin' the chillun. I set down once and told her how I thought we ought to bring them up or at least we ought to git together on her way or mine. Lord, she nearly blowed up!"

His patching finished, he shuffled over to the bed in the corner and carefully laid the pants on the clean white spread. From a wooden box wired to the foot of the bed he picked up a clock, gave it a vigorous shake, held it to his ear to see if it was ticking, then replaced it. "Ain't neither one no count," he commented pointing to another clock on top of the box. He moved the coffee pot to the edge of the stove before dropping into a rocking chair in front of the stove.

"No," he said, "me and the old woman never was together. She 'lowed as to how she sho' warn't goin' my way. She always let 'em chillun do things I didn't like at all. Sometime they'd ask her could they go places and she'd say so sweet-like, 'Go ask yo' papa. You know how he is.' I see what she up to. She's jest tryin' to pisen they minds agin me, and make 'em think I was the one to always say no.

"A broke up home is the worstest thing can happen. It's different 'bout sickness. That's somethin' you can't help. But jest to have a family and then everything go wrong, that's mighty bad. I know some say if you's equally yoked everything will be all right. But 'tain't so. My wife was jest a few years younger than me. It's foolish for ol' man to marry a young girl, less'n he's rich and spry and able to go round places where she wants to go. Sometime none of it works. I jest worried over my troubles so till sometime I couldn't sleep nights.

"But it don't make no difference how much you worry, yo' life jest goes on the same.

"I had a little home there in Aronsville I was mighty proud of. A fo' room brick house set up on a hill. We had city water and we had a well. One of these kind you let the bucket down in and draw up full of good cold water. The place was an acre square. Well, as I was go' say, when me and my wife busted up I told her whatever I had I'd give her a half of it if it warn't but a thimble full. She say she want money. So I turned in then and I mortgaged my home. Fo' hundred and fifty dollars was the mortgage. I give her the last cent of it. Didn't keep a penny fo' myself.

"Then I come down here to Knoxville and went to work to pay off that mortgage. I worked at the feed mill in South Knoxville nearly nine years. That was a mighty good job. I paid off the mortgage on my place. By the time I done that the bottom fell out of everything. I got behind with my taxes on my house. The city been wantin' it fo' a school house. Professor Jacobs come down here from Aronsville last summer and stood right there in the do' and talked to me 'bout it. I knowed I jest as well let it go. They'd sell it fo' taxes anyhow. I got a little out it. Nothin' like I'd got if my taxes had been paid up. The chillun could paid a few dollars a piece and kept up them taxes. Then we'd got a thousand twelve hundred fo' it. I worried and I worried over it. Things gits on you so you don't know which way to go sometime. Well, talkin' 'bout it don't do no good neither. But I jest gits to thinkin' sometime and wonderin' what was the trouble.

"My wife and the chillun lives here in Knoxville. All the children work. They mama stay home and

if'n she don't want to clean up, them girls falls in there
on Saturday and do it.

"You want the story of my life? I started to write
it once myself, but my house got broke up and I ain't
had my mind on nothin' like that since. Some I wrote
got scattered and the rest I tore up.

"What they go' do with this stuff anyhow?" He
leaned forward and rested his elbows on his knees.
"Gittin' ready fo' war? I'm too ol' fo' that now. Well,
let me see. I'll have to study a bit. My age is down in
the Bible. I think I was borned 'bout '80. Yes, I think
that's right. Out of a family of thirteen chillun, me
and my brother is the onliest ones livin'. I was borned
in Bedford County. The first original Fishers come
from Bedford County. My father was a farmer, jest
a share cropper and his name was Lester Fisher.

"Bedford County was a powerful wheat country in
that time. Why, the buyers would crib eight and ten
thousand bushel of wheat and corn, and the same thing
'bout wheat, cotton, and tobacco. But that didn't do
the po' farmer no good. The po' farmer lost all the
time 'cause he warn't able to hold his crop over for high
prices. Big farmers had warehouses and they could
hold they stuff fo' a big price.

"That reminds me of somethin' that happened when
I was in Akron, Ohio, in war times. Sugar was sellin'
fo' thirty cents a pound. I was workin' at a machine
shop, loadin' blocks fo' a floor. Well, they's a white
fellow there and 'course he wasn't doin' nuthin' but
layin' flat of his back whilst we's loadin' the truck. He
was a pretty smart man, though. I'll have to give it
to him there. He say, 'In ten days you can git all the
sugar you want fo' sixteen cent a pound. The big
shots has bought up the sugar and they'll hold it in

the warehouses and force the prices down.' Sho'
enough, in ten day's time sugar's sellin' fo' sixteen
cent jest like he say. Things can happen like that
when it come to money.

"Well, I lived on the farm till I was 'bout grown.
Country life is the best life they is. I went from there
to Aronsville where I begun public work. I made ice.
Then I went to work for a lumber company. I worked
fo' years in the lumber yard and five years firin' the
boiler at the saw mill. I went from there to Kansas
City. I served ten months at a icin' station. I iced
refrigerator cars.

"I was lookin' fo' better all the time. I served
eighteen or twenty months at two of the Big Fo'
Packers. Armour and Company, Morris and Company, Cudahey, and Swift is called the Big Fo'
Packers. The balance of the time I served 'round railroads. So I traveled seven years with race hosses,
carin' fo' them. Yes, I'm an ol' race hoss man. I
served two seasons with Gwinn's trottin' horses out on
Richards Pike. I spent several seasons 'round Walnut
Park.

"I worked hard all my life, but age is agin me now.
They tell me right away now that my workin' life is
too short to give me a job. They'll hire a boy 'fo'
they'll hire me, though I'm heap the best worker, mo'
settled and everything. A young fellow'll work a while
and then fool 'round where I'll work week in an week
out. But they say his workin' life is longer than mine.
Nothin' fo' ol' man to do nowdays.

"Didn't git to work but one day last week. Can't
lay brick in real cold weather. The mortar'll freeze
and when it thaws it'll pop and crumble out. Summer's
the season for brick work. I used to do some brick

work 'fo' I left home. I don't lay brick, though. I sets
grates sometime. My work is mighty hard. Carryin'
sixteen and eighteen bricks on yo' head sho' ain't easy.

"I'm tired, that's the reason I give up stewardship
at church. Let some of the men that's got wives serve
a while. I got to cook and wash and iron, patch and
clean up fo' myself. I don't feel like runnin' to meetin's
every night or two. I'm still a class leader and I belong
to Sister Wilson's Club. I believe its the Ever Ready
Club. I used to belong to the Masons but I'm un-
financial now. We had fun in that institution.

"I likes to read. I likes races, chicken fights, and
baseball games. I takes the paper enduring baseball
season. When its over I quits. I'm not much on football. I used to like to dance. I don't do that now.
The dance they do now ain't nothin'. We used to do
the square dance. You ain't never seen that kind of
dance is you?

"I could vote but I don't. I quit voting when
women started votin'. Hist'ry, I like them ol' hist'ry
books. In the European gov'ment some women has led
the country but I can't see nothin' good none of them
done. I have a hist'ry of England and a Greek hist'ry
too. Sometime I git lonesome here and I jump on 'em.
I ask a woman once where civilization started. She
said it started in China, but it didn't. It started in
Egypt. After she say she didn't believe the Bible, I
let her alone. People go to Egypt now lookin' fo'
knowledge. The reason they don't want to give the
'Gyptians credit is 'cause they's niggers. Shucks,
undertakers ain't learnt yet how to fix the body like the
'Gyptians done. Wish I knowed how. Make me a
barn full of money, mummyin' up the folks. Make
'em so hard and lastin' you could stand 'em up on the

graves. They'd be the corpse and the headstone all at once.

"My, you're jest sweatin'. Let me open this door. Why, I'm 'bout to burn you up. Chile, I believes in my fire. Yes'm, I must have plenty fire and a good bed to sleep in. I put me in two tons of coal the other day," he pointed to five big cans full of lump coal. "I had enough to last to Christmas left over from last year but I put more in. I still sleeps on my feather bed. I was born on one and I still own one. Winter and summer I has my feather bed. It don't git too hot. I can't sleep on a hard bed, and that's what them ol' mattresses is.

"It's funny how I got my feather bed. My bed was a chicken feather bed. My wife's feather bed was goose feathers. When they moved down here they got stylish and started sleepin' on mattresses. She give her feather bed away. I knowed if I ask her for it she wouldn't let me have it. They put it outside. I was up there one day so I ask my daughter what she go' do with that ol' feather bed. She say they'd give it away, but the folks hadn't come after it. So I told her I'd give her mine and a dollar to boot if she'd let me have it. She say all right. I give her the dollar and rushed on home, put my feather bed on my little ol' wagon and took it on over there and brought my goose feather bed back. She say 'bout a hour after I left the folks come after it. Chile, I was jist in time. Luck was with me that time. I'm sho' proud of my goose feather bed. She's a good-un, too. My daughter's got a little ol' radio she said I could have, but I ain't got no 'lectricity here to feed it.

"I didn't git much larnin', jest the primary grades. Well, to the fifth grade, but that's the same as the eighth grade now. Folks don't know nothin' now. You can take these college graduates and put 'em up to talk. Why they can't talk!

"All my chillun's got a middlin' fair education. Henry went to Fisk one year and quit. Him and Professor Jacobs was boys together and classmates. Now the professor is principal of the high school there at Aronsville. Hester, Jane, and Mary all went to the college there at home.

"One of my gals don't care for nothin' much but cookin'. She's a jim-dandy good cook. She can cook any kind of cake, jest git it out of her head. When they was going to school whenever they say, 'Papa I need a book,' I got it. Dollar and a quarter, dollar and a half, whatever it cost. When we broke up, they was a trunk full of books I'd bought fo' them.

"It's always been my desire to git to the place where when I got too old to work I could take care of myself. But I've had so many back sets. I had no hope of bein' rich but I did want to be comf'table when I got ol'. But this has been my bad year. All last year I made forty cent an hour, but this year I ain't made but thirty cent a hour. I pay six dollars a month fo' this house. It depend on what I want as to what I spend fo' food. Now, if I git a chicken or lamb roast or somethin' like that, it'll run 'round three or fo' dollars a week.

"These days I don't have no special one to work fo'. It's jest work fo' one and catch another fo' old Clyde Fisher."

LILLIAN C. LOVE
JAMES R. ASWELL

In Service Occupations

Plow Beams for Pills

A COUNTRY DOCTOR ISN'T NECESSARILY MORE HUMANE than the city practitioner, but he's likely to be more human. Knowing all about John Jones—how many bales of cotton he made last year, what losses he has sustained, what domestic difficulties he faces, how things are with him in general physically, financially, spiritually—the country doctor's approach is as friend or neighbor as well as physician. I don't hold any thesis for this approach, but there it is. Recently I was riding along a muddy country road when I saw Dick Johnson having difficulty getting some pigs out of the mud of the road back into the pen. I stopped my car to help Dick."

" 'You stop to help me with my pigs, doctor, busy as you are?' he asked.

" 'You need help, don't you?'

" 'Yes, but—why, doctor, several cars passed right on by before you come along, and didn't a one of 'em offer to stop. You reckon you can spare the time?'

"Sometimes it's as simple as helping pull a pig out of the mud; sometimes it's a far cry from the mundane —as far away as the next world. I was called over to a patient who had accidentally shot himself through the abdomen. He was in great pain; so I first made him comfortable and then proceeded to examine his wound.

" 'Doctor,' he said, 'I'm suffering a lot. Get me easy and then take me to the hospital if you think it's any use.'

"I looked him straight in the eye. 'It's no use,' I told him. 'If you're not a Christian, you've still got time to make peace with your God. You're not going to die right away, but I've given you something to ease your suffering, and you're going to sleep soon, and—you won't wake up.'

"He looked me straight in the eye, just as calm as I am now. 'I've got no fear. I hate to leave her'—his wife was standing at the door crying—'and the children, but I ain't afraid.'

"That's the only time I've ever told a patient he was going to die. I'm not sure we oughtn't to tell more of them, but we doctors try to subscribe to the 'as-long-as-there's-life-there's-hope' theory. In this case, I had to give the fellow his chance, after that shot of morphine.

"Sometimes it's fiction, in the doctor's day. A white fellow that I had known all my life came to me one day and said: 'Doc, you've got to give me somethin'. I've messed up a girl, and I've got to get somethin' for her to take, right away.'

"I told him I couldn't do it, that he must go ahead and marry the girl.

" 'I can't do that,' he declared emphatically. 'No suh!'

" 'Don't you love the girl?' I asked.

" 'Not partic'lar,' was his reply. 'You've got to give me somethin' to get her out'n this fix.'

"I kept after him about marrying the girl, and he kept insisting he couldn't do that. Finally he said: 'Well, if you don't somebody else will.'

"I knew it was probably true; so I temporized by

giving him something harmless, telling him that the suspected pregnancy was probably a mistake, and if so the medicine would bring the girl around. He came back after a few weeks and said: 'Doc, that medicine you give me ain't worth a damn! You got to give me somethin' better'n that.'

"Finally I talked him into consenting to marry the girl. The baby came, more than two months too soon, but I assured the man's mother who was helping at the delivery that it was a seven months' baby. She and I both knew better, but the fiction made for happier relations all around. The marriage has proved successful; they have as happy a home as the run of people. I have felt that fiction was justified too, when I discovered wives with venereal disease contracted from husbands. I've never told anything that I felt might break up a home. Instead, I say it's a bad appendix. Appendicitis has had to bear a lot.

"I studied medicine partly because I wanted to help people. I get a big kick out of it. I'm no saint or any of that kind of stuff, and I don't deserve credit for doing things I like to do. For example—drinking whiskey: I never take a drink, for I don't like it. If I hadn't liked helping people I probably shouldn't have studied medicine; if I had liked whiskey I probably should drink it. I was influenced toward medicine, too, by my association with an uncle who practiced medicine in my old neighborhood. When I was a boy I used to ride around with him while he made his horse-and-buggy rounds. A brother-in-law, Dr. F. W. Jenks, also influenced me.

"My father was W. I. Cain, and my mother, Ella Little. They lived on a farm in Beaman County, just across the Farthington line near Wayland. I was graduated from college in 1912 and from medical college in 1916, interning at two large city hospitals. Then I volunteered for war service and was appointed second doctor at an army training camp, later serving as Major.

"The first case of flu at the camp puzzled us. We didn't know what it was until fifteen were stricken; then we decided it was Spanish influenza. The men died by the hundreds. The worst cases were admitted to the hospital, and a temporary hospital was made out of the Y.M.C.A. building, where hammocks had to serve as hospital beds. We were simply swamped, and many cases went into pneumonia and died from lack of attention. There were so many deaths that the bodies had to be put on ice and kept in cold storage till they could be attended to. One of two men with identical names, it was told, died. When the body was shipped home, the boy's mother insisted on seeing her son's face once more. When the casket was opened, she discovered that it wasn't her boy at all. After that we devised a different method of identification.

"One day when I was vaccinating my daily thousand, from the line a man said to me: 'Doctor, don't stick that needle in my arm as hard as you did that nigger's just ahead of me.' I was about to bawl out the private for addressing an officer so, when I looked up and recognized Willis Jackson, a former class mate of mine. I pulled him out of the line, assuring him I'd settle with him later. Soon as I had a chance I asked him what he meant by saying I had just vaccinated a nigger. It proved to be one of the mulattoes from down around Anton that Roy and I both knew. Until our discovery, he had passed as white not only among the service men, but with white girls too. He was transferred, later be-

ing sent up North where no doubt he has passed successfully as white. Like that Jones-Miller crowd in
upper Farthington, there is a group of mulattoes in
Maddox that have practically no signs of Negro blood.
Many of them have clear blue eyes.

"From the army camp I was sent to New York for
two months and then to the Navy Yard at Boston for
four months. In the receiving office we sometimes
found as high as 2000 venereal cases in one day. One
sailor who wanted to get out of service shot his finger
so that it had to be amputated. He got his discharge
after we amputated. From Boston I came back to the
army camp in the South, leaving the service in 1919.

"I began the private practice of medicine in Wayland on September 1, 1919. There were the usual difficulties that obtain in private rural practice. *The
Horse-and-Buggy Doctor,* which I'm reading right
now, pretty well describes some of them, though not
many country doctors are as hardboiled as he sounds.
Most of us are a little soft I reckon. In 1919 to 1922
and after, many of the roads in Farthington during the
winter months were almost impassable. Why, right on
the main street of Wayland I remember a chicken got
stuck in the mud one day and couldn't get out. A
crowd of men around town bet Harvey Newton five dollars one day that he couldn't pull a road cart down
Main Street. Harvey put on boots, waded through
the mud pulling his cart after him, and won the five
dollars. I had to make most of my calls on horse-back
or by road cart during the winter, but I didn't turn
down calls on account of the weather or bad roads. I
always thought, 'Suppose it was my wife or my child
sick.'

"One night a colored man came for me during a snow.

It was a delivery case; so I told my wife not to look for me back that night. The baby came about eleven o'clock, but it was snowing so hard I told the colored man to fix me a bed so I could go to sleep. That's the only night I ever slept in a Negro's house, but I've been on the roads lots of nights going to and coming from patients.

"The lack of equipment was not as great a handicap in my early practice as were the rough roads, for in Farthington we have access to hospitals in a number of towns and cities—or we do now since there are hard-surfaced roads. One of my patients was a victim of bad roads. We called and examined him one night and knew he should be rushed to a hospital right then for an emergency. But we couldn't risk the hazards of the Farthington roads. Next morning we took him on the train, and he died en route. Because of the easy access to hospitals I've done very little operating. The operating I've done has been on kitchen tables and on beds. I recall one case following pneumonia, where we had to insert a drainage tube. To keep the tube from going too far in, we pinned a safety pin through it. The man of the house came home half drunk and was furious when he saw the safety pin. He went all around telling that we had sewed his son up with a safety pin.

"Bad living conditions in so many rural homes have handicapped the country doctor. Fifty percent of the people in Farthington County are ill-housed and ill-fed. About ten percent live in comparative luxury; twenty percent live moderately well; twenty, less well; the others, without the necessities of life. Since I've been county health doctor, I've had occasion to go in lots of homes, and I can bear testimony to the fact that one half our people do not have the bare necessities. I have delivered babies by oil lamps without chimneys. I have been in homes where there were no chairs—only blocks of wood and store boxes to sit on. Some of our houses do not have chimneys; stove pipes are stuck through holes in the walls so that smoke from tin heaters can escape. Some have no windows, only holes in the walls, with guano bags for curtains. One house near Maryton, our county seat, where I called to see a patient, has no flooring at all, only the dirt of the ground.

"Not only have I prescribed for patients, but in some cases I've had to nurse and to see about food for them. In labor cases sometimes, with nobody in the house but the husband and me, I've had to bathe and dress the baby. I was called to a pneumonia patient where everybody in the house was sick, and the little thirteen-months-old baby was crawling all over the mother's bed, with nobody but the sick mother to do anything for him, and no money to hire anybody. The mother needed food more than medicine; so I had some chicken soup made for her. I took the soup on my next visit, but it was too late; she died. A colored man very ill with flu sent for me. Living alone, he had nobody to look after him. I left him some medicine, but warned him what he needed most was plenty of cold water to drink and a warm room. There was no wood cut; so I went to the wood-pile and cut the nigger enough wood to last through the night, brought him a bucket of cold water, and told him how to take the pills I left.

"There have been amusing incidents in my practice too. On one occasion the girl who cooks next door to me got sick, and her mother sent for me. The mother was one of those strict old darkies who expected her daughters to walk the straight and narrow path she herself had always walked, and who had no suspicion of the trouble her daughter was in. Neither did I till I examined and found her pregnant. To get the mother out of the room a minute, I told her to go bring me a glass of water fresh from the pump so I could give the patient a dose of medicine. When she left the room I told the girl she was pregnant. She emphatically denied it. I gave her some medicine, telling her mother I didn't think the girl would be any better right soon, but to let me hear if she got any worse. It wasn't many hours afterwards that I was sent for again. The girl was in labor. I told the mother then what the trouble was, and she was the maddest woman you ever saw. She stood over the daughter, demanding the truth of her. The girl continued to deny she was pregnant. Between the labor pains, she emphatically denied she was going to have a baby. Even after the baby's head was in the world, right on till the baby cried, she denied she was pregnant. That mother was mad enough to kill the girl, but after the baby was bathed and dressed she stood over the daughter and said: 'Nigger, if you kill that baby I'll kill you.'

"One mother whom I had attended at the birth of her six children, without being paid, called me in for her seventh delivery. After it was all over and she was comfortable, she looked up at me and said, with the utmost sincerity: 'Dr. Cain, I've never been able to pay you nothin' for deliverin' my other six children; so I'll give you this one.' I didn't tell her I'd rather deliver six more for her free, than to accept this 'fee.' A husband, feeling very grateful after his wife had borne him a nice son, said to me on one occasion: 'Doc, I've got nothin' to pay you with, but I'll name my boy for you.' Years after that I saw the man in Anton one day. 'Doc,' he said, 'yonder's your boy—Robert Cain.'

"Another parent chose a more ambitious name. Lots of people believe if a baby is born with a veil over his face that he is born to see things. Of course there is a physical explanation for the 'veil,' but they won't listen to it; it means something supernatural to them. In one such delivery the parents rose to the occasion by calling their son and heir Saint Peter. I get a lot of kick out of colored folks. I'm their friend, and they know it; so they don't mind if I tease them a little. One old woman came to me the other day and said: 'Doctor, I'm sick. I'm sick bad.'

" 'Why, auntie,' I told her, 'you're tricked. Somebody has dressed you up.' The colored people say they've been 'dressed up' when they mean somebody has conjured them.

" 'I knowed it!' the old colored woman said. 'I knowed it. Tell me who done it.'

" 'There's an old man across the creek that wants to marry you, and—'

" 'How'd you know?' she asked wonderingly.

" 'And he's dressed you up so you'll have to marry him.' "

" 'Exactly so!' she confessed. 'Exactly so! Tell me what I can do to take de trick off'n me.'

" 'Pull a hair out of your head,' I advised her, 'and wrap it around a nail. Go to the creek and find a bla'gum, drive the nail into the tree right up to the head, and then start home the same way you went to the creek. But be careful not to look back.' I haven't heard anything else from the old lady; so no doubt she's cured!

"One of the most unusual situations I've had was that of the three sisters, all of whom were insane and had to be taken to the asylum the same day. One died, however, before we could get her to the hospital. The belief among the colored folks was that these three sisters had been conjured.

"An amusing thing happened to a friend of mine, who does right much doctoring among his colored tenants. Charlie usually goes to investigate the cases of patients on his farm himself before sending the doctor to them. He usually gives them 666 or castor oil and lets it go at that. A Negro tenant came to town to tell Charlie to send a doctor to the farm to see about his sick daughter. Charlie went himself. The girl didn't appear to be very sick; so Charlie told the mother to give her a big dose of castor oil, and if she wasn't better by next day he'd send a doctor out to see about her. Next day he asked the tenant how his daughter was. 'Oh, she's better now; the baby's come,' he said. We teased Charlie about his maternity case.

"The order of things has changed somewhat regarding the collection of fees. It used to be the rule not to charge widows any doctors' fees, but since the various relief agencies there is less charity, less private charity, and this has had its bearing among doctors too. A great deal of charity is still being done by rural doctors, has to be done, but they are accepting pay that is offered by their patients even though it is in produce rather than coin. I have been paid for 'medical services rendered' in molasses, hogs, chickens, eggs, corn, potatoes, hams, beans, all kinds of vegetables. The biggest item I ever accepted in payment for medical service was 200 plow beams. I still have some of those plow beams. An old doctor who had had a lot of rural practice once said to me: 'Son, make it a rule to take anything for pay that's offered you.' I took the 200 plow beams, but I balked on the baby!

"One of the reasons that I left private practice and went into public health service was because of my interest in farming. A doctor needs some outside interest, and lots of doctors in the small towns get pleasure and recreation from farming. But people complain about this. If they send for the doctor once or twice and are told that he's at the farm, they're likely to say: 'Well, he'd better give up practicing medicine or farming one.' Many times I've waited and waited for calls; then soon as I'd plan a day's trip somewhere, here would come a call that couldn't wait, and my family would have to go on without me. Of course the biggest reason I accepted the job as county health doctor was that I had a definite program I wanted to see carried through in Farthington County.

"I've been county health officer now for eighteen months, and during this time I have been able to inaugurate a program that already I know has done good. This broader field of service has changed some of my ideas that I thought were pretty firmly rooted. One was birth control. For a long time I felt that it was wrong to practice birth control, but after seeing so many frail women broken down from prolonged child-bearing with the end not yet in sight, so many helpless children neglected because their parents aren't able to provide even the necessities for them, I changed my mind. Women sometimes come to me asking for 'something to take' after they become pregnant. A woman came the other day and said: 'Doctor, I'm that way again. You got to give me somethin'. I don't want no more babies.' I tried to explain that it was too late now, that we mustn't destroy life after its inception. But it's hard sometimes for these overburdened women to grasp the difference between abortion and contraception.

"In the maternity clinics I find many cases of women who have had too many children and should be taught to practice birth control. There are six maternity and infancy clinics in the county which are held once a month in six different places. Four nurses are stationed at four more places to contact midwives and to bring in expectant mothers to the once-a-month clinics. These nurses instruct the midwives and supervise the delivery of the mothers who have been to the clinics. If on examination any kidney trouble or high blood pressure, etc., are found among the mothers, the nurses visit them and instruct them in pre-natal care. If we find mental defectives or abnormal physical conditions in patients, then with the approval of the Eugenics Board in Raleigh we have them sterilized.

"In our venereal program we have three clinics. By July we hope to have two more. Of those we have examined, twenty-one percent show positive. Only a few white people are represented among the 299 positive Wassermanns out of the 1500 tested. Farthington County, with twice the average of the United States, will probably continue to make a poor showing in venereal averages; for our population is three-fourths Negro, and low moral standards are prevalent among our colored people; some of the conditions that obtain would sound as far-fetched in print as some of *Tobacco Road*. It will take fifteen years to make a noticeable showing, to reduce the venereal percent in Farthington.

"The big colored element in our county is a health problem as well as a social and economic problem we have to solve. The colored birth rate is sixty-nine and one-half percent, with no decrease in the rate. I think our attitude has got to change a little. Recently I tried to get permission from the Board of Education to establish a clinic in one or two rooms in the unused school building at Dunstan. The ladies of Dunstan appeared before the board to protest against this plan, saying that they wanted to make the school building a community house and were unwilling to have Negroes come there for clinical purposes, even once a month. Yet they allow Negroes, many of them with positive Wassermanns, to come into their kitchens, to cook their food, and to nurse their babies. It isn't easy to pick up a negative servant in Farthington. Recently I found out the boy who milked my cow tested a positive Wassermann; so I took over the milking job myself.

"Then we've got to make provision for their education too. Recently a delegation of Negroes from up around Camp's Store met us, the County Board of Education, in Maryton, and petitioned us to furnish a bus for their children to be brought to the Poplar Spring School. They had $950 to invest in a bus; they asked nothing of us except permission to be routed. One of the members of our board said: 'Let the niggers go to school like they've been going.' The matter was left pending. You know what happened? The Negroes employed a smart lawyer, and he has been before the board with the demand that we give the Negroes a bus, with no $950 attached to his demand. What happened? We guess that the lawyer took the $950 and told the Negroes he'd get them a bus and it shouldn't cost them anything. Now if we grant this bus, all the Negroes in the county will demand one for their various schools, and Farthington would be broke.

"I serve on the county board because I've always been keenly interested in education. I was on the Wayland school board till I accepted the county appointment. I'm also a member of the Ruritan Club and other local organizations, local meaning Wayland. I have my office in Maryton, but continue to live at home.

"The TB program makes more showing than any of the others, in a short time. There has been a decrease of TB in the county by fifty percent, but there's too much of it still. In 1939 I skin-tested 6500 school children out of a possible 8000. Of these 1500 showed positive, with 250 latent and 46 active cases. We have tried to get the active ones in the Sanatorium, though the chronics have had to stay home, re-infect their families, and—die. Last summer we had a fluoroscopic clinic for the examination of adults, and we expect to continue this annually. Our goal is to establish a local sanatorium for TB patients, my preference being a tri-county hospital for Ritchie-Maddox-Farthington.

"As a group, doctors may be opposed to the socialization of medicine, but as individuals many are not. Dr. Jameson over in Anton tells me frankly that I'm all wrong, that I shouldn't practice as I do. Instead, he says, the county should provide the fund, and the local private doctors should be called in to treat the charity cases, with their fees provided from the county fund.

"No unusual diseases have come under my practice. Pellagra is all too common, but with the cooperation of the welfare board it has been possible to treat the pellagra cases with an approximately proper diet. In the Bolton School I found a case of chlorosis, or "green sickness," which was the result of a diet deficiency. We found the child had been subsisting on a diet of white potatoes for breakfast, dinner, and supper. She responded to changed diet right away. Otherwise, there have been the usual kinds of illness—flu and pneumonia, the infectious kinds, and still a little typhoid though vaccination has reduced it to a minimum.

"I'm proud of our program. Farthington is the only county in the State that has a maternity and infancy clinic like ours. But it will take time to show the difference a comprehensive program can make in the health of a county."

BERNICE KELLY HARRIS

Business Is a Pleasure

IT WAS A GLOOMY MORNING AND I FOUND HIM SEATED at his desk in the back of his store studying some old ledger accounts. At first he wasn't inclined to talk. At last:

"Well, suppose you drop around the house some night, where we won't be interrupted by customers dropping in. Come in tomorrow and I'll try to tell you what night will be most convenient."

I dropped in next day. His partner was up front on the lookout for trade. Instead of naming an evening hour for me to interview him, he motioned me to a chair, pulled his own chair over and opened up. What he gave me was more a history of his times than of his personal life. It is hardly possible to disassociate the two, so I give you his story just as he gave it to me. Pull your own chair over and listen in:

"It was the year of the total eclipse of the sun—1900 I think was—when I went to work for R. A. Budleigh's Store. I worked mornings and afternoons before and after school, and the full day on Saturdays. I was sixteen years old. My pay was $1.50 a week.

"My principal job was cleaning spittoons. Spittoons were important fixtures in all stores in those days. It seemed to me that most men chewed tobacco and many women dipped snuff and were not ashamed of it. Many of our women customers used those spittoons freely.

"Shopping was different in those days. There were no automobiles. The farmer took a day off to come to town. He would leave home around daybreak, spend the greater part of the day in town, leaving town after noon and getting home around sundown. He didn't come to town often and his shopping list contained many items. Often as not he brought his wife with him. Stools were provided at regular intervals in front of the counters for the convenience of patrons. And between stools were oversize spittoons. We didn't call them cuspidors. There were twenty-two spittoons in Budleigh's Store, including the spittoons in the office.

"In front of every store were hitching posts for the convenience of our rural customers. It was not unusual for a farmer to drive up with his horse and buggy, or horse and cart, at nine o'clock in the morning and leave his horse tied until he had finished his business in town at three or four o'clock that afternoon. At noon he would put a bundle of fodder and eight ears of corn down for his nag, give her more rein and let her feed. The horse droppings were prolific and as soon as I showed up at the store in the afternoon, if I didn't think of it first, Mr. Budleigh would suggest that I should clean up after the horses.

"The streets were not paved. In places they were knee deep in mud in winter. In dry weather every passing vehicle stirred up clouds of dust. The merchants in our block had combined to build a water tank in the neighborhood from which ran a one-inch iron pipe providing spigots on every store front. With a 50 ft. length of garden hose we sprinkled the street twice a day and kept down much of the dust. Part of my job was sprinkling the street in front of the store.

"Stores were lighted with kerosene oil lamps with bright metal reflectors. Most stores opened early mornings and closed at nine o'clock at night. It was part of my job too to keep the lamp chimneys cleaned and polished.

"I was employed at Budleigh's less than two years when Burton and Jones hardware store just across the street offered me $1.50 a week. Their offer appealed to me because they had fewer spittoons to clean and fewer hitching posts, which meant less chambermaid work for fewer horses.

"A handy method of cleaning spittoons was to take them down to the public dock on the street where there was plenty of river water to wash them out with. One day a neighboring merchant, who had fewer spittoons to clean, said he would give me ten cents a day to clean his spittoons. My employers were willing for me to take on the extra work. Boy! I felt rich. I had so much money coming in that I bought a bicycle.

"My next job was with Murray, Pleasants & Co., dealers in dry goods, clothing, notions, hats, boots and shoes. I was getting along. It wasn't long before I was offered a better job with Prince's Shoe Co. I left

Prince's Shoe Co. in 1907 to go with L. M. Butterick, at that time the largest and busiest department store in town. I was a full fledged shoe salesman then. I was with Butterick's for seven years, until 1914, when I engaged with my partner in the present business which we have carried on ever since.

"I've seen a lot of changes in merchandising and social customs in my thirty-nine years of mercantile experience.

"Thirty or forty years ago most women made their own dresses and under garments, or employed neighborhood dressmakers. Most boy's clothing and man's trousers were home made. Yard goods, including pants cloth, were in great demand. Women's ready made coats and dresses were in little demand and the men's custom-made clothing business was still feeling its way. Silk hosiery was a luxury, sheer silk and chiffon hosiery unknown. There was no such thing as a woman's custom-made hat. A woman bought a frame, so much velvet, so many yards of ribbon, certain feathers or flowers, and a milliner designed her hat to her individual notions. The array of such fanciful headwear in a church auditorium on a Sunday morning was a sight to behold.

"Hour-glass corsets, bustles and bust forms were the height of fashion. Women even padded their coiffures with rolls of hair called 'rats.' They wore skirts that trailed the ground and a man had to wait for a rainy day to get a glimpse of a feminine ankle. A man never knew what sort of figure he was courting in those days. But once matrimony admitted him to the privacy of his lady's boudoir, what a kick he got out of seeing the lady go through the ritual of disrobing! There were no bathrooms or dressing rooms in the average home to which milady might retire for this intimate business.

"It took countless buttons, hooks and eyes and pins to put a woman together in those days. Even their hats were held on their heads with long stiletto-like steel or brass pins. The other day I was on an automobile ride, with five women in the car and I wanted a pin. There wasn't a pin among the five of them. The modern miss releases a snap, shrugs her shoulders and drops her clothes with the nonchalance of a moulting hen giving herself a shake and dropping a feather.

"A lot of water has gone under the bridge since I first went behind a counter. The merchant used to get his goods in wooden packing cases. The wooden packing case is almost a thing of the past. Almost everything today comes in paper cartons. Where we used to wrestle with a heavy nail puller, we now use a pen knife.

"It isn't safe for a small merchant to buy in heavy packing case quantities any more, on account of the changing styles. Take shoes for instance; the traveling salesmen used to come twice a year with their sample lines. We bought our fall and winter shoes in the spring, our spring and summer shoes in the fall. We can't do that any more. The manufacturers are developing new styles every few weeks. No one can tell what the trade will demand in shoes three or six months from now. The shoe salesman drops in now every sixty days. The same with woman's hats, coats and dresses.

"Even men's shoes are subject to ever changing styles. A man's shoe that may be the rage today, may be obsolete another season. And yet I well remember when the prestige of a store was gauged by the quality of the brogan shoes it sold. Remember those brogans? Made of thick cowhide; stiff cowhide uppers, devoid of linings; heavy cowhide soles, not sewed on but pegged with wooden pegs. Brass tops on the toes, iron rims imbedded in the heels. Guaranteed to wear a year in barnyard manure. That was the type of shoe rural people and the working class people in town generally wore thirty or forty years ago. Today we have no calls for brogans and, to tell you the truth, I wouldn't know where to buy them.

"It seems to me that the old brogan shoe was a pretty good symbol of those days, when life was hard compared with what it is today. Forty years ago—certainly fifty years ago—there wasn't a bathtub in the whole town, no piped water in any home. The telephone and the electric light had not arrived. Automobiles were unthinkable, and when they began to appear early in the century they were regarded as another rich man's toy.

"Why, I remember the sensation caused by the first barrel of gasoline that was brought to town. Lee George, who ran a small grocery and fruit store, bought a peanut roaster to be heated by gasoline. He had to order his gasoline from Baltimore. When his barrel of gasoline arrived, he had it carted up from the steamboat wharf and placed back of his store. News of the arrival of that gasoline spread like wildfire. Gasoline was thought of as a highly inflammable, explosive and dangerous article. What was Mr. George thinking of, to bring a barrel of that deadly stuff to town and set it down right in the heart of the business section? Did he want to blow the whole town up?

"The town council was hurriedly called into special session. The mayor and councilmen, with white, tense faces took immediate action. An ordinance, effective pronto, was enacted prohibiting the storage of gasoline in greater than one-gallon quantities in the city limits.

Mr. George was ordered to remove that barrel of gasoline to the outskirts of town, where he built a shelter over it and drew out a gallon at a time as needed for his peanut roaster.

"Only as far back as 1914 merchandising was relatively easy. Many men with good characters and little capital had established grocery stores and made money in the grocery business. With little capital, but with good credit and some years of experience, we started our little dry goods, clothing and shoe store and made money from the start.

"First the telephone, then the automobile and, more lately, mounting taxes have played their part in revolutionizing business. The advent of the telephone ushered in an era of buying 'on approval.' It was so easy for a woman to call up Butterick's, for instance, and ask for several pair of shoes to be sent up for 'approval.' The goods would be obligingly sent up and perhaps several days would elapse before the lady made her selection. All the time the goods were out of stock. A lot of bookkeeping was involved. Mitchell's with a turnover of less than $75,000 a year, employed three bookkeepers. Our merchants organized about 1916 and put an end to that expensive trade practice.

"Imperceptibly at first, but rapidly enough, the automobile revolutionized all business. Sales became smaller and more frequent. The farmer who used to come to town once a month or once in three or six months with a list of supplies to last him until his next trip, now runs in any day in the week and buys a pair of shoes, a suit of overalls or a plow line and is on his way. The stools in front of the counters have gone with the spittoons. Nobody has time to sit and shop any more. Spitting is tabu. But, remember, grandma used snuff, daughter sucks a cigarette.

"But the automobile has otherwise affected all business. It has increased the tempo and the cost of living. With the fixed charges of their automobiles, higher rents, higher taxes and other advances of modern living, the masses seem to find it increasingly difficult to meet all of their obligations. Darn few people seem to be able to adjust their desire for things to their ability to pay for things. We have thousands of dollars in bad accounts on our books that are forever uncollectible. All credit lines have had to be tightened. We send a bill collector out once or twice a week now, instead of the first of the month only.

"I never let my automobile embarrass me financially. I have owned one car in fifteen years and it is still giving me good service; a model T Ford, 1924 model. I bought it on May 3, 1924. I waited until May 3rd because tax listing time is up May 1st. I let the dealers list it for taxes before I bought it.

"For several years now I haven't felt able to buy a new car, and that old buggy takes me where I want to go and brings me back. She looks ancient but there's a lot of 'get up and go' in her yet. Another thing, I've got a boy coming on; he's president of his high school class, popular with the younger set and if I had a new car it would take a lot of gas for him. He never asks me to lend him the old bus; he would be ashamed to be caught in it. His daddy ain't.

"Again, the automobile has made the larger stores and bargain days of larger city stores available to the average man or woman who formerly had to buy at home or resort to a mail order catalog. Every day we see cars full of people passing us by to go to Norfolk or Richmond to buy. Often as not they could do as well at home, but they enjoy the excitement of travel and the contacts with the larger city life. But down the line, the smaller country merchant is seeing car loads of his old customers going by his door, heading for ours.

"The chain stores have complicated things for the independent merchant too. Their specialization in cheap, flashy merchandise, attractively displayed and carrying easy-to-read price tags gets the business. We independents have to hand it to the chains! They usually have more attractive stores, know how to dress their windows, make shopping so easy, and have so systematized their business that they can get by with the dumbest, cheapest help on earth. We independents have to depend much on personal relationships and know our customers. Once we forget a man's name or neglect to inquire about the health of his family, the condition of his crops, or about his hobby, we are in a way to lose his business. Our customers are interested in us and love to come our way because we are interested in them.

"Yes sir, it's the personal contact that counts. When you don't see me around the store, you know I'm out drumming up business. I make the rounds of our manufacturing establishments once a month, regularly. I'll go out to Eichorn's mill on a fair day at lunch time when the hands are gathered under one of the sheds for the lunch. I pass among them showing a suit of overalls that we sell for a dollar and a pair of workshoes that we sell for a dollar and a half; give them each a pair of shoe laces and a piece of advertising matter. They know where to come the next time they need work clothes or shoes.

"In one of our machine shops the other day a workman dropped a hammer on his foot and was laid up for several days. That gave me an idea; I am taking a pair of shoes with metal toe caps—something new on the market, designed to protect a workman's foot in just such accidents—over to that machine shop and leaving them for the men to examine at their leisure. I'm going to get the jump on other dealers with that line of shoes."

I had noticed a beaver hat and a funny little low-crown Yiddish derby on a shelf in the back of the store. I asked him to tell me about those hats.

"That beaver was given me by a man who was once prominent in politics in our town. It was good as new and I guess he thought I might find a purchaser for it. But I had another idea. Whenever there is one of these womanless weddings that schools and churches get up as a money making stunt, that hat goes out to help outfit the groom, and everybody knows it was loaned by us. When a certain Postmaster General bought himself a new car some years back because his old car was too low for his silk hat, I put that stovepipe on my head, climbed into my model T and rode all over town. Had everybody laughing about me and the Postmaster General. That was good advertising.

"Now, about that Yiddish derby: My boy used it in a Yiddish part in a school play. That gave me an idea. I brought it down to the store and it has been making sales for us ever since. I work it like this. My partner gets hold of a tough customer and isn't selling him. The customer was out of sorts when he came in. I get down the Yiddish derby, take off my coat, snap a pair of red arm bands over my shirt sleeves, tuck a red bandana in my belt, prance up to the customer. Nine times out of ten it gets a laugh, puts the customer in a good humor. My partner backs off and after a little bit I bring the customer around to the merchandise he was interested in, and sell him.

"I guess my brother Pat was right. Someone once asked my father why I was so talkative and Pat so quiet like? Father couldn't answer but Pat spoke up and said: 'They used a phonograph needle to vaccinate him when he first went to school.'" And then, in a serious vein, he returned to the subject of business generally. He said:

"No, we are not making easy money any more. Our overhead is steadily increasing. Taxes are higher and higher. We are not complaining about the interference of government in business; it doesn't affect us little fellows like it does the big ones; where the government hits us below the belt is in doling out overalls, work shirts, bedding and countless other commodities to thousands of so-called relief cases who shouldn't be on relief at all. We personally know a number of working people who are practically living out of WPA Commodity Stores to the loss of merchants who are expected to pay the consequent tax bill.

"The sales tax? That doesn't bother us; we rather like it. The public doesn't like it, so we never mention it; we just tack it on to the price of the merchandise. Sometimes we have to mark a 25 cent item up to 27-cents, because to mark it 26-cents, just a cent more to cover sales tax, would be a little too obvious. A nationally advertised article that the manufacturer puts a retail price of $1.00 on, and which we formerly sold at 90 cents, we now mark down to 97 cents only, making four cents more on the article than we made before the sales tax was inflicted on us. If the public only knew what the sales tax is actually costing them, they would howl!

"No, we are not making what you might call good money any more; we are not doing the volume of business we used to do; we used to employ two clerks when we could have got along with one. The NRA drove us into that economy. The only clerk hire we indulge in now is a clerk to help take care of the extra trade on Saturdays. My partner and I take care of the trade now.

"And, say! speaking of the automobile; when I saw what it was doing to our business I put it to work for me. When I built my home, the small bungalow type of home had not come into style. We built a large roomy house with rooms to spare. We put a sign TOURISTS WELCOME out in front of our house a few years ago, and now it's turning in a nice little revenue every week. It means a little more housework for the wife, but I help out at night, acting as night clerk, and get down stairs in time to start breakfast in the morning. A dollar twenty-five for a room and forty cents for a breakfast isn't to be sneezed at.

"You hear a lot of belliakin from little business men these days; you're not getting a squawk out of me; I trim my sails to the winds as they blow, and when they don't blow for a spell I put out my oars. I once dreamed of getting a lot of money ahead and living on Easy Street. I don't have any such dreams any more; I just take life as I find it, live within my means, find my social life in my church and Sunday School, and with the old friends who stick by us year in and year out. You see, business isn't just business with us as it is with the chain stores, it's a pleasure. And not one of the least of the pleasures in doing business today is in the general

improvement in the quality of the merchandise one
sells. Whether it's the pinch of competition, improvement in manufacturing and processing techniques, or
an awakening of conscience, I don't know; but I do
know that merchandise generally is more dependable
and more fairly priced to the merchant than it ever was
in the earlier years of my business experience. One of
the pleasures of doing business today is the increasing
high regard that manufacturers and jobbers generally
seem to have for the integrity of their products; it is as
if they had discovered that honesty is not only the best
policy, but the only policy insuring permanent success
for either an individual or an institution."

W. O. SAUNDERS

Gold Tooth

I FOUND HIM LIVING IN A COMFORTABLE HOME IN
what was in times past the fashionable residential
neighborhood of the town. Indeed, next door was the
fine old Colonial ancestral home of the most distin-
guished white citizen the county had produced. Old
white families have died out or built themselves more
modern homes in the suburbs and Negroes have moved
in until what was once the town's social center is today
a Negro neighborhood.

He is a professional man—a dentist—and his office

and reception room occupied two of the rooms on the first floor. He seemed surprised to see me. "When white people want to see me they usually 'phone me to come to them," he said, guessing that I had noted the surprised look on his face when he had come to the front door in response to my bell.

"I have come to ask you if you will tell me the story of your life," I said.

"The story of my life!" he exclaimed. "It would take a million words," he said. And then: "I think I should be glad to talk to you, but I would have to have time to think about it; could I see you in, say, a week from now?"

I assured him that I could wait a week. Just one week later he walked into my office and told me that he was ready for the interview.

"But I was wrong about it taking a million words to tell the story of my life," he said; "I have been thinking it all over since I saw you and I find that there isn't so much to my life after all. It's going to make mighty poor reading."

"We'll see about that," I said. "We are alone; I think you know me to be a sympathetic listener and one with a minimum of racial prejudices. In this story I am going to write about you I want you to be perfectly frank. If you've got anything you want to get off your chest, out with it and don't be afraid of me. Talk to me as man to man, not as a colored man to a white man. Begin with your family background."

"My father was a Methodist minister," he said; "but before he was a minister he was a carpenter. My father was born in 1867, just after the Civil War, and life was hard for his parents who had been slaves. He told me that there were many times when he had to go to garbage pails to get his food. And he told me that the first hundred dollars he made, he spent it to build a home for his mother who had never had a home of her own. The hundred dollars went for timber and hardware; he did all the work.

"When my father felt the call to preach he did not lay aside his carpenter tools. It was years before he gave up his manual labor; by that time he had been given the degree of Doctor of Divinity by Livingston College in recognition of his earnestness and influence.

"My father said I was born for the ministry. He told me that I had all the attributes of a leader and that it was his wish that I should be a bishop in the church. I couldn't see it his way and I chose the profession of dentistry. But I haven't been happy; I have made money, but it hasn't brought me satisfaction or peace of mind. As I grow older I hear the call to preach that I couldn't hear when my father was alive.

"My father was a righteous man; my mother a saint. I remember when I was a little boy I found a nest of hen's eggs in an old cemetery. I brought them home and my mother asked me where I got them. When I told her, she said I must take them right back and place them back in the nest exactly as I found them. I told her that even if those eggs did belong to somebody else, they would never find them. 'But if those eggs are left in the nest the hen that laid them will hatch them out and lead her biddies back to their rightful owner,' she said.

"I remember too when once I fought a girl. When my father learned of it he beat me and lectured me, lectured me and beat me. 'I am ashamed of a son of mine who would stoop so low as to strike a female,' he said; 'you are lower than the animals, commoner than a dog. A dog does not attack a female of his kind; a lion does not attack a lioness; men are made to be the kings of the earth, women its queens.' And so he lectured me between lashings until he was nearly exhausted. You see, I had the right sort of training when I was growing up.

"I was a tough boy. My father used to call me 'All Face,' saying I was like an Indian because I never suffered from cold. When I was 12 years old I used to get up at five o'clock in the morning, make a fire in my father's room, make a fire in the kitchen, fetch a pail of water and then take a milk pail and walk three miles in the country to milk a cow that my father kept in the country because he had no place in town for it. Did I say walk three miles? I didn't walk it all; I would run a mile, walk a mile to get my second wind, and then run the other mile. I didn't know what it was to get tired.

"At thirteen I hired out as an apprentice to a barber. After milking the cow, bringing the milk home and getting my breakfast, I would go to the barber shop, sweep the place out, clean the spittoons and then hurry off to school. I would go back in the afternoon, shine shoes, wait on the barbers, brush off the customers. I got ten cents a week and what I could make shining shoes. Later, when I learned to use a razor and clippers I got a dollar and a half a week. My barbering helped me to get my education. I got what I could from the public schools and denominational schools, and then went to Howard University where I finished in 1917 with the degree of Doctor of Dental Surgery.

"I established myself in the practice of dentistry in this city shortly thereafter, being the first dentist of my race to establish himself in the field. I was successful from the start; not that the members of my race knew anything about dentistry, but they all wanted gold crowned teeth.

"I tried to talk to them about oral hygiene and dental prophylaxis. It didn't mean anything to them. They were not interested in saving good teeth; all they wanted was gold shells, even for their clean, sound teeth. They would come to me and insist that I file down perfectly good teeth and crown them with gold. They might have gone hungry and suffered from cold all winter and gotten hold of a little money in the early summer for work in the potato fields. But they would spend their last dollar for a shiny gold tooth.

"In 1919 I resolved not to take another dollar from a member of my race for gold unless a gold fill was absolutely necessary to save a decayed tooth. I lost money and saw my former patients go to other dentists who were not so conscientious. I had to give up a fine resolution. I have made $150 to $175 a week; I have made $40 to $60 in a day; and most of it was for gold shells. A bootlegger, flush with money, came into my office one day and ordered $42 worth of gold work at one sitting. And his teeth were as clean and sound as a hound's. It is only in the last few years that the more enlightened people of my race have begun to show some apprehension of the connection between oral hygiene and general health."

But I wanted to know about his feelings toward the white people. "My relations with the better class of white people have always been pleasant and often helpful. When I was younger I had many unpleasant experiences with the lower class of whites, but I am not bothered by that class any more because I have learned to avoid them and not give them any opportunity to

insult or provoke me. If some ignorant white man
makes some slurring remark about 'the damn niggers'
in my presence I pay no attention to him. He doesn't
hurt me by his cheap opinions. What I do suffer is
the envy and jealousy of members of my own race."

"But you must have some grievances against the
white race?" I pressed him.

"I only ask of the white people that they give the
Negro a fair deal. When I pay first class fare on a
railroad train or a passenger bus I want accommodations comparable to those of the white passengers. I
want my children to have the same educational opportunities as white children. And I object to the dis-
franchisement of Negroes on purely racial grounds;
if there are lots of Negroes who are not capable of voting intelligently, so are there a lot of white people who
should be disfranchised on the same grounds. But we
colored people have to be patient; the white people
have the jump on us in the matter of civilization; we
must admit that a lot of us are not far removed from
the jungle. And we are going to need the leadership
of white men for a long time to come, or until we learn
the white man's lesson of cooperation. I'll try to give
you an illustration of what I mean:

"Winter before last I saw from my office window
little Negro children in rags going to school. I noticed
that some of them had only remnants of shoes on their
feet. I learned that four teachers had been dropped
from our colored schools because the attendance of
colored children had dropped off, because they didn't
have clothes to wear. Some, indeed, had to stay in bed
on bitterly cold days to keep from freezing to death.

"There was a meeting of our community club. I attended a meeting at which the leaders were stressing the

need of a playground for our children. The white children had a playground; the Negro children should have one too.

" 'Don't let's argue for a playground,' I spoke up, 'until we have put first things first; what we need more than a playground is means to provide for the under-privileged children of our race to get the benefits of the education that is available for them. There are hundreds of colored children in this town who haven't sufficient clothing and who are underfed. They need clothing and food to enable them to go to school. I told them that if they would subscribe any amount of money to help these children I would raise an equal amount, if I had to pay it out of my own pocket. They wouldn't listen to me. In desperation I determined to do what I could on my own account. I put 42 milk bottles in every colored place of business in town, with an appeal for donations for the aid of indigent children. I would ride all over town after office hours to collect the coins from those bottles and I was fortunate if I got so much as sixty cents a day. And then I called on the white mayor of the town for help. He came out to our club one night, indorsed my plan and told them that he had talked to the city fathers and that they would agree to match our funds dollar for dollar, to give the indigent colored children a chance. Well, sir, some of our leaders who had given me no cooperation at all fell all over themselves subscribing a substantial sum for the work. It took a white man's indorsement to get anywhere with a plain common sense program that should have appealed to our people from the start. That's why I say we are going to need white leadership for a long time to come.

"Of course I am not insensitive to some of the slights

that one must suffer on account of the color of his skin.
I resented the action of a theatre owner who wouldn't
let a Negro chorus appear on the stage of his theatre
for a white benefit. I regret that I am denied the
privilege of hearing big men and fine musical organizations that come to our town with messages and pro-
grams of uplift. I smile when I pass the big white
church up town with the words carved over its door,
'A HOUSE OF PRAYER FOR ALL PEOPLE.' I
know it doesn't mean MY people.

"But the white man has given us the radio, and the
radio knows no color line; if we are denied admission
to the halls of white men where fine speakers and fine
music are to be heard, we can twist the knob of our
radio and bring their voices and their music into our
own homes. I am sorry to say, however, that most of
our people find in the radio only another instrument
of jazz and swing."

"And what of the future for the colored man?" I
asked.

"Right now it looks pretty dark. It's my idea that
it will be a hundred years yet before our people will
find their place in the sun. Race prejudice will lessen
as our skins grow lighter and lighter. You will have
to go to Africa to find a black man a hundred years
from now. Our darker skinned business and professional men are choosing light-skinned wives. I attended an Elks Convention in Atlanta a few years ago.
In one hall we had 7000 delegates and visitors; in another hall 5000; I saw but only three black women in
that whole assembly.

"Later in our National Medical Association in
Richmond I counted only five black women out of 4000
delegates and guests.

"At St. Louis in 1928, at the General Conference of the A. M. E. Zion Church of all states and Africa, I observed that every bishop had a mulatto wife, and the higher up a minister's station the brighter his wife.

"And not only by intermarriage of black men with mulatto women is the color problem fading; our darker skinned people are spending enormous sums on hair straighteners and complexion aids. I have seen women of my race who have changed their complexions several shades lighter since I first knew them. As I see it, the race problem in America is just going to fade out in a hundred years or such a matter.

"In the meantime we can not pay too much attention to our indigent children. Our preachers and teachers generally are not helping them. Their parents are working hard for a bare living and don't have the means or the time to help them. They roam the streets, get into mischief and many of them land in jail very young. Jails don't help criminals; jails breed criminals. It would be a fine thing if we had a farm of 75 or 100 acres with a staff of intelligent right-minded teachers and overseers to take these unfortunates, teach them the principles of right living and the dignity of work; teach them how to do for themselves, how to keep physically strong and morally clean.

"As to social equality, I don't think any intelligent Negro seriously wants it. We who think realize that our people have got to do a lot of cleaning up and brightening up before most of them would feel at ease among white people if they were accepted as social equals. That's why my first interest is in children; we've got to start them right to save them from hoodlumism, buffoonery, and vagabondage. They need a lot of drilling in thoroughness, faithfulness, good manners and the virtues of right living."

The doctor looked uneasily at his watch. "I'm afraid you'll have to excuse me please; I have an appointment with a patient about this time," he said.

"Another gold crown?" I asked.

"You guessed it," he replied; "she's a school teacher who discovered a cavity in one of her front teeth the other day. It made her happy as a child; she's going to have gold in her mouth now."

W. O. SAUNDERS

On the Road to Sheriff

"ALL I EVER STUDY ABOUT OR EVER WANT TO DO IS TO be kind to all in every way and do my duty as First Deputy of Brundage County."

"Well, in some ways deputy work jist can't be beat. You git to go so many places. It ain't confining like mill work and they's not any hard hand labor, day in and day out, to wear a man down. You git a better salary than farming and it's stiddy money, too. Dry spells and wet spells and smut and rot will set a farmer back. But a deputy don't have to worry none. His business is always good.

"When you're in deputy work, you have some drawbacks, though. Look at my hours! May git a call any hour, day or night. Never know jist when the county will need me. It seems like it needs me mostly when the weather's the worst. I don't know why, but I git a sight more calls in cold rainy or sleety times than in good weather. And don't let nobody tell you the work ain't dangerous. You risk your life every time you make an arrest, every time you serve a warrant or raid a still. That's what I go through all the time to keep this county peace-abiding.

"Far back as I can remember I always wanted to be on the side of the law. I'm the only one of my family ever went into this business. My father was Horace Squires Marshall and my mother was Betsy Naomi T. Farley Marshall. All of my people has been farmers all the way through and that's the way they started me out. My brothers farmed and I guess I'd be messing with farm work right this minute if they hadn't been that little certain something in me that put me on the side of the law.

"I always had a lot of patriotic feeling. So when the war come along I was right ready and was glad to go when they drafted me. The government then trained me to fight and sent me overseas. Well, I sure done my best in that war. I stopped a bullet and got wounded. Stayed in a hospital till she healed and went back at them Germans. So they laid for me and give me a dose of gas and I was out for good that time. Government sent me home and I spent two years in hospitals. That old gas is sure hard to clear out of a man's system. But they finally got me shet of it and I come home to Brundage County.

"Well, I jist knocked around for a couple of years. Didn't feel like fooling with farm work. It was jist one thing I wanted to do—deputy work. But I couldn't git on. Then in nineteen twenty-four I got a place. Served my county and its good people ever since except between nineteen thirty-two and nineteen thirty-six. In that time they had a sheriff that him and me couldn't noways git along. So I jist knocked around until we got a good man in here again and he give me my job back.

"Here's how I make my salary. Well, I don't guess you'd exactly call it salary, either. It's commission work. I mean, I git my money all according to how much arrests and subpoenas and warrants I do. So, you see, it keeps a man hustling on his toes to make a go of it. You've sure got to hit the ball. If business is dull, go out and look some up, I say.

"Now whenever they's a funeral anywheres in this county, like as not you'll find me there, specially if its back off the road somewheres. Most usually they's lot of drinking goes on at country funerals. The family drinks so's to drownd their sadness. Them that comes out of respect for the deceased drinks so's they won't git too low in mind from watching the women folks carry on. And then they's lots of young bloods comes jist for the pure fun of it and gits lit up. You can look for a fight before it's all over. If nobody gits to fighting, then you can grab somebody for having liquor on them or in their car or wagon. Any which way it is you carry them before a justice of peace and he fines them and you git your fee. If they can't pay the fee, it's the county road for them and the county pays you your fee. You can't lose on a funeral.

"Next to a funeral is a political speaking and a barbecue. Always drinking then and fights. Almost any gathering where people git together may mean you can pick up a fee. Auction sales where they're selling

off a mortgage-due farm is good. The man that's being
sold out may git ugly and try to start something and
then I can step in and put it on him. Lots of times
you can do business at a revival meeting when somebody
makes trouble over what they believe. Oh, they's a heap
of ways to do if you keep hustling. But I wish they'd
give me a regular salary along with my fees.

"I keep right at it, doing my duty. I aim to rise in
this work. Right now I'm on the road to Sheriff. If I
live and nothing happens you will call Elmore Marshall
sheriff before many more years.

"The largest raids or work we usually have now is
stills. They's several we've got spotted now to gather
in. We'll be going in again in a very few days. Usually we get our tip-off when it's least expected and have
to go in all kinds of weather. We almost never find anybody there, but they's always signs of them. The still
worm still hot and the mash boiling. But they have
time to see us coming and run, no matter how much we
try to slip up on them.

"We raided a still a short time ago and found it
directly on the Creighton County line, we thought.
But we found after we had busted and shot it all up
that it was all in Creighton County territory. You
jist don't seem to be able to make people quit making
liquor. They'll go to jail for it and come out and go
right back at it. But still raids is gitting to be pretty
tame. The birds is flown usually.

"We haven't had a mob since the time they got the
nigger that killed Buck Starwell. The nigger had always worked for Mr. Buck and knew him well. Well,
he had a sudden spurt of gitting drunk. They wasn't
no living with him, that's all, when he got drunk. Bad
nigger then. So he got in a lot of trouble and hid in an

old house on Mr. Buck's place. Mr. Buck was then
sheriff of the county—you remember when that was.
Well, we tried after that nigger. He shot a lot of men
when we tried to run him out. Mr. Buck says, 'I'll go
git him my own self.' He walked right toward the
barn. The nigger shot him before he got to the door,
in cold blood murder.

"They gathered a mob and went after him. Practically everything in town joined it and shot it out with
him. He was holed up in the barn and with plenty of
ammunition and it didn't look like we was ever going
to get him out till all the ammunition had give way.
But some of us got enough of that. We got together
and rushed him on all sides at once. He hit a few of
us, but none serious, and we got him that time.

"Well, he got such wounds he soon died without living to be hung. The mob come pouring in when we'd
disarmed him and jist riddled his body when they got
to him before we could stop them. Niggers was in on
this hunt as well as whites for they all loved Mr. Buck,
a friend to black and white alike.

"About the hardest shooting scrape we've ever had
or the toughest customers is the Garners. Them
Garners is into everything happens and always gitting
out, too. They was caught cold-handed, almost, in the
robbery of the Ten-Acres Postoffice sometime ago. But
they got out of it. Some of the Garner girls has served
time in prison for stealing and various things. Well,
they jist don't seem to be anything much they haven't
done, though no proof of murder has ever been put on
them.

"One time the boys, Boyd and Skipper, refused arrest and after most of the ammunition in town had
been shot, they hid in this log barn with the rest of

the family and shot it out.   It lasted several days.
We'd finally captured them all but Boyd and he
jist wouldn't give up.   He shot two or three deputies
and city officers.   Finally, though, his mama seen he
would be riddled by bullets if he kept it up.   She run
in front of our men to the barn begging him to give
hisself up for her sake and the girls.   So he did or
otherwise we wouldn't never have taken him alive.   He
already had a bunch of wounds, but he was a crack
shooter and fought it out to the bitter end almost.

"We've caught them Garners several times since then.
They's always wanted for stealing in other counties.
We've found the goods on their land, but they always
worm out of it somehow.

"Once I let a man git away in a still raid.   I was new
on the job and kind of skittish of shooting at a man.
Well, this was down near the river.   I went down there
and was watching.   We slipped up on them and they
had their backs turned and we didn't see their faces.
They all run jist as we yelled at them and we shot over
their heads.   One run and jumped in the river.   He
stayed under so long I thought he was drownded and
when he swum out right almost at my feet I was so
happy that he wasn't drownded I jist stood there and
didn't ever recognize who he was or say a word to him.
Jist stood with my mouth hanging open, a stone's throw
from him, and let him go walking off down through the
woods.   The other deputies was chasing the others and
I let him git clean away.   Could have caught him if
I'd tried.

"One time Joe Mumpower shot Rae Barfield.   He
was a high yellow and so was she and she was a cook
here in town.   They accused him but couldn't find the
body.   Finally I went to his place and searched and

seeing a fresh looking place in his barn, he told me that it was a hog had died with cholera and he'd buried it there. I become suspicious and made him dig there. Well, he uncovered the hog right straight. I told him to keep on digging. And it wasn't long till I soon saw the body of the woman. So I forced his confession there. We put him in jail and he hung hisself with his belt.

"Another branch of the deputy work is this. Lots of cold checks is passed and we have to run them down. We serve subpoenas and warrants and arrest people for failure to pay debt. All in all, it's a pretty hard day's work. It's hard to serve a warrant on or arrest a man who is your personal friend. Have to do it, though, even when it's your own neighbors and friends. We must do our duty by so doing.

"About the only criminal assault case in this county by a Negro on a white was a porter at the hotel. We got him for assault on a white girl here. But it later come out showing she was crazy and only trying to git some money out of the management of the hotel.

"Well, I like my work here among the fine people of Brundage County. They's nothing I'd rather do than serve them as their sheriff and I aim to run in this next coming election. I never was blessed with no children in my married life, but if I had a boy I would tell him, 'Git on the side of the law, work for the good people of this county, and they will gratefully reward you some day like they done your Dad when they made him sheriff of this fine county.' "

NELLIE GRAY TOLER
JAMES R. ASWELL

. . . And Costs

"DON'T YOU KNOW THE SPEED LAWS, SON?" ASKED Squire Porterfield.

"Yes sir, I reckon I do."

"I reckon he don't!" said the deputy.

"I guess I just didn't notice," the man in the leather cap and jacket said. "That truck I'm driving rambles along mighty easy and I guess I was going a little fast. But I'm always careful."

"Well," Squire Porterfield decided, "that will cost you five dollars and costs. That'll make twelve-fifty in all. Do you want to pay it?"

"Yes, sir, I want to pay it but I don't see how I can. I was out of work for five straight months. I just got this job—this is my fourth week—so I won't have any money till I get paid Saturday night."

"Who you drive for? How much you make?"

"Keefe and Company. They give me twelve dollars a week. I've got a wife and two children to support, and I'm afraid getting arrested for speeding will just about cost me my job."

"Larry, what do you want to do about this case?" Squire Porterfield said to the deputy. "However you want to handle it is all right with me."

The deputy called the driver aside and talked to him several minutes. They returned to the squire's desk. "Well, Squire," said the deputy, "he says he can pay the amount of a dollar a week. Suppose we let him handle it that way. I don't want the boy to lose his job over it."

"Okeh." The squire made an entry on the warrant with his fountain pen. "You can go now."

A shriveled little old woman, accompanied by a girl of about fifteen or sixteen, approached the squire. The girl asked him if he thought they needed a lawyer.

"No, I don't think that'll be necessary."

"What did he say?" querulously asked the old woman. The girl shouted the reply with her lips close to her mother's ear.

"They tell me he's got one!" shrilled the deaf woman. "Some thinks we ought to have one, too."

"Well, maybe if that is the case it might be better to get one," the squire shouted across his desk.

There was a discussion as to what lawyer they would get. Finally one of the lounging deputies suggested an attorney and gave directions to his office. The couple left.

"That," said Squire Porterfield, "is one of the most pitiful cases ever come to my court in a long time. A case of violation of the age of consent. We got the young man in jail now and his trial comes off tomorrow. That girl isn't right bright and she and her ma are poor people. The boy took advantage of her under promise of marriage. Then after the girl's doctor'd told her what was coming and she told the boy about it, that boy right off and married another girl. He was married day before yesterday and we picked him up last night. The only thing to do is bind him over to the higher court. They'll probably give him two to five years in the pen. That is, if the girl's story is true. I'll have to hear the evidence, of course, and decide on the merits of the case. It's a shame, though, for a girl like that to get into that kind of trouble. Why she's just a little over fifteen with a mind of a child of ten.

"Excuse me," as the telephone rang. "Hello. Yes, we garnisheed him, but his boss says we'll have to get it a dollar or so a week. There's already two garnishments ahead of ours."

The squire paused a moment, then continued, "Yes, I thought that was better than nothing at all, but it'll be some little time before we get it all. Okay, we'll do our best.

"Nothing but grief on these garnishments," he observed, returning to his chair which he immediately tilted against the wall while fishing in a package of fine cut tobacco for a fresh chew. "We handle dozens of them every month. There's a fresh batch of them going out now." He pointed to a pile of addressed and stamped envelopes lying on the desk.

"The poor devils don't get work enough to live on, let alone pay back bills," he stated, spitting with remarkable accuracy into the sawdust-filled frame which surrounded the base of the oval-shaped iron stove, a good ten feet away from where he sat. "But we've got to handle them. I make it as easy on them as I can and let them pay off in small amounts from week to week as they get paid. Sometimes the creditors become impatient and we have to tighten up. But, tell you what, I don't like to do it and I don't only when I have to.

"Come in, come in!" the squire called to a woman standing before the open door. Hastily he hurled his cud of fine cut toward the sawdust box at the stove. "What can I do for you?"

"You remember me, don't you, Squire? Katy Newberry that used to be?" she said. "You married me and Randy Pilchers right here in this office.

"Laws-a-mercy!" the woman chattered on, rolling out her words so fast it was hard to keep up with her. "Hit don't seem like hit was any time at all since I was standing right there in front of your desk and saying 'I do,' but I didn't promise to obey, did I squire? Randy's made me a good man, though, at least as good as most, and—"

Here the woman had to pause for breath and the Squire took advantage of the fact to get in a word. "Yes, yes, I remember you now, Katy. What do you want now, a divorce?"

"La, no, Squire! I guess I'll hang onto Randy for a while longer. You said for better or worse. It's not been much better and it could been a lot worse so I ain't complaining, but that low-down Ott Motlow that used to hang around some with Randy borrowed my guitar about six months ago and never did bring it back and now I hear he's sold it for five dollars when I paid twelve and a half for it brand spanking new not more than a year ago and I want to get it back and can't I sue him or get the law after him some way, Squire? The scalawag, he never was any good for hisself nor nobody else. A more no-account shiftless worthless scrap of humanity I never did see—"

"Wait a minute, Mrs. Pilchers," the squire broke in, holding up his hand. "Did you lend him the guitar yourself?"

"No, Squire, I'd never let him have it, knowing him like I do. He got it from Randy one evening when I wasn't home and he come there and Randy says he just picked it up and said he was going to borrow it awhile and Randy, he said—"

"Tell you what we'll do, Mrs. Pilchers," suggested the squire, seating himself at the big table which served as his desk. "We'll get out a warrant for him charging him with petty larceny and have him brought in. Do you know where we can find him?"

"Why, yes, Squire, he's been laying up with that Opal Fillmore and you'll likely find him there most any time of the day or night, why, La me, it's a sin and a shame the way some people carry on, now ain't it? I remember when—"

"Just sign right here, Mrs. Pilchers." The squire shoved a paper toward her and handed her a pen. This she took and scrawled her name on the indicated space. Meantime she continued her story without interruption. Finally, she was persuaded to leave after the squire retreated to the rear room, from which he emerged a few moments later after a cautious survey of the room showed that she was gone.

"My God! I sure as hell pity Randy!" said one of the deputies.

The squire shook his head. "It was a sad day when I married her to him. Usually my marriages turn out pretty good. In fact, marrying people is one of the more pleasant duties of a justice. I marry lots of couples here and I enjoy performing a ceremony, especially for young people who are well equipped to start life out together. Always try to give them a word or two of helpful advice and it's most generally appreciated. I remember one time a good many years ago a boy and girl come to me to be married, but I was a little dubious about them making a go of it together. I knew them and their families, too. Both were highstrung and hot-tempered and I hesitated about performing the ceremony on that account. I questioned them rather close and they vowed that they would make a go of it. So I said to them, 'Well, I'll marry you if you'll make me a promise and agree to live up to it. That is that you, John, are to decide all the major or important questions that come up between you, and you, Sally, are to decide all the lesser questions. Do you agree to follow this rule?'

"They promised faithfully that they would, so I married them. Well, they moved to Cincinnati shortly after where John got work. I kind of lost track of them but often wondered how they made it. Well sir, just a few days ago I run into them on Gay street. They had three of the finest children I ever saw and both were looking well and happy. I asked them how they were getting along and they said 'Just fine' and then I jokingly inquired as to the agreement they had made and whether they had lived up to it. John laughed and said that was easy to live up to because there hadn't been any major questions so far. So I guess they'll make it all right.

"But some of my marriages don't turn out like that, unfortunately." The squire leaned back in his swivel desk-chair and stared out the window. "Couldn't expect them to. Some break up almost before they're started, especially forced marriages. I've had several shotgun weddings in my time but none of them ever amounted to anything.

"One was a bright young fellow and a very attractive little girl whose pa brought them to my office with a shotgun under his arm. I believe he'd have used it, too. I made him give it to me and we all sat down and talked it over. It was just another of those cases that happen now and then in the best of families. Instead of reasoning calmly with the young people the old man had started blustering right from the start. Both the boy and girl got their backs up about being forced into marriage. They were going through with it because they had to.

"Well, I talked with them alone and found they really had cared for each other, but the attitude of the father had killed what regard they did have for each other. I married them but they never lived together. The girl, now a grown woman, still lives with her folks, and the boy left the country and was later killed while hoboing his way on a freight train. I've often thought how different their lives might have been if the girl's father had used a little common sense.

"Come in, Luke!" he shouted to a tall man in faded and patched overalls who had just entered the door. "Come in and take a chair. How's Mamie and all the folks? What's on your mind?"

"They ain't so good, Square," was the reply, as the man came stumbling into the room and perched on the edge of a chair. He twisted his old hat in work-worn hands. After describing in detail the state of health of the various members of his family, with solicitous comments now and then from the squire, Luke finally got down to his business.

"Square," he said, "they's a set of squatters a-living up on the ridge in the old Jennings clearing and they been a-cutting timber off'n my forty and I want to law them about it. They ain't got no right to cut my timber and I want to stop them. Can you see to it for me?"

"Well now, Luke, I guess we'll have to see about it. How much they cut and what're they doing with it? Making crossties?"

"No, they hain't making anything but fire wood

out'n hit. I guess they's cut about six or eight trees altogether."

"H-m-m-m," mused the squire, drawing down his bushy white eyebrows. "Were they green or dead trees, and how big were they?"

"Well, Square," Luke said hesitantly, "they was dead timber. I don't jest rightly know how big they was but I reckon they was pretty good size. Anyhow it was my timber!" Luke sat forward on the extreme edge of the chair, while his hands fanned the air and his worn hat tumbled unheeded to the floor. "I want to law them about hit!"

"Now, let's see, Luke." The squire lay back in his chair and put his fingertips together in front of him. "Do you know these people? Know what their circumstances are? Ever been to see them?"

"No, I don't know them, excepting they's jest squatters. Ain't got nothing and no place to put hit if they did have. I've seed them from a distance. They's a passel of children that I seed a-picking berries last summer. But that hain't got nothing to do with them gitting my timber, Square."

"Look here, Luke!" The squire suddenly sat up and squinted at the other. "Maybe them people needed that fire-wood to keep them from freezing. Maybe they haven't got enough to eat or enough clothes to keep them warm. How would you like to see your children go through something like that? Bet you they cleaned up around the few dead trees they cut, burned the brush, and slicked up good before they left, didn't they? You got more dead wood on that forty than you'll ever use, haven't you, Luke? You'll not suffer any because somebody cut a few dead trees off your land to keep warm, or maybe sell a load or two to get a little some-

thing to eat, now will you, Luke? Maybe those people
are all right, Luke, just a little down on their luck,
maybe, like all of us are liable to be most anytime, and
here you would go lawing them because they're trying
to get along without asking help from anybody. Had
you ever thought of that, Luke?"

"Well, no, Square. What do you think I ought to
do, Square?"

"Why, Luke, if it was me I'd take Mamie along and
you and her go and see these people and find out something about them. See what kind of people they are.
Maybe you can help them some way. Maybe when you
talk to them you won't want to law them. Tell Mamie
I said to take along a can or two of her fine peaches and
a piece of side meat or shoulder and get acquainted, and
then you can talk to them about your timber. After
you see them, then come back and let me know how you
come out and we'll decide if they really ought to be
lawed. How about it, Luke?"

"I'll do it, Square. You never advised me wrong yit,
and I'll do what you say. Much obliged, Square.
Come out and see us sometime and eat with us. Mamie'll
be right glad to see you." Luke left the office.

"That's one of my marriages," said the squire, filling
a cob pipe and tamping the tobacco down with a stubby
forefinger. "Honest as the day is long. Hardworking
as they make them and a good man to his family. Bet
he goes over to see those squatters and takes them a
load of vegetables and stuff out of his cellar. Luke's
like that, and Mamie, too. Never saw a finer couple
when they stood up before me. Knowed they'd make a
go of it when I married them. Somehow I can always
pretty near tell.

"Well, with one thing and another I keep pretty

busy." He leaned back and gazed at the ceiling. "I guess the criminal cases, alone, will average a hundred a month. Then there's dozens of garnishments and replevins and a good many civil cases. I don't like the civil cases, though. They're more trouble and grief than all the others put together, them and the garnishments. In civil cases no matter how you have to decide them you always make an enemy of the one it goes against. I don't handle them any more than I have to. I like criminal cases best—they're not so much bother. You either bind them over to the grand jury or higher court or turn them loose."

At this point the squire was summoned to the telephone which had been answered by a deputy. "Hello! Hello! Yes, Squire Porterfield speaking." A pause of two or three minutes during which the squire listened intently, beating a subdued tattoo on the desk with a pencil. "Can't you people settle things like that without going to law about it?" Another long pause. "Well, we'll send out and get him, but you've got to be here and prosecute him. Yes, we'll let you know when to come."

The squire resumed his seat near the stove. "That's another one of our grief cases. A family fight and the woman wants a warrant for her drunken husband. Jack," he addressed a deputy, "better go out and get him, I guess," and gave him the address.

"We'll bring that fellow in," continued the squire, "and I'd be willing to bet two to one she won't show up. That's the way with the biggest part of such cases. They want their men arrested and held until they sober up and that's all. They very seldom show up to prosecute and, of course, all we can do is turn the man loose again.

"Speaking of cases that are not prosecuted, we had a murder case right here within a block of the office a few weeks ago where a Negro woman killed a Negro man. Cut him all to pieces with a butcher knife. Some of the neighbors come running up here and we went and brought her in, but do you know we couldn't find a single person to testify against her. We held her in jail under a charge of murder and spent days trying to get evidence enough to try the case, but we couldn't get a thing. The murder was committed at a Negro blow-out and must have been at least a dozen eye-witnesses, but those Negroes didn't know a thing about it. They just won't testify against each other.

"Afraid they will be jumped on later about it. Well, we couldn't do anything with the case and called in the Attorney-General's office, and after about a month they gave it up, too. Had to turn the woman loose. She's still around here. I saw her pass the office yesterday.

"We get lots of applications for peace warrants, but we try to sidestep them every time we can, unless we know the party who makes the application. These Negroes would have us running our legs off serving peace warrants if we'd let them. Every time a Negro looks cross-eyed at another it's a case for a peace warrant.

" 'He threatened to kill me, Square, and I wants to put him under a peace bond,' " he mimicked.

"But that's like the murder case I told you about. We never can get enough evidence to warrant a peace bond. As a result, we have all our work for nothing and nobody to pay our fees. We simply tell them to bring in their witnesses and then we'll issue a warrant, but they're pretty nearly never able to bring them in.

"Well, it keeps us pretty busy, all right. I've got

eight officers working out of my court, five white and three Negro. They don't all work steady, though. I've got four steady men while the rest work just when there's something for them to do, but they're kept pretty busy at that."

The telephone rang and he reached for it.

"Squire Porterfield's office. Yes, this is him speaking. The case is set for four o'clock this afternoon. Yes, they say they're ready for trial. Well, it looks like you have had plenty of time to locate your witnesses. When do you think you can have them ready? But, Larry, the boy's been in jail three days already. We ought to try this case and get it over with. All right, make it four o'clock Friday then, but I'll expect you to be ready by that time."

He banged the receiver on the hook. "Those lawyers give me a pain sometimes. They can think up more excuses for delays than a Negro can for not testifying. That was a case of a young fellow we arrested for assault with a deadly weapon. Hit another fellow with a piece of gas pipe in a fight. So far as I can learn, the other fellow started it and was going to use a knife when he was knocked out. There's always somebody having trouble of some kind though.

"Well, they tell me the General Court Sessions bill passed both houses and is now up to the Governor. He'll sign it, of course, but there's some who say it's not constitutional. I understand there's a move on foot to contest it. If it does go through it will take the biggest part of our business away from us. All these cases will then be handled by the General Sessions court. It's going to make it hard on some of the defendants, though, because as it is now we try to be fair and give a man a chance to pay his fine, or garnishment a little at a time and help him along that way when he needs it. But with the other court he'll have to pay up or go to the workhouse and work it out at the rate of a dollar a day. I don't believe in being too hard on those who are unfortunate.

"Several years ago I used to get a lot of the Southern Railroad business—vagrants, trespassers, and so on. One day they brought in thirty out of the yards and charged them with vagrancy. I could have sent them all to the workhouse but I didn't. I turned them all loose, poor devils, but I found out later there was one in the bunch who was wanted for bank robbery somewhere up in Michigan. There was a big reward out for him and I let him slip right through my fingers. Since that time I always look them over pretty careful, but I've never run onto anything like that again. That's just my luck. What a man gets for being too kind-hearted in the J. P. business."

RAY R. HUMPHRIES
JAMES R. ASWELL

Trucker and Builder

JOHN MERRITT HAD HAD SEVEN HOURS SLEEP IN THE past two nights. He would get about four more hours when he got to Milton after midnight. Then he would get up early to deliver his vegetables and fruits to the Milton grocers. This done he would start the hundred and sixty miles back to Richmond where he would arrive early in the afternoon, buy another load, and get back to Milton in time for four or five hours sleep—if everything went right.

When driving like this John Merritt sometimes pulls to the side of the road and lies flat on the warm concrete under his truck, completely relaxed. Five minutes of this and he can drive on as if he had slept. He drinks coffee and Coca-Colas to stay awake but doesn't use or trust such aids as No-Doz. When he started driving four years ago he weighed 165 pounds and has since gained fifteen pounds. He has never had a wreck.

John Merritt owns, or owns with his three brothers-in-law, four trucks, three of them half-ton pickups and one a ton-and-a-half job, all Fords and all but one thirty-five V-8s. Every day except Saturday and Sunday he takes one of the pickups to Richmond. Doing this five days a week makes him feel all wore down sometimes, he admits, but it's a competitive business and the Milton grocers know his stuff is fresh. The Richmond trips net about fifteen or twenty dollars each. The big truck, driven by one of his brothers-in-law, runs to Norfolk and nets more. The big truck requires a helper, whom they hire. It gets ten miles to the gallon, loaded or unloaded; the lighter trucks get twice that unloaded and about eighteen loaded. His first truck was a '26 T model and he has traded in for a succession of newer models ever since. Fords, he thinks, are as good as you want for your money.

Two of the brothers-in-law stay in Milton and get advance orders and deliver with one of the pickups. Their market is Milton though they sometimes help supply Richardsonville and the University of North

Carolina at Chapel Hill. They are all younger than John, who is thirty-three.

His load on a mid-September night consists of tomatoes, roasting-ears, black-eyed peas, stringbeans, and peaches. He also carries two dozen eggs for his own home. Most of this stuff, he says, is raised close around Richmond. The other truck gets vegetables and fruits grown in the back country around Norfolk and on the Eastern Shore or even brought in on ships. He follows the markets and has hauled about everything that grows.

Last winter he hauled fruit and vegetables from Florida. This winter he is going to do it again, but as a driver for a Milton fruit dealer instead of as an independent. At least he thinks he will get the job which will pay him twenty-five, maybe thirty dollars and expenses. He says last winter was the toughest he ever saw. He was paying on three trucks, his baby was born and his wife wasn't working. The competition was bad, too many trucking. He knows the Florida markets and is a close buyer and he will be able to save his employer money on the stuff. He will start about December first and will store his own trucks. He rarely goes further into Florida than Jacksonville. There he can get anything he wants.

John Merritt likes the uncertainty and chance of trucking but he is getting tired of it. The life of a truckdriver, he says, is six years. He thinks this winter may be his last on the highway. He can always get something to do around Milton or he may go back and stay on the farm with his mother and father and take care of the place. Besides, he has an income from his houses and he will have a chance to build more.

Houses seem to be a passion with John Merritt. Be-

fore he finished high school he was getting three dollars
a week from a house he had built almost entirely with
his own hands with lumber he had cut on his father's
farm and had had sawed. He never followed carpentry
but studied it out, and it's not hard, he says, to learn
something you really like. He built his first house in
Milton during vacations and spare time, and he did
all the work except some of the finishing. Now he can
almost completely build a house by himself. Altogether, he has built four houses, three of which he still
owns. He says he could have gone to college but he
figured that after four years he would be just beginning
while if he didn't go he could have a house or two built
and be getting three dollars a week rent from each.
And he was restless and wanted to do things with his
hands.

If another panic comes he says there's nothing better
than houses if they're clear and paid for. The next
house he plans to build is to be on a lot he owns in the
Negro section of Milton, near the large Freeman's
College for Negroes. Nigger houses, he says, are the
best paying. He plans a three room house which will
have only electricity at first but there will be a bathroom later and eventually he will put in water. Now,
there's a well near by.

The house he lives in is one he built. It has five
rooms. They have two beds but when his brother was
married and came there to spend the first night there
was only one bed, and John Merritt and his wife spent
the night on a cot. Their own honeymoon had been to
Asheville on twenty-six dollars.

He married five years ago. His wife was from
Milton. She works and on Sunday plays the organ
at their church, Methodist. She took music for nine

years and they have a piano. His daughter is eight months old. A man, says John Merritt, hasn't known anything until he has a child. They plan to have her go to college and he has begun to set aside something each week in an account for her. They tried to sell him an endowment policy which would have paid her two thousand dollars when she becomes eighteen but he said to hell with that. That way he couldn't touch the money before she was eighteen and he may want to take it out and build her some houses before then.

Though he likes the house where he lives he feels that the farm up in the northeast corner of Orange County, adjoining Milton, is really home. He was born there and home, he says, is the place where you spend your childhood. But he would hate to leave the house he has built and lives in. He doesn't like to think of other people moving into it. He would almost want to go off and, like the fellow says, leave it empty with a fence around it. But it would rent pretty good since houses are hard to get in Milton.

On the farm his father, who is 61, and his mother and a couple of younger brothers live. The boys are getting ready to leave and the old folks will be alone. His father always talks of building a house and moving to Milton, but John is sure that he will never be satisfied anywhere except on the farm. He may go and live there with the old folks until they die. He doesn't know whether he would want to stay after that.

His father had 367 acres—he used to say he had 365, an acre for each day in the year. He sold over a hundred acres to the husband of one of the daughters. He settled the place about the time John was born, but he was from just a mile and a half away and the neighborhood is full of relatives. John Merritt doesn't have any trace of his people very far back but they have been there a long while. He has English, Scotch-Irish, and some French blood. The Merritts are Baptists and Democrats. The section is about two-thirds Democrat and a third Republican.

There were ten children, six boys and four girls. One girl died. They were born, twin boys, then John, then a girl and a boy, girl and a boy, girl and a boy, and a girl. One of the twins is manager of an ice plant in an eastern North Carolina town. He was the one who spent the night at the house. One of the girls teaches school in Jonesburg. She went to the Womans' College of the University of North Carolina at Greensboro and graduated at Duke. She was always smart in school, he says, while he had a hard time getting by. She always made between 90 and 100 at Duke. The youngest girl is entering Greensboro this year.

His father never had to hire anybody because there were always plenty of younguns on the place. Now he occasionally takes on a helper but he doesn't do much farming. John Merritt figures that his father is worth about $11,000.00 cash. He made his money on the farm during and after the war. The farm is pretty good land and there is standing timber on the place.

His mother was in the hospital a year or so ago for removal of a gall stone and an operation for female trouble that was from his birth. It cost $800.00. She always said she had more trouble bringing him into the world than any of the others. And he loved his mammy —he loved his daddy, too—but he was his mammy's youngun. He always stayed close to her.

John Merritt thinks Franklin Roosevelt is the best Democrat of all. He doesn't think Hoover was so bad; he had a Democratic Congress and just gave up. He always held it against Wilson for getting us into war after promising to stay out.

John Merritt believes in Christ because, he says, as the saying goes, Christ raised such a stink. However, he wonders if the Bible is written as God meant it to be. He hates to believe that anybody thinks more of God than he does but he just believes there are lots of things in the Bible God didn't mean to be there. When you think about it, he says, man is little, mighty little. We don't know where we came from or where God came from.

John Merritt is not a drinking man, nor does he fool around with women. He doesn't cuss or at least he didn't until he started driving, but you have to cuss some of the people who are on the road, he says. He doesn't follow foreign doings much but he says about the Germans that God scattered the Jews and man is going to scatter them.

On Sundays and on his days off John Merritt doesn't go riding. He works around his house. He is always doing something.

LEONARD RAPPORT

The Grand Ways

LEOLA PRENTICE, HOUSEMAID AND COOK IN THE LARGE two-story brick residence, flashed a broad smile when she opened the front door. "Hello, there and come rat in. Mis' Rutherby she gone out. Ain't nobody home but me and Precious. He's another one them Pekinese pups Mis' Rutherby got since the last un died of pure meanness."

She led the way through the house.

"Yes'm, this a new uniform I got on. Mis' Rutherby she make me change every day. I wears first one color and then 'nother color, 'cordin' to how she want me to. Sho' is glad she ain't got onto no black for house uniforms yet. Maybe next time she go somewhere and see the maids dressed in black, she come back, she say, 'Leola,' she say, 'I'm go' put you in black now. And then she give me a whole new set of uniforms—caps, aprons, and all. Ain't never give me no red uniform to wear yet, though. Wish she would. I laks that red. Me bein' light complected, I can wear most any color they is, but it's red that makes me becomin' mo' than anything. My ol' granny use to make me dresses out of colored figgered calico. She say high colors sets off a light complected colored girl. She give me these earrings I wears daytimes. Make me look a Indian or a gypsy. Mis' Rutherby give me that pair of long dangly pearl-like earrings she use to wear. I sho' proud of 'em. Come on downstairs where we can talk and I'll show 'em to you.

"Maybe it was my grandma," Leola chattered on as she went down the back stairs toward her basement quarters, "that put it in my haid to quit that cotton pickin' and come to Tennessee and git me a good job. Her name was Carolina, so everybody call her Ol' Aunt Carolina back down there in Mississippi where I comes from. She all time tellin' my mother that I was 'the biddablest of all the ten Prentice chilluns.' She'd say 'Leola, you is smart. You ain't lazy. You don't belong to walk on no plowed ground all the days of yo' life. Why don't you learn maidin'? Why don't you git a good job and be a lady lak you's borned to be?' We knowed some women, and men too, what was cotton pickers and come to Memphis and got theyselfs good jobs. One of 'em got me this job. That's how come me livin' here. Been with the Rutherbys ever since I come, and that was four years ago."

Leola turned the key and opened the door to her room—a combination living room, bedroom, and bath. The walls were papered with clusters of wild pink roses entwined in a design of old fashioned garden trellises against a white background. Scatter rugs, made from old carpets that had done service upstairs covered a rough floor which Leola had painted a chocolate brown. "If'n I'd had my rathers, this flo'd been some other color," she explained. "But it's so dirty in this city. I couldn't keep it clean nohow.

"You lak my furniture? So does I. This set use to be Mis' Gwin's but they got new furniture for her room when she come back from New York. It's curley maple, they say. I think it's awful pretty. Granny Carolina she'd cackle if she could see me in a room lak this, with my bed lamp and magazines on my table and flowers, even if they is paper flowers. Lord, if she could jest see them pink Swiss curtains at my windows! Mis' Rutherby she say she won't have no maid in her house she don't take interest in her own room and keep it nice. Say if you is ontidy in yo' own room how can I expect you to keep the house red up proper?

"But I always was tidy-lak. Don't lak to have a mess about me nowheres. I takes the same care of my clothes I do my room. See 'em things hangin' in my closet? They's mostly old clothes the white folks give me. I make 'em over and mend 'em here in my room nights. Do it all with my fingers. They ain't a sewing machine in this house. Don't reckon they's ever been one. White folks nowadays don't have they clothes made up for 'em lak they use to. They buys from the sto'. Bet they ain't a week Mis' Rutherby don't have a carload of clothes sent out from the sto'. Now, she don't *buy* all them clothes! She jest like to try 'em on befo' the mirror. She strut 'round in 'em. Then she send 'em back.

"That woman's all time studyin' 'bout style. She mighty quick to learn me. Don't make no bones, neither, hoppin' on me when I makes a mistake. When I stops to *re*collect how us Prentices had the grab habit at the table, most everything we had to eat all in one pot on the hearth or kitchen table, and now me steppin' 'round lak a bird on sore claws, passin' eats one at a time, and cleanin' off table the same way, I thinks to myself, 'Leola, Granny Carolina was right. You is goin' to be a real lady.'

"That's my grandma's picture on the wall. Took by one of them travelin' picture makers, jest a year before she died. I sho' loved that good ol' woman. She was more lak white folks than any colored person I ever knowed. She wasn't raised by white folks, but worked fo' 'em all her life till she got the rheumatics so bad she couldn't work no more. She come to live at our house when I was a baby. I'm jest twenty years old now, but I can recollect jest as well how she use to talk to me when I was jest a little bitty thing. If'n I'd cry or was sick, she'd take me on her lap and nuss me.

"Granny Carolina, she read the Bible to all of us, too. She an awful good woman. But let one of us younguns sass her or pay her no mind when she called us, and she'd take and wash our mouths out with lye soap and maybe whoop us with a willow switch. Didn't hurt none. But that ol' lye soap! Ever taste it? Worse'n castor oil. She knowed the switch wouldn't hurt much less'n she take and flip-flap, wam, wam, on the bare laig. When she do that you might as well had a burn from the fire. Her rheumatics didn't make no matter when she took it into her haid to give us a good switchin'.

"Granny, she kept a ol' cow bell by her chair on the flo'. When she want somethin' or somebody to come, she take and ringed that bell, bing, bing, bing! Three times jest lak that. When she do that and out in the field we'd hear three rings, most generally meant she want me to come to the house. They all say 'Leola, Granny's callin'. Better go see what she want!' Then when I get to the house, she say to me, 'Come on in the house out'n that hot sun, chile. Time fo' you to rest.'

"You see my mama bein' a widow woman and havin' ten chilluns, every one of us had to pick cotton when pickin' time come. We went from field to field, everywhere they needed some extry hands. Didn't work fo' no regular man, though. And cotton pickin' wages was all we ever had. Some of the colored families down there use to move around like circus folks. If they was too far from they home when they got through the day's pickin' they sleep in folkses barns. But we never done that. My mammy never would agree fo' us to do cotton pickin' in a field that was too far from our house so's we couldn't walk back that night. She say, 'I keeps my family together. Don't git in no mischief that way.'

"Some days when Granny'd call me back to the house, when I was still so little, she'd set me to making fire-lighters out of scraps of paper. Matches was scarce. She say, 'Now Leola, you can work for yo' grandma a while. I pay you with a cookie.' She made the best gingerbread cookies I ever eat. Well, maybe not as good as the ice box cookies I've learned to make since I come here. Mis' Rutherby's so proud of 'em she 'stributes 'em 'mongst the neighbors lots of times. Granny never heard tell of ice box cookie. Neither did I till I come here. Never even heard of a ice box 'cept the froze-over wash tubs, sometimes, or the wash pans and buckets left outside on shelves by the back of the house. Never did have much ice and no snow either back where I come from.

"Another reason my grandma would call me back to the house was 'cause she was 'fraid I'd git a snake bite. You know them ol' cotton-mouth moccasins is poison. They quile up under the cotton bushes and you stick your hand or your toes under there, and he bite you right now. Nobody in our family ever got snake bit, but they was a boy once. He was workin' in the same field we was—that was after I was 'bout twelve years old and went to the fields all day with the others—and he was bit. Took him to our house and Granny fed him fat meat so fast it most choked him. Cured him, though. Granny say she hope don't nobody else 'round here git bit by a viper. That's what she call a snake. She say, 'Fat meat's too scarce.'

"Most any kind of meat was a treat to us. At hog killin' time, we'd git a ration of meat for helpin' neighbors render they lard. We jest had common food, dried fruit, and garden stuff, and lots of black molasses. I lak that a heap better'n honey. Sometime when Mr. Rutherby go off on a huntin' trip, he'll bring back some comb honey from a farm. Nobody else here laks it much but me and Mr. Rutherby. He takes what he want and give me the rest.

"He was brought up on a farm. Mis' Rutherby she say, 'My husband was reared on an old Southern plantation.' He don't talk no foolishness lak her. He talk about his boy-time days on the farm. And she say, 'Arthur lived on a plantation.' It don't make no diffunce to him. He let her talk and do lak she pleases and go on talkin' 'bout that farm.

"I wonder do duchesses do the way Mis' Rutherby do? Seems lak she sho' do have the grand ways. Most too grand, too, fo' her pocketbook. Leastways, that's the way it look lak to me. Ain't never raised my wages since I went to work for her fo' years ago. Mr. Rutherby he did once. He give me a dollar raise. He come in the kitchen one day. He say to me, 'Leola does you think you could use another dollar a week from now on?' But, the Duchess," (here Leola smirked, shrugged her shoulders, and mimicked the manner of her mistress) "the Duchess she didn't lak that. Not her. She jest give me more work to do.

"When I first come here, they was jest three in the family, not countin' the dog. They give me three dollars a week then. That look lak good money to a cotton

picker. Pickin' cotton ain't no job fo' a lady. And
here they furnish me with this nice room, and my food,
and the clothes they give me ain't ragged lak I was use
to down in Mississippi.

"When Mis' Gwin come back from New York—you
know she been there three years studyin' somethin' or
other—she give me a lot of pretty clothes. Heap mo'
style to 'em than them Mis' Edith and her mother give
me. Me and Mis' Gwin has got the same kind of taste
in clothes. Sometime, when I go out on my afternoon
off, folks don't know at first whether it's me or Mis'
Gwin. That don't make me mad. But it'd make her
boil. She's been good to me, and I lak her, but she's
got her mama's temper. If she knowed folks thought
we look alike when I git all dolled up in her clothes,
she'd have me fired right now."

Leola chuckled, and got up from her chair to give an
imitation of herself stepping out of the house. It was
a clever impersonation, graceful in movement, and an
exact reproduction of Gwin's gestures. She completed
the portrayal by representing herself as leaning on the
arm of her escort at a midnight ball, just before the
unmasking, when all that she would say to her escort,
who kept asking 'Black gal, who is you?' was 'Black
boy, jest call me Mis' Gwin-nia!'

"Does you dance? Lord, I could jest die dancin'.
Give me some of that good ol' swing music. Give me a
slick floor and I can shake my feet all night long and
never git tired. Our club—we calls it the Twentieth
Century—give a dance once every month. But I got to
be back here next mornin' by six o'clock jest the same.
Sometime when I late and maybe the alarm clock didn't
go off or I miss a car—I spends the nights with a girl
friend the nights our club has a dance—I git a good

scoldin' and then have to work on my next afternoon
off to pay fo' it.

"Mis' Rutherby she scold me a heap. Most the time
I don't pay no 'tention. Jest let her talk herse'f out
and then I go 'bout my work. Reckon she knows she
couldn't git nobody else to do all the work I do fo' fo'
dollars a week. I'll tell you what all I have to do. You
see, they's a bigger family now than when I first come.
Mis' Gwin is back from New York. Mr. Arthur come
home from college and now Mr. Rutherby's mama come
to live here. She's an ol' lady, more'n seventy, and she
been an invalid most her life. She's rat fretful, and
always so particular 'bout her food. Maybe sometime
when I take her breakfast tray to her room she claim
the coffee too strong, or too weak, and I have to traipse
back down stairs and make her a fresh pot. I take
breakfast trays to all their rooms, except Mr.
Rutherby's. He gits his in the dining room by hisself
at six-thirty of a mornin'. On Sunday mornin' he'll
eat in his room. I takes up six breakfasts every mornin'
and each one is diffunt. Every one of them has to be
fixed fresh soon's they ring the bell. Don't none of them
eat at the same time. Mostly Mis' Edith and Mis' Gwin
sleep until 'bout eleven o'clock. Then they don't want
no lunch. Mis' Rutherby has hers about eight-thirty
or nine o'clock. And Mr. Arthur—well, neither the
Lord nor the Devil know what he go' do, ever! That
boy a plumb sight. His daddy don't know he stays in
bed some days till after lunch. I bet some of these
times if Mr. Rutherby come home *on*expected, and he
find Mr. Arthur quiled up in that bed, he take and drag
him out by the hair!

"I go over this whole house with the Hoover every
day, and dust every crack and corner good as I can.

Answer the doorbell and the telephone. Sometimes I have to laugh. Folks can't tell my voice from Mis' Rutherby's and they start talkin'. Thinkin' it's her answered the 'phone. Good thing we got an extension or I'd run my feet off answerin' that 'phone. Specially when all the young folks is at home. Lots of times, though, they git invited out, or they spend the day at the country club playin' cards and golf. And they all have a lot of company here too fo' meals. Mis' Edith's sorority meets here every other week, and Mis' Rutherby's card club meets here every Thursday. That's the day most servants has off. But I can't git off 'cause that's her card club day. She give me Tuesday afternoons. I usually git away around one-thirty or two o'clock.

"Then I do a considerable washin' and ironin'. I lak that kind of work. The girls lak to have me do up their best things. Sometime I wash shirts for Mr. Arthur, or wash one of his sweaters. Better not shrink it, though! Once I scorched one of the ol' lady's pet handkerchiefs. She lak to never got done talkin' 'bout that. Seems lak ol' people whine so much and act like they put upon. Why that ol' lady's livin' in clover. But she don't know it. Least she don't act lak she do. But they's one blessed God's truth, and that is she ain't allowed to go monkeyin' with bossin' the house. I don't have to take orders from nobody but Mis' Rutherby.

"Speakin' 'bout handkerchiefs. I do up all Mr. Rutherby's to keep 'em from bein' tore up in the laundry. Once when they was one missin', Mis' Rutherby say she have to take it out of my wages. But then when she learn that she jest hadn't counted right, she say she sorry. She's good to 'pologize if she thinks she done you wrong. They's a heap of good in her, 'spite of her bein' so fidgity 'bout things.

"Seem lak, since she's so particular 'bout me keepin' my room tidied up she'd learn the girls some such manners. Wish you could jest see their rooms in the mornin' with all they clothes on the floor jest where they dropped 'em the night before. Lipstick, paint and powder all over everything and the dressers a-gaum, and hair left in they combs and cold cream smeared on the mirrors and all that sort of thing. And they shoes! Bet both of the girls has a bushel of shoes all messed up on the closet floor. I have to pick up after 'em always twice a day.

"Then they's the downstairs lavatory and three bath rooms upstairs to red up mornin's. Mr. Rutherby he don't make no mess shavin', but look out for that Mr. Arthur! He no more thinks to red up after hisse'f than that little pesky Precious, down there in the kitchen all time under my feet. And I does the window washin' and washin' curtains for all over the house. But, of course, not all at one time. I be dead if I was to try to do that. They's two double windows in the library, one in the reception hall, two in the dining room, and two windows in every one of the five bedrooms upstairs.

"I makes out the laundry list to go with the week's washin' and count everything when they come back. The special dining room linen I does up myself. Clean the silver once a week, too. They's a university student live in the other basement room, which they gives him for firing the furnace. Sometime if he git back late, and the ol' lady git chilly, I have to go fix the fire. But don't do that much.

"What do I do between jobs? Well, I listen to the

radio when ain't none of the family 'round, and read the funnies in the newspapers before they git out of bed. Same thing in the afternoon, when the papers come befo' the family all gits back from wherever they's been. And I talks to my boy friend on the telephone. And I reads the story magazines and looks at the pictures in the style books.

"Tell you the truth! The thing I hate most is takin' Precious for a walk afternoons. Mis' Rutherby treat him jest lak a baby. She talk baby talk to him all the time. But he don't git no sweet talk from me. And he don't lak me, neither. He's so mean to run and pull at the chain. Hurts my hand tryin' to hold him. Once he got away from me. Saw a cat and he lak to had a fit. I couldn't hold him. Well, he got lost and they didn't find him fo' two or three days later. Mis' Rutherby took on terrible. She never said a word about firing me, though.

"I know plenty servants has a harder time than me. They all the time changin' jobs and never seem satis-fied. Plenty ladies on this block right now would take me if I'd go to 'em. They tell me any time I quits Mis' Rutherby to let 'em know. Course, Mis' Rutherby, she bossy, but most of the time she don't bother me, as long as I git my work done right and on time. We has a schedule. That makes it easier. That Precious is my abomination. He my cross. No use wishin' he'd die or git lost fo' keeps. She'd jest git another one. She got to have her pet.

"Yes'm, it's gettin' time for some of the folks to be comin' in now. Them that's comin'. This Mr. Rutherby's night at his Smoker Club, so he won't be home. And Mr. Arthur and Mis' Gwin is havin' they dinner at the *ho*-tel with them friends of hers from New

York. We don't have much for dinner nights Mr.
Rutherby ain't here. Mostly left overs, and maybe one
hot dish and some coffee. I'll go up with you and see
if the afternoon paper has come. I got to see what
Tarzan's got into today. Saw him in the movies once.
But I lak the paper pictures best.

"Next time you hear from me guess I'll be rat here.
Don't know, though, as you'll hear anything 'bout me
gittin' a raise in my wages. Way I looks at it, the two
girls'll marry pretty soon, and the ol' lady may go to
California to stay with another daughter, or down to
Florida to git the sunshine. And the work won't be so
hard. And when I gits married all I learned here will
come in handy to run my own home. Then maybe I'll
play lak I'm a Duchess, too, and git a girl to work for
me. Won't I make that girl step, though!"

DELLA YOE

JAMES R. ASWELL

I Can Read and I Can Write

THE NEGRO HOUSES ON JACKSON AVENUE ARE STRUNG
out like ragged clothes on a wash line. Unpainted.
Run down. Lee Lincoln's house—centering the East
side of the Seventh block—stands lopsided from added
rooms. One room takes care of Lee. Home-made book

cases, racks, stands, tables, piled to the limit with books, crowd the room.

"I can read and I can write and I can figure," Lee said. "Every day I am thankful that I had a chance to learn. A man can't get anywheres much these days without schooling."

Lee wore the blue overall uniform of freight packers on the L. & N. railroad. His powerfully built frame tallied with his occupation. Lee pointed out his books with pride. He talked slowly, carefully.

"I'm fifty-three years old, still studying. Still buying books. I have almost five hundred books here on all kinds of subjects. Lots of them I have read from cover to cover."

He took a pair of silver rimmed spectacles from his inside coat pocket and fitted the hooks to his ears.

"My parents didn't have time to fool with schooling for themselves or any of us children. They were share-croppers. By the time we would get five or six years old the cotton field got us. I can remember playing about Pappy and Mammy and the older children when they were making the crop and at picking time, wishing I was old enough to help. Before long I was right there slaving too."

Lee pulled a dark oak rocker to a clear space in the center of the matting rug for his visitor. He settled in a straight chair.

"We didn't make much money. Not ever enough to get along easy. But from year to year we'd manage to get by some way. Corn pone, sorghum and sowbelly was the most we had to eat. I didn't mind. I like 'em to this good day. Going to the meeting on Sunday or to some neighborhood shindig at night was the way we had our fun."

Lee took off his glasses and polished the lenses with a clean white cotton handkerchief.

"Mammy died when I was sixteen. Then I pulled out for myself. I worked around for different planters for a couple of years. Then I got a job on the L. & N. Railroad at Memphis trucking outbound freight. It was the best job I had ever had and I was set on not getting fired."

He sighted the glasses for clearness.

"That was the job that learned me a man's got to have schooling to get anywheres. Signboards were posted on the freight cars with the name of the town where the car was to go. You had to know how to read to know what to load up. When the boss would say, 'This truck-load goes to the Nashville car,' I'd ask one of the truckers on the quiet—'Which one's the Nashville car?' One day the Boss heard me. He called me over, picked up a freight bill. 'Read what that says, Lee,' he said pointing to the words, 'The Louisville & Nashville Railroad.' I was scared stiff. I knew it wasn't any use to give a guess. Mammy and Pappy had learned me that a lie always got you in a fiddle. 'I just don't know, Boss,' I said right out. 'I can't read a line.' "

Lee shifted his weight in the chair. A smile of satisfaction spread over his honest face.

"Next day at noon-time the Boss brought a first reader book and a tablet and a pencil. He commenced to teach me to read and spell. I was mighty tickled when I could tell him what some of the words were. At noon-times while I was eating my lunch and every night I studied. Before long I could read most of the signs that said where the freight went. I learned how to write my name. I learned to copy and read back everything in the primer. My, I was one proud Negro!

Boss was tickled, too. I never will forget him. Never. He was the best man I ever knew. I've got a little picture of him. I never have framed it. I got a lady artist to fix it on a card for me and I keep it for a book-marker."

Lee left his chair and went to the iron bed in the far corner of the room. He pulled back the clean quilt—tucked at the head over the pillows—and found the book with last night's reading place marked. He left the book face down on the quilt and brought back the boss' picture.

"There he is. Fine-looking, don't you think? I never will forget him, because he was so good to me and learned me to read and write. I worked at that freight trucking job until the railroad transferred me to Nashville. That was a big promotion. I was made a regular officer. I had a badge with 'L. & N. Railway Police' on it. I worked all up and down the line on excursion trains and in the Nashville yards. I was about thirty years old then. I knew I never would have gotten that promotion if I hadn't picked up what little education I had. I kept right on. I went to night school two or three terms. For more than two years while I was an officer I got a white man to come to my room two nights a week and teach me. I paid him fifty cents a night and there wasn't a night that I didn't learn more than a dollar's worth. He was real educated and had a lot of patience with me. Pretty soon I could read newspapers good as white people and books too. There were a lot of words I didn't know the sense of, so I got me a dictionary. I paid twenty-two dollars for it."

Lee went to the center table and straightened the

scattered newspapers and books. He dusted off the large dictionary for display.

"My teacher told me this was a good one. It is, too. Wish I knew just half the words in it. He was all set on me getting good books. One hour of my lesson he would teach me words and reading and the other hour arithmetic. He would work up all sorts of simple problems he thought I'd have need of in work. He never did just stick to the book. I never will forget the night he told me how to take the carded weight of a carload of coal, figure how many tons and bushels was in the car. Then how much it would bring at so much a ton. Now that was fun. Just as much fun as reading those freight car names. I got so at lunch hour I'd pick out a car of coal in the yard every day, maybe more than one, figure up tons and bushels. He showed me how to figure lumber, too. I planned and figured ever' bit of the lumber for my coal house last fall. Figured it all by myself. I was right proud when my figuring came out just exactly like the lumber man's."

Lee got things on the center table settled to his liking. He rubbed his large hands clean on his pants legs and came back to his chair.

"I know I can read and figure better than I can write. I got to worrying about people not knowing what I meant if I put it down, so I got me a typewriter. They can read my letters now. I am secretary of my union and that typewriter is a big help there. Minutes look nice. Most anything makes a good show when you get it fixed up like print. I use it to make out my rent receipts. This house here I don't use but one room— this one. I pay the whole house rent and sublet all but this room. I've got two families here now. They're good renters, pay on time. The difference in what I pay rent and what I get from them helps me a lot since I lost my good job."

Lee slowly buttoned up the brass buttons of his overall jacket.

"About three years ago I got cut off from the railroad police 'cause I was the only Negro officer left on the system. They put me back to trucking freight, though I mostly packs freight in the cars to go out. I watch for thieving on the platform. I don't get paid for that, just paid for packing freight. They told me I'd have to take this job or nothing as they had to cut expenses. I took it. There were a lot of white men officers that didn't have thirty-two years experience behind 'em like I did. Not easy to pick up a job when you getting along in years—I had to take it. Everything that had been coming in for so long went out sooner than I got it. My wife, now, was one to help a man save. She could have helped. She was a good woman. I spent more'n two thousand dollars on doctor's bills for her. Maybe they eased her some. I don't know. Anyway doctors didn't save her."

Lee rammed his hands deep in his pants pockets.

"Since she died I never have come across a woman I felt like I could trust. We didn't have any children. I never was much on raking up relatives, so I'm going it by myself. I do my own cooking, most of the cleaning too. One of the women that rents does my washing. I had a little saved together from my officer's salary after I got the main of the doctors' bill paid. I had it in a bank. It busted along with the rest of them. The bank got all I had but wages—and those about a fourth of what I got as an officer."

Lee took off his glasses. He unbuttoned the top buttons of his coat and stored them in the inside pocket.

"If I can just keep my job I'll be satisfied. I'd rather work for what I get. There's lots better folks than me out of work now.

"I ain't going to have a preacher telling me I lost my officer's job for some wrong living. I didn't. I don't hold much with churches and less with the preachers. I loaned my preacher twenty-five dollars more'n two years back. I haven't heard a word about it since. If a man lives best he can he'll get along. I'm getting along. You can't do a big lot of things on sixty-five dollars a month but you can live and help a few out besides. A preacher's after my money a sight more than he is my soul."

Lee left his chair and went back to the dictionary. He was silent while he hunted a word.

"I thought so. Not any such word. That Methodist preacher tried to trip me on it last time he came here snooping. I seldom go to church. I do like a good moving picture when I'm not too tired to set. I go to union meeting once a week. I'm secretary."

He closed the dictionary noisily.

"I'd rather get a good case of beer and settle right here with time enough to read on any book I pick up than anything I know of in the world. I remember when I used to have to drink and play poker and shoot craps to make me feel big. I don't now. I don't crave going around a lot like I used to."

R. R. HUMPHRIES
JENNETTE EDWARDS

Snappy Feeding

M AUREENA MURPHY—LOBBY!"
Evelyn gave a hitch to her slacks as she waited
for an answer.

"It's this putrid paging that gets you up when you'd
rather be down."

Evelyn was slender and attractive. Her blonde
bobbed hair was neatly finger-waved. She left the desk
and walked to the hall leading to the Y.W.C.A. reading
room. She megaphoned her call "Mau-REEN-a
MURphy!"

"Miss Murphy isn't in. Would you leave your number? . . ."

She settled in the revolving chair behind the desk.

"I've spent some of the best years of my business life
answering some sort of racket. Telephone bell. Auto
toot. The first job I had when I came to Memphis was
being curb hop for a drugstore. And I mean I hopped.
My salary was five dollars a week. I bet I ran off ten
dollars worth of heel caps that four months. I was
fresh from the country. Aiming to please. Half the
time it would be trotting out to see what some old man
in a big car had his chauffeur sitting on the horn for.
A penny box of matches, maybe. I'd be there and back
before he could have struck one."

Evelyn shifted her position to get the telephone receiver.

"She'll be back in her office in the morning. Mrs. Gordon's not keeping desk now. It's her rest period. . . ."

The receiver went back to the hook.

"That sounded like a board member to me. I can always tell by the way they ask for one of the secretaries. Right-that-minute, please . . . urgent. The last one of those board ladies work as hard keeping this Y going as if they got paid for it. And they don't get one red cent for all their work. Not a penny of pay. If you ask me it's pretty swell of them to do it."

Evelyn let one leg dangle comfortably over the chair arm.

"That curb hop job taught me plenty. If you get food to the hungry in a hurry they aren't so snooty about what they're getting. Seems to taste better when they see the tray running to their mouths. I was just tickled to death with myself when I got expert. Ten different orders in my head without getting coffee crossed with Coca Cola was going some for a country girl!"

She tilted the chair back.

"I'd been curb hopping for four months when a call came in to the Y for a girl to wait on tables in the lunch side of an up town drug store. Wanted some one under twenty. Seven dollars a week for trotting trays— breakfast, lunch, supper. I was thrilled to death to get a shot at it. Believe you me, I didn't lose use of my legs. Rush hour at lunch time made curbing look like rest period. The food they had and way they had it just got me at first. We didn't have a lot of fancy food in the country, but Mother was a fiend about germs. She'd have died off if she had seen how the trade gobbled up stuff she'd thrown out the kitchen door to the chickens. I ate it too and it didn't kill me. Saddest looking sandwiches with wilted lettuce. Tuna fish that wasn't so young. Well, my stomach did sorter do the ocean roll when I stopped to think about what I was putting inside me.

"But we had the trade. The kind that pay the punch on the check with the tips they didn't leave. Lots of room I've got to talk. I could count the tips I've given in my long life on my nose. I guess most of our customers streamed in because the food was cheap. The crowds we'd have! I thank my lucky stars for that job. It gave me a break that was a honey. Made me what I am today. When the manager got a store of his own he needed waitresses. Took a few of us girls along with him. We got right in on the ground floor. He thinned out the old gang that was there. Made me fountain manager. Believe you me, I know something now about why you've got to stretch food if you manage to manage. I'm not giving a dollar's worth for a quarter but you can park the baking soda when you eat with us."

Evelyn reached for the receiver of the ringing phone.

"You have to fill out a room application blank. . . . Depends on your salary. . . . Everybody has to have a room mate. . . . I can put her name down here. They'll mail her a blank."

She wrote the name and address on the pad as the receiver went back to its hook.

"A fountain manager's got to make fifty percent profit on all fountain sales. Got to—or out you go. Well, I'm still in. What the customer don't know isn't going to make him change feeding places. Just get the food to him quick. Hot if he wants it hot. Cold if he says cold. And give him a good line while you're getting it there. One thing I can't stand is to see a girl look like she could chew a nail in two when she's serving people.

"Being a waitress let me in on a bunch of fountain manager tricks. I was about a post-graduate when I was promoted. A crushed ice Ph.D. Dilute drinks. Really spread spread. Fake filling double dips. The first thing I teach new help's how to roll an ice cream dipper to air proof the filling. If they're still digging deep after the first week they're fired."

An elderly transient came to the desk for her room key.

"Here you are, Mrs. Wilson—303. I bet if you boxed that number in stocks, bonds, and races some Friday you wouldn't be stopping at the dear old Y the next time you came up from Atlanta. No, I am not going to tell you how—because as long as I'm here I want you to keep coming."

Evelyn put the keyboard back in place.

"She is simply adorable. Heavenly days, it must be nice to have enough money to get out of the way of your family when you are that age. I felt like the idle rich when I first got to be fountain manager. Eleven dollars a week. I've cleared enough this year for the fountain department to get my salary up to fifteen. I never will get more than that no matter how long I make supplies last. Sometimes I get so sick of stretching food I wish I could land a whole gallon of frozen malted milk in the face of a certain somebody that signs my salary check. Just sometimes.

"I work thirteen hours straight five week days and Sunday. Anywhere from eight to ten that other day. After the fountain's closed it's up to me to stay there and get it cleaned up for the morning rush. That place was filthy before we took it over. Just plain nasty. I got my hands in the worse shape. Still do. It's going to be kept clean as long as I'm there if they put me in the caboose for cruelty to roaches and water bugs. The sanitary inspector said for me to just let him know if the old gang that was there ever tried to get their jobs back. He said none of that slop crew would nose me out as long as the city health department had anything to say about eating places. They were all set for closing the fountain when we took over the store. If you're hipped on trench mouth or the bad disease, drink with us."

Evelyn twirled the chair in the direction of the wall clock.

"Plenty of time before I have to shed my slacks and get dressed for work, praise Allah! I'd like to sit here a lifetime. I'd do desk duty whether they cut something off my room rent or not. I feel just like I own a hotel when I'm behind this desk. And believe you me, it's a heavenly feeling! There were eleven of us children at home. Nobody ever had a bed to themselves, let alone a room. We lost the farm after Father died. I don't ever remember living in a house big enough for six people much less twelve after then. I guess Mother was a genius to get us all as far as high school. I got two years in the county one before I landed in Knoxville to get a job. I'd rather soda fountain for the rest of my life than to raise and educate eleven children off of butter and eggs and milk money and sewing cheap for everybody in the country.

"I keep thinking I'll get around to improving myself. Getting a better job. The Y has classes in about anything you want here at night. Public speaking. Personality courses. Scads of courses you can get high school and college credit for if you're one of these hard-working ambitious girls who are cut out for the higher things in life. Well, little Evelyn's brain may go to wrack but the old body isn't! Not as long as there's a swimming pool. And a badminton court. And all those new contraptions in the health club to jiggle up your pep.

"One of the girls in my room just can't see why I don't take a business course. Be a secretary. She says there's just two do's to it—shorthand and typing and one don't—chewing gum. Well, I could do the don't. But I just can't feature sitting at a typewriter all day trying to make out what some long-winded big shot made me Gregg down. Now getting him in a good humor with a sandwich and a cup of coffee, I adore that. I just plain get a kick out of feeding people. I'd bawl my eyes out if I thought I was going to lose my job.

"I would like to make enough money to have a room by myself. I'd just as soon it would be in the Y as anywhere else in the world. You do get fed up on the rest of the bunch in the room digging into your cold cream. Making off with your lipstick. And borrowing the very dress you'd planned to wear. But I'll take living in the room with ten girls to going back to the farm. The Y's heaven compared to being stuck in the country."

DELLA YOE
JENNETTE EDWARDS

Prayer Done the Work

A FOUR ROOM CABIN IN BLACK BOTTOM IS ANDREW
Jonas' home. His widowed mother and nephew
Jamie constitute the family for which he is responsible.
The house is their own and is free from debt. There
are few comforts but the family manages to get along.
The "sittin' room" has a fireplace that Andrew enjoys
more than anything else. At night the family gathers
around it and sometimes the neighbors join them by the
comfortable blaze.

Ella, Andrew's mother, is old and quite feeble now.
Once she was a good cook and her services were always
in demand. Now she stays at home and "makes out"
with the help of Jamie to cook and wash for the family.
She pieces quilts from scraps brought to her, and often
at night while Andrew stretches his tired withered legs
to the warmth of the fire, his mother nods and sews,
humming glory tunes between nods. Jamie studies his
lessons stretched out on the floor, his wooly head turned
to the fire, and asks questions which neither Andrew
nor Ella can answer.

The Jonas' have no garden. The little yard around
the cabin is bare except for a few flowers. Occasionally
some neighbor comes and helps Ella "rid up" around
the place. These days are a great joy to Ella, who sits
in a cane-bottomed chair and directs the work while

she puffs on a corncob pipe and carries on an uninter-
rupted conversation with the worker.

She loves to talk about old times and to tell of her
"white folks." Ella says she warn't the best cook in
town, but she shore was a stomp-down good'un in her
day. She is very proud of the fact. She remembers
the long ago days when they all lived on the Griffin
plantation and she had the pleasure of preparing "rilly
sumpchous" meals. One Christmas, she recalls, Ole
Marster gave a party for all the "help." For days before that wonderful Christmas Eve Ella washed and
mended. She greased the Sunday shoes with suet and
rubbed each shoe until it glistened. All the children's
heads were washed and also rubbed with grease, and
stocking caps were pulled snugly over the shiny heads
at night to keep them smooth.

The afternoon before the party each little child was
scrubbed with all the strength behind Ella's pride. She
would have no "dirty niggers" going from her house.
The wash tub stood before the open fire in Ella's room.
Buckets of scalding water were ready at hand. As each
child was groomed he was admonished to "go set down
somewheres and mind out where you set," and when all
thirteen had been prepared, Ella said, she was so wore
out she doubted if she would take much pleasure to go
herself. When candlelight had come the children grew
impatient, so a start was made for the big house.

A great tree stood in the main room, glistening with
tinsel and many candles. "Land," said Ella, "you
never seed the like! Them chillun looked plumb
baffled 'bout so much glory. They just stood peerin'
at that tree like hit didn't belong to be. Ole Marster
had the gifts all 'stributed round and after a while
brung out the lemonade and cake. Every once in a

while he'd say to one of the men, 'Go see kin you find Tom,' and that meant 'Git yo'sef a dram, nigger.' Then us all sang songs, and Andrew, he hopped his brash se'f up onto one of Marster's good cheers and flopped his hands to his sides making a racket like a rooster, and squalled out,

'De rooster crowed, de rooster crowed,
He flap he wings an away he goed.'

"Marster laughed fit to kill, but I never was so shamed 'bout any thing in all my life. I snatched that nigger down and promised to wear him out time we got home. Old Marster, he say, 'Don't you do it, Auntie, Andrew's goin' to grow up an' be your dependence.' "

And so it turned out. Andrew is now the family's sole support. He makes a good living for his mother and Jamie. He is a bootblack and has a paying business of his own. Each morning he starts out early. He has more than a mile to go from his home to the boot-black's booth in Hunter's Shoe Shop. He covers the distance on crutches. Sometimes he is given a ride but more often he makes the journey back and forth un-assisted. He works hard and his earnings amount to around ten dollars a week. Carefully spent, this pro-vides for the family.

Every one likes Andrew, and tries to help him. In-variably he is polite and cheerful. When asked to tell about his life, he replied "Who in the world do you reckon wants to know about old crippled Andrew.

"Well, I've had my ups and downs same as a heap of other folks. 'Fore I got crippled I had me a lively time, but now I just sits and shines shoes and talks. Course I hears about all there is to hear 'bout whats goin' on, but I can't get nowheres no more 'count of crutches bein' so troublesome to go on.

"There's just me and Ma left at home now, and little Jamie, Sister Pearline's boy. You'd think with Pa and Ma havin' fifteen children there'd be some of 'em to care for us now, 'sted of its bein' me carrin' all the burden, but that ain't the case atall.

"There was twelve boys and three girls. Now there's only three of us livin'. Sister Pearline is workin' for some white folks in Augusta, Georgia. She promised if Ma and me would take Jamie to care for so's she could get free to work, she'd send us money for his keep. But do she send that money? She do not! I's the one providin' for Jamie.

"He ain't no trouble, and seems like Ma gets a heap of comfort out of the little fellow. He helps too, when he ain't at school. Ma can't get out no more, so Jamie's company for her. I got a brother Sam somewheres, but we ain't had no word from him in quite a spell now. Ma grieves. She say she knows he's daid, but if you knowd Sam like I do, you'd say he was a-warmin' some jailhouse more likely.

"When us was all chillun, we lived at the old Griffin place, down on Pacolet River. Pa worked on the plantation, 'ceptin' grape pickin' time. Then us all harvested in Mr. Robbie's vineyard till the crop was all gathered.

"When us got started of a mornin' us looked like Pharaoh's army comin'! Ma got up before good day and cooked rations. Twarn't no fancy cookin', neither. Fatback and grits, pone bread and coffee, anything she tuck a notion to give us for the lunch buckets to carry to work, she put in, and seems like pore as it was it always tasted good when noon come. Mr. Robbie'd blow a long blast on his old huntin' horn, and us niggers would get in the shade somewheres to eat and rest.

"Ma always tried to do better by us when night come. She'd cook up a big pot of greens with corn dumplin's, fix sausage and gravy to eat with the yams, and maybe bake a sweetcake, if she had time, or pies. And come Sunday she shore put the big pot in the little'un, and sort of made up the difference for the whole week.

"Sat'day nights us would go 'possum huntin'. Lawd, I can hear the dogs now, youp-youpin' over the hills! And the niggers shore got their fill of hollering after them.

"Harvest time, after grape pickin' was done, us went to the fields for Mr. Griffin, and law me, the good eatin' we done then! Boss sure believed in feedin' his help. He say to Pa, 'When your family gets through feedin' there shore ain't much left to give to the dogs.' Mr. Griffin say niggers can't stand up to work on no empty stomach. And he never seed us go ign'ant neither. We had a school house. Boss had one set up on the plantation and sont away for a teacher. Us niggers had to go there and learn, too. Boss didn't take no foolishness.

"Hits sort of pitiful now, now there's just me and Ma and the little'un left at home. Ma grieves a heap for the old days, and about me having to care for her, crippled like I am. But I do the best I can and look to the Lord for the rest.

"Before I got pa'lized I was sure a likely worker. I helt my own with the best. Rich folks come to Hillcrest and took a likin' to me, seems like. I knew all the prettiest places to drive 'em and the best camping spots. Then some times they took me with 'em when they went away, maybe to cook for 'em or again it was to drive the hosses.

"One time I went way out to California. That year I was house boy to Mr. Ames. Lord, that was a fur piece from home! I'd get to studyin' over it some days and be scared plumb to death. I sure was glad when I made it back to Hillcrest again. Mr. Ames used to say, 'Andrew's a honey, he is,' and I hated it so bad when he took sick and died. Seems like I sort of belonged to Mr. Ames. I never did work for no better man in my life.

"I tuck infantile p'ral'sis in 1914 while I was workin' in Chicago, and seemed like Andrew's days was done. I've noticed though, that them as wills to do, does. For a mighty long time I just lay in the bed an' worried 'bout what was to become of me and Ma now. Folks would come to see me after they sent me home to Hillcrest from the hospital, and say 'What you goin' to do now Andrew?' Lord, I just didn't know. I studied a heap about it. Some days I'd just moan and pray. Prayer's what finally done the work! After a while I hushed up that moanin' and set to studyin' 'bout what I could do to get along.

"One day after I'd got used to my crutches I sent for a carriage to come after me from Mr. Millard's stable. When he come, I say take me back where you come from. The man he look sort of 'stonished but he he'ped me in the carriage and turned the horses 'round and we went back.

"Mr. Millard was propped in a chair agin the side of the stable. I can see him now just same as if it were today. He was chewin' on a straw and sort of half sleep. When he looked up, there I was. I ast him the best I knowed how to put me back to work.

"Mr. Millard seem like he couldn't believe his own ears at first, and he say to me, 'Why, nigger you can't drive no hosses.' 'How come I can't!' I answer back. 'Didn't I drive 'em good before I got cripple?'

"Well, Mr. Millard sort of turned this over in his mind and after a while he say, 'Doggone if I don't let you try. I bet the Yankees will take to this cripple business.'

"He gimme back my team, and just like he say, folks'd want me to drive. It was 'Send Andrew to drive. We don't want nobody else in his place.' Me and Mr. Millard shore done well right up till the time of automobiles. Then he had to close up the stable on account of 'em and quit the business.

"I never did have no runaways nor much trouble, 'cept just one time. I was comin' home to the stable late one evenin', just studyin' 'bout how good I was gettin' along, when here come Mr. Jarrett drivin' a brand new car.

"I don't know to this day how come us to get so tangled up. First thing I knowed I was down in the road all mixed up with the lines and the buggy was on top of me. The hosses was just a-rarin' and trompin' all over me, and it sure look like Andrew's time was up once more. First I'd holler at the hosses to 'Stan' still!' Then I'd holler at Mr. Jarrett to 'Do come he'p me!' Folks come a-runnin' when they heard me holler and he'ped me get out.

"Mr. Jarrett was still a-settin' there like he's cripple, too. Seems like he couldn't get organized, somehow. But in a day or two he come and gimme a nice Sunday suit and some other things, and he say he shore was sorry I got so skunt up. When time come for him to go he gimme a dollar, too, and say 'Nigger, if anybody ast you what happened, you say you don't know.' And I done like he say.

"When the stable closed for good seemed like I was shore out of luck one more time. I tried to do odd jobs, but seems like a man can't do much good to work hampered up with crutches. I found me a place at last helpin' in the kitchen of a nigger rest'runt. The man gimme my board and a little change. Ma she was a-workin' at the hotel since I got out of work, and she stayed on long as she could.

"While I was settin' around I got to studyin' 'bout making me a bootblack box. Well, me and the boys rigged one up, a right good'un too. Sunday mornin's I'd crutch it up to Main Street and shine shoes for the white gentlemen. After bad weather set in Mr. Hunter let me rig up this corner in his shoe shop, and I'm doin' right well. I try to give good service and seems like folks are mighty good about comin' here to old Andrew to get their shoes shined. I been here a long time.

"Some of the Burns Chapel brothers come for me and Ma on Sundays, so we can get to church. I sure love goin' to meetin'. Looks like there's a heap of comfort in religion, and I shore believe in prayer. I aim to make out just the best I can, and put my trust in the Lord."

ADYLEEN G. MERRICK

Easier Ways

YOU SEE, MY PAPPY KILLED HISSELF WITH HARD work. Hard work and exposure. It ain't good for a man to git out in all sorts of weather, no matter how good he feels. Well, Pappy worked like a slave in that saw mill. Made good wages. But what happened to Pappy? Hit killed him, that's what!"

"I jest don't care nothin' about a stiddy job myself. Ain't cut out for hard work. I gits by in easier ways. I's nobody's fool. I make hit good enough to suit me. Why, they ain't a time in the year, or mighty few of them, that I don't have plenty somethin' to eat. Usually find me a place to sleep and clothes enough to git out on the street in. I jest tends to the wants of white folks. Colored folks is made to give a hand to white folks. And I does it. I don't see where schoolin' could git a nigger like me. Niggers ain't got enough money for more than a half-way education. When they git it, it jest messes them up to where they won't have the jobs they can git once they's out of school. Hit takes money, plenty of hit, to turn out a doctor or a lawyer. A preacher now—from some I's heard in the pulpit hit takes less for turnin' out a preacher.

"Well, the schoolin' I got is plenty for me. I can write my name to anything put up for me to sign. I can read enough to git a heap of pleasure out of newspapers. You ain't goin' see no newspaper left on the sidewalk if I's around. Don't have to be that day's paper. Any old paper will do. They's a sight in the old ones that's new to me. I's glad folks that's got money enough to buy papers and magazines ain't got sense enough to take keer of them. Most every room I's had I's been able to pretty up with magazine pictures. I moves right smart but hit ain't been a time hardly when I didn't have some good ones tore out to cheer up the walls. Flower and tree pictures rest a body jest to look at them. They ain't never had to work hard.

"Why, I've never had more than two stiddy jobs in my life. But like I said, I don't want for nothin' the year around. Only thing frets me is when I don't have no 'baccy money. Then I has to git out and sharp-eye the gutter for some cigaret and cigar buttses. Anyhow, in winter I gits a dollar a week for keepin' up furnaces. They's five or six white folks here in Knoxville thinks I knows all they is to know about keepin' they houses temper'tured. Some that don't git me to fire calls me in to tote out ashes. Spring come along, then I gits first one job and another of house work. Washin' windows and helpin' out with cleanin'. House work ain't too hard for me. Leastways, that I gits paid for ain't. But come to workin' for yo' food or a place to sleep and womenfolks goin' to work you 'twill yo' tongue hang out. In summer I gits a run of lawn mowin' and weed hookin' off lots that's growed up. Now, that's right hard work. Don't let nobody tell you weed hookin' ain't hard work. Ain't goin' to take them jobs no more 'less hit ain't no other thing in sight. When hit's gittin' late for grass cuttin' and too early for firin', things gits pretty scarce with me. But them times is few. Could be fewer and suit me better.

"Oh, white folks always takes keer of me pretty good. They ain't goin' to let a nigger starve when he mind his manners and keep his place. Some niggers nowadays ain't got no manners nor no sense, neither. White folks work hard to git where they's got in this world. I mean work hard with they heads. Them or they Pappies and Mammies has had to do that sometime or other. I tell you I knows when a man is more than jest a Mister. And I ain't goin' to be callin' him no Mister if he served in the army or up to the courthouse. Times when I's short of work I's extry particular about doin' some of them things I ain't got no notion of askin' pay for. Why, I's had Jedge Matthews and that Captain Potter give me a dime many's the time jest for gettin' them in they coats. Hit holps out when jobs that you is strong enough to do is scarce.

"Now they's one thing you got to be mighty keerful about when you is doin' for white folks. Don't never tell them nothin' that they don't want to hear. You hear some bad news about yo' white folks. Maybe somebody say for you to tell hit to them. Well, don't never do hit. Keep a shut mouth on that bad news, no mind if hit most chokes you tryin' to git out. Let them find out they own bad news. But if hit's good news you hears, why jest bust a leg tryin' to git hit to they ears. They mostly will give a man a dime for good news. Suppose you don't hear no kind of news about them. Then you makes up somethin' nice and tell them. Don't make up nothin' big that they's like to find out ain't so.

"Jest sort of say, 'Mister Granger, dog if I didn't hear a man say somethin' good about you today.'

"Mister Granger say, 'That so? What was hit?'

"You says, 'He say you is a comin' man around here.

He say you don't let no flies light on you. No sir!
That what he say.'

"Mister Granger say, 'Who say that?'

"I say, 'Well sir, I couldn't see the man's face. Jest
saw his back of the head. He looked like a mighty big
somebody.'

"Mister Granger laugh. He don't really believe me
but hit make him feel good jest the same.

"Yes, I git along. I makes hit pretty good in the
easier ways. Well, where I sleep ain't always all I
want. But I moves around. I tries to git the best
folks has to offer me. I ain't never paid a dime out in
my life for a place to sleep.

"The room I's got now is warm in the winter and nice
and cool in the summer. They's things about hit,
though, that I ain't goin' to put up with much longer.
Hit's in the basement of the house where I does the
firin' in the winter. Ain't really no extry room there
for me scrouged between the furnace and the coal pile.
Miss Ann always gits the coal put in in June because
hit's cheaper then. That means both me and the coal
is there all the time. The worst part about it is that
roof leaks. Ever hear of a basement roof leakin' before? This one do. Hit's a leak in the top roof and
hit runs down through the walls. Keeps that basement
messed up and wet more than half the time. Mighty
bad on a man with the rheumatics. Well, I's woke up
many's the time and found the whole place plumb
flooded. I's had to lay planks to git dry footin' from
the bed to the furnace. And that water, hit's loosenin'
them bricks in the walls, too. Hit can't go on always.
Sometime I's goin' wake up mashed to death. I's
spoke to Miss Ann about hit time and time again. She
say the landlord's been promisin' her he'd see to that

leak. Well, he better! I ain't goin' to put up with no
place like that to sleep in. I can be independent as a
hawg goin' to the wars when I wants to.

"The air down there ain't none too good, neither.
Dust from the coal in the summer and smoke from the
furnace in the winter. Hit near stifles you. I has
trouble with my breathin'. Doctors says one reason is
all this spare weight to my height that I carries around.
I's five foot two and I weighs some over two hundred.
Well, ain't nothin' I can do about that. Lord made me
that way. All I's goin' to do is try to rest myself somewheres I ain't goin' to choke to death. A man made the
wrong shape like I is ought not to work too hard,
neither.

"I guess hit's a good thing I never made enough to
support no regular woman. She'd jest married me to
git her livin' and then laugh behind her hand at me for
bein' potbellied all over. Another thing, women wants
so many things these days. They ain't never satisfied
with nothin'. Hit's gimme, gimme, gimme and more,
more, more with the women. Some of them that picks
at they vittles when you is courtin' them is goin' to eat
you out of house and home once they got you where you
is hitched. Only thing a woman is good for is
cookin'. I ain't never had to do my own cookin', nohow. But I ain't got no woman and hit's boardin'
houses and restaurants and more folks with homes than
I could count up that's glad, more than glad, to give me
a little somethin' to eat when I drops around. Ain't
always leftovers, neither, though them's fillin' if you
is really hongry. I washes up the dishes and gits the
kitchen in some sort of shape for them that puts out
extry for me.

"White folks keeps me in clothes. Shirts, underwear, pants, and coats. When I gits a spare supply, I trades them off or sells them. I jest takes anything anybody want to give me.

"Now, with all them good clothes they give me, one time I took a notion I'd git me a new suit so I'd shine at the frolic up to the dance hall. And I done hit. Hit dug into what I had saved up but I figgered hit was worth hit. I don't take no part in the dancin' but I git a right smart fun settin' there on the side of hit makin' the girls have a good time. Lot of them figgers they can have more fun settin' there chewin' the rag and cuttin' up with a man with a head full of sense than shakin' around with some of them young bloods. They's all fools, the young bloods these days. A new suit can trim a fat man down to where the woman won't pass him up whether he's dancin' or not. Mine done it for me. Women buzzes around me like bees on watermelon rinds when I's got on my new suit.

"I put that money back I had to pay for my suit. You see I saves most every cent I make firin' furnaces. Gittin' my food and my clothes and a place to sleep without costin' me nothin' holps out. A man jest has to think about them things when he ain't cut out for hard work. And I ain't. The Lord cut me out in the shape of a man that's naturally made to have a good time. But he didn't give me the money to have that good time. Still, I gits by and hit's mighty few times I want for anything."

DEAN NEWMAN
JENNETTE EDWARDS
JAMES R. ASWELL

On Relief

Them That Needs

"SORRY. I AIN'T ALLOWED TO MAKE NO CHANGES. . . .
Keep the line moving, please. . . . We ain't got
no salmon. Fat bacon's the only kind of meat we got.
It's good for seasoning. Meat's too high priced for
the city to give away. . . . We got enough stuff here,
such as it is, to keep folks from starving."

Slim Jackson shoved supplies across the table to the
city's needy with the speed of a well-oiled machine.
He stuck the last relief slip on the filing pin. The frail
looking woman who handed it in packed canned goods
carefully in her split bottom market basket. She
parcelled out the sacks of potatoes, flour, meal to the
three small boys with her. She could take her time
getting in moving order with no line shoving her now.

"Thanks," she said as she walked to the street door.

"Not a-tall."

Slim did not look up as he gave a hurried straighten-
ing to tiers of corrugated boxes filled with canned
goods. He pushed back the stacks of flour, meal, potatoes that lined the concrete floor of the basement supply room. Work finished, he pulled a chair close to
the table and sank down to get the weight off his feet.
His elbow rested on the table as he talked.

"She'd be polite if I give her sawdust. Some's like
that. Got manners. Some's had it so hard they've
forgot how to be polite if they ever knowed it. That

365

woman that got so fussy when I wouldn't swap for salmon, she's had it hard. Five little children and a sick ma to take care of. No money to do it on except what comes from taking in washing. Her husband took off and left her before the last kid was borned. She don't even know where he's at. All the kids is just to the size to be under her feet. Not a one big enough for helping. Lives more'n three miles from here and has to walk every step of the way here and back when she comes for supplies. That's hard on a woman.

"The way I look at it is this. This is a rich country. I figger it ain't going to hurt the government to feed and clothe them that needs it. Half of 'em can't get work, or just ain't fixed to handle work if they get it. I imagine this country's worth near on to ten billion dollars. We've got the money. Plenty of it. No sense in the big fellows kicking about a little handout to the poor. Matter's not if some ain't deserving.

"I'll admit there's some don't deserve a nickel of the government's money. Lot of them that comes here, why I'd sooner give them a kick in the pants than shove 'em out supplies. But you got to take the good with the bad. Or bad with the good, whichever way you've a mind to put it. Most that comes here are poor and can't help it. Needs help. Needs it just same I need this job. Always going to be more poor folks than them that ain't poor. Now take me. I've always been poor and I guess I always will be. I ain't saying that's the government's fault. It's just a downright truth, that's all.

"There's a lot of things I'd like different in the world. But I can't say I got so much to complain of. If I'd had more education like as not I'd be getting more pay. Maybe, I wouldn't. Not getting no schooling is my

own fault. Poor or rich, humans is faulty one way or
the next. Time I got to the seventh grade I got the
making of money in my head. Wages looked to be
about the best thing in the world. Well, I had a run
of good jobs. Made fair money for a year or two driving trucks. Took a turn at auto fixing, too, around a
filling station. Just first one thing and another. Jobs
was easy to get then. That's before women got set on
going to work. That's what caused all this depression
business. I'm not saying that the women don't need
jobs now. They does. But they got themselves to
thank for the fix the world's in. They started out taking jobs from men when there wasn't no sense in them
working. Them men lost out on good jobs and dropped
right down and took ours. Just wasn't no jobs left for
poor folks.

"Folks that ain't never been poor just don't know
nothin' a-tall about doing on nothing. I get so all-fired
full of laugh when some of these women from the higher
ups comes down to the Welfare Department. Nice
ladies, but it ain't a salt spoon of sense about poor folks
in their heads. Pretty little thing come last week to
tell the women come here about cooking. Before she
started spieling, she seen them cans of salmon I took
from the big case and put on that shelf back there.
That give her a start. She aimed to tell them how to
make up a pot dish from salmon. We ain't really got
no salmon here. Just a cheap grade of canned
mackerel. She sailed in. 'Brush the baking dish with
melted butter,' says she. If she hadn't been so pretty
and so young, I'd liked to asked right off—'Where they
going to get the butter? Ain't two in the rooms got
butter for their bread. You'll have to shift to a skillet
for the cooking. That's about the best they got for

greasing up.' Of course I didn't say no such to her. She was just plumb wore out time she got that salmon out of her head and into the cook stove. When she come to tail part of the talk giving them leave to ask her questions, she looked to me about ready to fall off the box I'd drug out for her to speak from. It's a blessing the Lord made it easy for some. A blessing. And I'm glad He done it.

"My wife's one ain't got no easy going. She do all the house work. Washing. Ironing. Sewing. Cooking. There's eight of us counting me and her. Six children. Me and Ella took a marrying notion when we wasn't to no age. Without a penny laid by. Two that age ain't got no sense about what's to come. Ella ain't never throwed in my face talk of things she ought to have. Things I ain't been able to give her. She's been poor all her life. She ain't got as much schooling as me. No further than the fifth grade. Same year we's married our first young one come along. They's come two years part regular since then. All boys but the last one. We got the sharpest little girl baby I ever seen. Born past July. Suits me alright. I'm proud to have one like her. Girls mostly have a hard time. Ought not have too many. Especially when thing's like they's now. Me and the boys can take care of sister. I aim to see she gets a shot at schooling. I'd like to get that little farm I'm set on while she's little. Give her just the kind of playing and eating she ought to have.

"Lord, there's one thing a man with a wife and kids got to do—hang on to some sort of steady work. Get the most pay he can. When we's first married, I was carrying freight all over the state. Trucking for a big concern. I just throwed up that job. Thought

I'd pick up another one in no time. I'd just got plumb sick of sleeping and eating in cheap boarding places. Being away from Ella all the time. I just quit.

"Well, I wasn't as smart as I thought. I'd get first one thing and next for piece time. No steady work. The depression come on. I really wasn't trained to do much of nothing except drive a car and do mechanics round filling stations. And in them two lines looked like I couldn't find nothing. I said to Ella, 'I ain't no fool and I ain't proud. I'm going to get something steady if it's digging ditches.' Look like the Lord know'd I meant what I said. Next week I got wind of the janitor job over the City Welfare Department being open. They seen hard work wasn't no matter to me. I didn't ask one thing or another about all the things they aimed for the janitor to do. I just said, 'I wants that job and I needs it.' They give it to me. Driving the car for the Director was throwed in extra to the cleaning and such. And I was plumb glad it was. I come right up from that job to where I'm now. I'm in charge of supplies and keeping track of the stuff that comes in and is give out. I still drive the car for the Director. It ain't good for a man to spend most of his time in a hole damp and dark as this basement. Driving that car give me a shot at a little fresh air and sunshine. And I needs it.

"Just goes to show the Lord'll work things out for us if we give him a chance. When I come down here I thought to myself—'Well, I'll put up with it till things takes turn for better.' Why it's just drug us along through hard times! I get my transportation. Food supplies. Clothes. They leave me take the pick of them sent in for poor families. Take shoes—you just try to keep shoes on growing kids. See what a hole it knocks in your cash. I'm glad I'm in on the ground and gets the first drag at what's sent in. And working for the city I don't have to pay my own house rent. Now that to me's about the best part of the job. Sickness come along like as not a man'll take rent money for doctoring and time comes to pay up he ain't put it back for rent like he thought he would. Out he and his goes. Unless he's got a mighty fine landlord. There's a few of that kind. Most is in the business for the money, though, and nothing else.

"Asides from groceries and rent and clothes there's ten dollars a week wages. I figger our spending, all told, about twenty dollars a month. Things we got to have that ain't give us is bought on the installment plan. Cost more that way. But what you going to do when things got to be got and there's no spot cash to hand! We's pulling long through debt right well. Just fifteen dollars owing on the furniture and about twenty-five on the washing machine. Lord, that washing machine's worth ever cent we paid for it. I told Ella if I ever seen another thing that'd be as big help to her I'd buy it if I had to bust a bank. It don't take her half the time used to to get all them youngun's clothes did and the house things and such. Ella keep everthing from the kids to the kivers clean as a pin. House the same. We keep our kids close to home. Don't let them run round with just any trash. I got the last one of ours insured for burial—except sister. I'll get her fixed time she's year old. I pay twenty cents a week on me and Ella. Ten cents for the two oldest boys, five cents for the others.

"Thing that worries me most about a large family is the feeding of them right. I know ours don't have what they's supposed to. Not if half's right I hear

them ladies who come here to talk says. We can't
manage the milk we should for them. If we get Grade
A they ain't enough for more than a cup around. I
guess that cheap canned milk's good enough for cooking. We uses what they give us. Them things con-
cocted for the place of butter ain't as cheap as you'd
think. I ain't strong like I used to be. And with all
this talk I hear floating round I wonder if its the
things I ain't had to eat that'd done it.

"I aim if we ever get out of debt to study about
things like that. Give our kids ever fool thing folks
says they ought to have to miss miseries that might
take them off. I want to buy me about three acres of
land. That'd be much as I could work. Build me a
nice little house on it. I'd raise chickens, have a garden,
two or three good cows and some pigs. I seen advertised
in the paper where you could pick up acres of land
round here cheap as ten dollars down and ten months
coming till its paid for. How a man's going to live and
bring up a big family on what the higher-ups call
'minimum wages' is something to study about. I tries
to do the best I knows how. I guess the Lord don't ask
more of nobody than that. But I'd be a lots easier in
my head if I could get together enough to buy that
little farm for me and Ella and the kids. A lots easier."

DELLA YOE
JENNETTE EDWARDS

Till the River Rises

As much sand and gravel as they is about here, you wouldn't hardly think nothing would grow. But it does. Every house down here, they's a spot for a garden near it if them that lives in it ain't too trifling to put it in. We have plenty of corn and 'taters and cucumbers and tomatoes in season. We shares with them that ain't got any if they's been down on their luck. I has flowers, too. Them seeds over there in the drying box is every one of them flower seeds. I save them from one year to the next."

Fan Flanigan sat against one of the crooked sapling poles which supported the driftwood joists of the porch. She was a small wizened woman, brown, gnarled, with thin gray hair. A washed-out shapeless house dress had not been pulled low enough to hide her large bony feet.

"It's all right here," she said, "and I like it pretty fair as long as the river don't start acting up. We don't have no rent to pay, jest sort of squat here betwixt the railroad tracks and the water and build our places out of what we can git off the dump and the wood we can ketch floating down the river. Me and mammy been here sence nineteen and thirty-two, that hard old year."

She puckered her eyes against the strong sunlight and glanced over the thirteen stilt-set shanties which straggled along the banks of the Tennessee River between the approaches to two of Knoxville's bridges. Most of them faced the railroad tracks where strings of coal cars and empty boxcars stood. Beyond the tracks was a high deeply eroded embankment crisscrossed by foot paths and littered with rusty cans, bottles, and other rubbish.

"You kind of grow to like this place," said Fan. "You'd like any place, though, if you live in it long enough, I reckon. A rich man up to Knoxville give this whole strip betwixt the bridges for poor folks to build they houses on. Them that come first taken the pick of what they was here. Ma done that. She come right after Pop died. We use to live in that biggest house over there. My brother-in-law lives there now. Him and Sis had sech a flock of children you couldn't stretch a leg without tromping on one. So me and Mammy moved out. This one room here we has is fair size and plenty for us. Mammy owns that brother-in-law house. She don't own a stick of this one.

"When you git your claim that rich man don't care what you make your house of. But they's one thing about it, the outside, I mean the roof, is got to be tin. That's the law. No way to put out a fire in Shanty Town. So it's tin roofs here or you can't put up a house."

An old woman appeared at the door. She wore a broad-brimmed man's hat, full skirted brown calico dress, and a sweater with the elbows out. Toothless and stooped, she was as wrinkled as a dried apple. Without a word she walked to the far end of the porch, dragged the wooden box near the edge back to the wall. She pulled the hat down over her eyes as she settled on the box for a sitting nap.

Fan jerked her head toward the old woman. "It sure looks to me like my uncle might know Mammy likes to drap down for a nap now and then the same as anybody. He's got a broke back-leg and can't work none. He lives on 'tother side of the house and he gits lonesome and comes around here and sets and sets and talks and then gits hisself settled on Mammy's bed. It always musses up the bed having him drap down on it. Don't you think Mammy looks awful old? She ain't, really. Jest about seventy. I guess me and her both looks more age than we is. That's the way it is when you can't keep no meat to your bones. You jest shrivel up like a simlin hit by the drouth. Folks is always thinking I'm past the age I says I am. I don't keer, though. Gals that's always studying about they looks want to fool some man into marrying them. I'm forty-seven years old and I ain't never been married. And Lord a-living! I don't want to be! I ain't hardly strong enough to live single.

"I may look bullhide strong, but I ain't. Mammy can outwork me two to one. My lands, she works out in that garden from sun-up till night come without stopping for more than a spitting spell. She's plumb stone deef. Couldn't hear you if you's to beller it right down her ear. But she knows every word I say when she can look at me talk. Every word. No matter, she's company for me and I hope the good Lord sees fit to let her live to be a hundred. She is got an old age pension and gits eleven dollars a month. It's what we live on. Besides that, we git supplies off the relief, stuff out of the garden when a drouth or a rise don't hit it.

"But Great Day! When the river rises they's no chance for a garden then. High water will drown a garden right to death. And we do git high water here off and on and the water kivers the whole place. This house is sot bout as high as any of them—ain't but one sot much higher. But you can't git away from high water. Git yourself, maybe, but not your house. The boy that's building that high one there has got hisself a city wife. He figgers he's smarter than the rest around here and he's perching his house a foot or two higher. Well, that bride ain't going to be no drier than the rest of us when the river rises up and starts flooding. Day of Judgement! She's going to be wetted down and mudified like anybody else.

"Oh, I tell you I've see that old river come up. And the gov'ment never sent us no notice of what the water was going to do. We jest set and see it come up. See it and know what we's in for. When it begins to git in the houses, we take and move everything up on the bank across the railroad tracks, and we camp there all on top of each other. Well, city folks come trotting up there gitting under our feets. Coming with soup kettles and kivers and half of them wouldn't no more set foot in your house low water times than nothing at all. I ought not to say a word against them and I know it. I 'preciates what they does. But it's mighty hard for them that's had it easy all they lives to know what 'tis to be poor.

"They's always one saying to another, 'Do you suppose them people's got little enough sense to go back to them shacks when the river goes down?' And that's jest the little sense we've got—to come back to where we got a spot for a garden and a house we've built to live in without putting out rent money when you ain't got money for eats, much less rent. Yes Lord, we'll always go back to Shanty Town till the river rises some day and forgits to go down.

"But, mercy on my soul, it's a mess when the waters run off! You got to take and rake and scrape mud off of everything. Half of what you got is plumb ruined. Oh well, when you been through it time and time again, you can git things in some sort of housekeeping shape before you know it. Then you can start pulling over the garden and seeing what ain't washed up for good. And see if there's no flowers left where you's worked nussing them like babies.

"I has right pretty flowers in the summer time. Nothing left now but that old hanging basket of moss and them mole beans. Castor beans, some calls them. They's supposed to keep a mole from rooting up your ground. No moles round here I ever seen, but them beans stands the worst hot weather. They's something green to have around. My nephew trimmed them stalks up that way. He says they looks just like palmettos— them's things that grow down in Florida State. The carnival my nephew works for shows in Florida most of the time. He's a show-hand for it. When they lay off for winter, he comes back here with us. I jest count the year around till the time he's to come. He's my favorite nephew, the only one I've got.

"Mammy's a heap of company but Darcy ain't never one too many for me. He's awful good to me and ma. Gives us money now and then. He carries all the water we use and he gits the driftwood floating in the river. Brings it right to us for stove woods. They's lots men around here picks up money from selling driftwood. Darcy could, but he jest gives it to us like it ain't worth nothing. It's hard for him to git to before somebody else snatches it. I've see men fight till they drop over

whose to git a few driftwood planks. Folks around here
have to make out jest every way they can. At times
they has right smart luck fishing and you can always
sell fresh fish. But then they make you have a license
to fish and you got to pay for it. Leastways, men do.
Womern don't, so at times they take womern along in
the boats when they go fishing. And the Law can't
say nothing, not a dadblamed word, if it don't know
who made the catch.

"Womern is a big help to men more ways than one.
Stretching a little money to go a long way and fixing
up men's homes for them. I wish you could see that
fern Jack Long's wife got off the undertaker. He had
it left over from a funeral. It's so pretty. I jest like
to go up there and set a spell to look at it all I want to.
And Jack's got as much sense as she has about gitting
the best that's to be got. He was a regular carpenter
before hard times drug him down here to live. When
it come to setting up his house, he know'd how. Got
good lumber for doing it, too. The way he done it
was to go down there to Henley Street where they's
building the bridge. He picked up every stick of the
wood they throwed away. Got enough for everything
but the walls and ceiling. That didn't stump Jack
none. He jest went over to a dump heap in South
Knoxville, and there he run into jest what he wanted.
It was a lot of emptied out sheet-iron barrels. First
he knocked the tops and bottoms out. He split the
barrels open down the sides and flattened them out for
the walls and roof. Right in that same dump he picked
up two hundred paint buckets. They's supposed to be
empty, but he scooped out about two gallons of paint.
It was a plenty for spreading over his house. The
colors ain't the same, but that don't matter. It's paint.

See over there how he kind of worked the different kinds into stripes and wherly cues? Makes a right pretty sight, don't it? Well, then he tooled and nailed some great big split cardboard boxes for the inside walls and pasted paper over that. Then he tinned the top, for the roof has got to be tin down here in Shanty Town.

"Good Lord! Look who's headed this way! Poor Mrs. Rosson!"

A thin woman dressed in black, with a white apron tied around her waist, was hurrying along the beaten foot path in front of the row of shanties. Her fingers nervously picked at her apron as she came.

"Most of the folks in Shanty Town is kin to each other," Fan said. "Mrs. Rosson is the onliest one ain't got a speck of kin around here. She's a widow womern. She ain't like the rest down here, noway. Low class and poor. When she come, all she had left was three or four dollars. Some of the men folks built a house for her from leavings and pick ups. She's scared most of the time. She lives to herself and jest always scared something is going to happen. She's been worse ever since that man tried to kill hisself jumping off the far bridge yonder. I seen him drap. I was setting right here and looking toward the river when he jumped. It didn't kill him right off. But I heard since that he's died."

The woman had reached the yard of Fan's shanty.

"Come on up and set a spell, Mrs. Rosson," Fan invited pleasantly.

The woman made no move toward the porch.

Fan said in a low voice, "She's got it in her head that the wind is going to blow that feller up out of the river. She thinks the wind troubles his sperit. Well, that body, it ain't here, I've told her time and again that Pleas Newman pulled that feller out of the river. He was as live as I am when I seen them carry him off. Pleas never did git a red cent for doing it, neither. Well, one thing he didn't need the money like most around here does. Pleas had a plenty. He bootlegged. Got his liquor from boats that come up and down the river. He was doing so well when he got killed. Making good money. His nephew up and shot him. Fairda never would have killed his Uncle Pleas if he'd been at hisself. Never in this world!"

Mrs. Rosson stood silently, staring at the river.

"It was jest the four of them living in a old houseboat up the river. Pleas, his little gal of about eleven, Fairda, and the woman who done they housekeeping. All of them was drinking the night of the shooting, except the little gal. I knowed Fairda never would shot Pleas unless he'd been crazy drunk. And that mean woman living with first one and the other of the two jest about egged him on. She's a whore. If ever was one she's it. Poor folks ain't got no chance to head the Law to the right one. No chance at all. If they had, I'd hike myself right up to court and tell them folks the straight of it. Git her burned to a crisp in the chair, instead of Fairda."

Mrs. Rosson turned away from the river. She walked to the foot of the steps and stood looking up. She spoke in a faint and worried voice.

"It's wavy today, Fan. The river's awful wavy, Fan. And the wind's up."

She did not wait for Fan to reply. Turning, she walked back in the direction she had come.

"She's gone to lock herself in," said Fan. "That's the way she does. Closes up everything tight about the house. Well, I've got the best pot of soup back there on the stove. I had Mrs. Rosson in my head when I throwed it together this morning. She's going git a good hot dip or two of it if I has to bust down the door to git it to her. I won't have to, though. She'll let me in. I'll tote it to her in a little tin bucket with a top to it. I keeps it for toting things fit to eat to them that's sick or hungry. When she gits some of that nice, warm soup in her stummick, maybe it'll get that wind out of her head."

DELLA YOE
JENNETTE EDWARDS

I Couldn't Be What I Wanted to Be

WELL, I'LL BEGIN AT THE BEGINNIN'. I WAS BORN August the fourteenth, nineteen-one, in the country about seven miles from Fort Mount, Alabama. That's in Courts County. My father was a tenant farmer. I was born in a two-room rough lumber cabin. The livin' room and bedroom was combined, and there was just a shanty for a kitchen. No, it wasn't a separate buildin', it was just worse than the other room, so I called it a shanty. I was the first child. I later had five brothers and one sister—that lived, I mean. Two others, a boy and a girl, died in infancy."

"My father just made a livin'. Mother also worked

on the farm. She picked cotton. I remember distinctly mother takin' me to the fields when I was just a little fellow and placin' me on a blanket or in the cotton basket while she worked. I played with frogs and things while she worked.

"I started to school when I was six. Had to go about three-quarters of a mile across the fields. One distinct thing I remember was my first day at Oak Knoll school. Mother fixed my lunch that mornin'. I remember she put fried flapjacks and a bottle of ribbon cane syrup in a tin box for me, and I trudged along with it under my arm.

"My next memory is a Punch and Judy show that came to the school. You know off in the backwoods like that we didn't have much in the way of entertainment and it was a big event. They had the show on a little porch attached to the school. You might say that was my first contact with the theatre. Another thing that occurred at this time—and I have a knot still on my head to show for it—was a fight with another boy about my age. I don't know what we fought over, but I remember he hit me with a brick and knocked me clean over a well. No, I don't mean that I just fell on top of the well-box but that he knocked me all the way across it.

"Along about this time too I had my first sweetheart. She was a girl there in school; seven years old, the same age as me. I thought she was the most wonderful thing in the world. I'd get all flushed and goose-pimply when she'd notice me.

"I can tell you, too, when I got my first conception of the value of money. I had to go every day to a lady's house who gave us buttermilk. One day I found a nickel in the road comin' back. The next day my father had been makin' charcoal. You know how they do that? He'd stack up some pine logs in a tepee fashion and bank it with pine straw and clay, and set it afire from the inside. Of course he'd leave a vent and let it burn slowly for several days. Well on this day the landlord told me he'd give me a dime for all the bits of charcoal I found left lyin' around. He'd use it in the blacksmith shop.

"Well I picked up all I could find and he gave me the dime and then I had fifteen cents. Daddy was goin' to Fort Mount next day. I always thought that was a marvelous thing—goin' to Fort Mount. We'd travel in a two-horse wagon. Well I went with him and I bought enough cloth there with my fifteen cents to make two shirts.

"And while I think of it—when we paid a visit to my grandmother's, who lived about twenty-five miles away, it was an *occasion*. We'd start out early in the mornin' pulled by a mule named Jude. 'Course we'd take our own lunch along and eat it on the way, and when we got to my grandmother's we'd find she'd cooked up a lot of good things for us. I don't know how she always knew when we were comin'; I guess we sent word days before by somebody goin' that way. Both me and the mule saw our first automobile on one of these trips and she ran away and nearly wrecked the wagon. I just stared at it wide-eyed.

"Grandfather had been rather successful. He had a surrey—or a hack. You'd better call it that so people'll know what you mean. I thought it was the grandest thing in the world. He wasn't exactly rich but I thought he was quite well off. And he *was*, compared to us. He owned the first Edison gramophone I'd ever seen and that made him seem wealthy to me. It had cylinder records—cut records, we called 'em—

that fitted on a steel bar and spun around. Of course
Father had taken me to town and I'd seen those machines the men had on the street, where for a penny
they'd let you stick little tubes in your ears, like a
doctor's stethoscope, and listen to the music. But my
grandfather was the only person I knew who *owned* a
gramophone.

"Yes, I remember some of the tunes he had. One
was called 'The Preacher and the Bear.' I don't remember all the words, but it went somethin' like this:

'The preacher went out huntin' early on one Sunday
    morn' . . .'

And then I forget what goes in between, but it ended
up with:

'O Lord, if you can't hep *me*, please hold that bear!'

O yes! there was one line about 'O Lord, you saved
Jonah from the belly of the whale.' I remember when
my mother's sister got married at my grandmother's, all
the people were sittin' around in the parlor after the
weddin' and they had that record on the gramophone
playin'. Well the needle got stuck on the word 'belly'
and it kep' playin' 'Belly-belly-belly-belly-belly.' It
was funny.

"Other songs I remember were 'Over the Waves,'
'Just Before the Battle, Mother,' 'Uncle Josh Billings,'
and 'Cohen at the Telephone.' That reminds me to
mention some of the songs my mother used to sing to
me. You'd probably be interested in them. They were
'Barbara Allen'—that's an old English folksong—and
'Old Black Joe.'

"My great-grandmother (on my mother's side)—I

remember her. She cured a knot on the back of my neck once by puttin' three grains of corn in a handkerchief and rubbin' them on the knot and then makin' me take 'em out and bury 'em in the ground. She said the knot was a beginnin' cancer, but I guess it wasn't because she died of cancer herself. She'd talk fire out of people, too, when they'd burn themselves. She'd take their hand, or whatever part they burnt, and blow on it and whisper and mumble somethin' to herself and just talk it out.

"My ancestory? Well my father was born in Barrow County, Georgia. My grandfather (on my mother's side) was born there too. I heard my great-grandmother say my great-great-grandfather stowed away on a ship and came over from Ireland. I don't remember where he landed, but he came straight to Georgia. That was in the late seventeen hundreds. He got a job with John Howard, who owned a big plantation. He was a blacksmith; made plough stocks. That is, he was supposed to. He really didn't know anything about it, but he had an old Negro helper there on the plantation who did. So he got by. In fact, he was so successful that he finally married Howard's daughter, my great-great-grandmother, of course. My father's people were Pennsylvania Dutch stock but I don't know much about them.

"My change from farm life came when I was nine years old. Dad moved away and rented a farm instead of bein' a tenant. But he didn't farm seriously any more. He'd become ill from Bright's disease. It was a hard life he'd led. I can distinctly remember him comin' in at the end of the day all tired out and eatin' our scant meal of cornbread, peas, and cane syrup, and then goin' right to bed. Well he'd saved a little money, so he wrote to some publishin' company and got the agency for sellin' Bibles, New Testaments, and the New Select Speaker, tryin' to add to the family income. I especially remember the Red-Letter Testament he sold.

"My father was, you might say, really a literary man. He wasn't really meant for farmin'. He always cared a lot about books—good books too. I remember some of the books he read to me. They were *Peck's Bad Boy, A Slow Train Through Arkansas,* and the *Story of Jesse James.* By the way, as a child I had an impediment in my speech and I remember there was a tongue-twister he'd make me say. It was Thistle ma thostle as thick as my thumb, put him in a coffee-pot and beat him like a drum.

"Well he went around through the country in a horse and buggy takin' orders. He swapped one of those big, old-fashioned Bibles—a $25.00 one—for the horse and buggy. The horse was so poor it could hardly stand up. I remember father comin' back with it and the buggy the day he got 'em. He said that all the way home he'd have to get out and pull the horse or push the buggy.

"Well, after workin' at it awhile he decided it was a good business, and since he couldn't do any more farm work we sold the farm interests and moved to Cedar Grove near Valette. He had a brother there who'd done pretty well raisin' peanuts and pigs. He'd feed the peanuts to the pigs. No, not all of 'em; he'd sell some of the peanuts. We lived with him a month.

"We went to town once in a while. Town was Jefferson, Georgia. I remember goin' to town once, and comin' back I fell off in the road and the two-horse wagon ran over my chest. Just one wheel. But it was so sandy along there that it just pushed me down in the sand. They thought I was killed. I remember how they carried on. But I was only slightly hurt.

"Well, as I said, we lived with my father's brother for just about a month, and then there was family differences. They had a big quarrel, so we moved to Jefferson and lived with some of my relatives on the main street, which wasn't very main. Then we rented a house of our own, my mother and father and three brothers. My sister hadn't been born yet. I started to school. We lived near the railroad and I remember my chief recreation was watchin' the trains go by.

"I had my first initiation into sex along about then. My cousins were responsible. They showed me how to masturbate. I don't know whether I really ought to bring this in or not, but it was somethin' that really affected my whole life and it's important. It had a psychological effect on me that lasted for years. Yeah, I'd heard all the old stories about how it makes you go blind or gives you heart trouble or drives you insane. It had a terrible effect on my religious life, but in a way you might say it was a good thing because it made me think—really *think*—about God for the first time. Oh of course my mother had made me pray and everything, but this got me to thinkin' about Him on my own I mean. I felt that I was awful—evil—and wicked— just horrible. I thought I was just too sinful to live. I got me a cross from somewhere—I don't know where —and I'd get down with it and pray to God to give me strength not to do it again. Oh! how I'd pray that He'd make me stop it. I'd make all sorts of promises and tell Him He could kill me if I did it again, but I always did it again and then I'd beg Him not to kill me that time but to do it the next time. I was only ten-and-a-

half years old then. It ain't right that a kid has to feel
like that.

"Well the next event I remember was that father
decided we might do better in a factory town. So we
went to Dogwood, Alabama. He had another brother
there. Father went first. He went to work right away
in a cotton mill as a quiller (that's operatin' a machine
that winds thread into quills for looms for heavy duck
cloth). He came back in a few days and he got a
wagon from my uncle—borrowed it—the one we'd been
livin' with in Cedar Grove. We loaded all the house-
hold goods on it and went back with him.

"Well for a few weeks we shared a house with my
uncle in Dogwood. It was a company house owned by
the mill. My father and my uncle and my cousin
worked in the mill there; eleven and twelve hours a
day. My uncle's house had the first electric lights I'd
ever seen. We lived just three hundred yards from the
superintendent's house, and I thought it was a mansion.
It was a big house, or at least I thought it was big
then, and it had grass in the front yard. All the other
houses just had dirt yards. He had an automatic
water pump in the well, too. It pumped the water up to
a tank and when the water got too low I could hear the
pump throbbin' when it started up. You might put in
that this was my first introduction to mechanics. I
know it's when I first got interested in what makes
things work; machinery, y'know.

"We lived with my uncle a few weeks and then there
was again family differences. So we moved to another
house, another company owned house. I went to the
mill school, but I left the seventh grade just before I
was eleven and went to work in the mill. The age
limit was eleven years, but my mother signed me up as

bein' eleven. That was so if the law or anybody questioned it they'd have this paper to show she said I was
that old. My mother was already workin' as a spooler.
A spooler winds the thread on big wooden quills which
were goin' to the twisters where they were made into
big thread which then went to the creeler and warpin'
rooms.

"My first job was pickin' up dropped quills in the
spooler room and sweepin' the floors and separatin' the
clean waste from the dirty. A waste-picker and sweeper
they called me. I worked five-and-a-half days a week
at sixty-five cents a day. Eleven hours a day. The
thing that was abhorrent to me was that all the men
and women chewed tobacco or snuff and I'd have to
separate the lint by hand and it'd have all the spit and
phlegm from their throats in it. I was always afraid
of gettin' some disease. Sometimes it'd make me vomit
to handle it, and I'd always gag.

"In my spare time I got books from the library.
It was owned by the mill too. I was a devout member.
I read lots of history and all the magazines. *Life*
magazine—the old *Life* with its funny cartoons—the
Literary Digest, and things like that.

"I stayed at the mill till I was seventeen. I'd got
to be a doffer boy—takin' off the full quills and puttin'
on empty bobbins. I got quite proficient and could
'run' the other doffers in. That means I got through
before they did. We'd each get on a row and start
down the line throwin' the quills off and puttin' the
bobbins on and we called that 'runnin' 'em in.' I made
eight or nine dollars a week at that.

"Then they taught me to spin. It was a woman's
job, but they were short of women spinners. So I didn't
like it. And I didn't like the bosses. They were mean.

If you got behind they'd come down the line and whistle at you. They'd put their fingers in their mouths and make a shrill, piercing whistle that let everybody in the buildin' know you were behind. So I became contrary and decided I could lose my job by bein' unruly. But they were short on labor and so they didn't fire me. They just pacified me by transferrin' me to the cloth room. That's where you examine the cloth through a magnifying glass to see how well it's woven. And there's supposed to be a certain number of threads to the inch, dependin' on the kind of cloth it was. The job paid fifteen dollars a week. It was easier work, cleaner work, and I felt like it was a white-collar job. I had some authority, too. I could lay the cloth aside and call in a worker and have the boss bawl him out. I could make 'em and break 'em. Of course if there was a worker I liked I'd say good things for him.

"From this time on I was anxious to get promoted and in my spare time I studied the job of the calendar man. The calendar man pulled the cloth over a machine that made a record of its width and length— every piece of cloth manufactured in the mill. This fellow wore a collar and tie and I distinctly remember the pencil behind his ear. Well I wanted to be like him. He didn't have to work; he had a Negro boy who watched the machine and he just took it easy. I decided that was the kind of job I wanted. Finally, by my diligent work, I attracted the attention of the overseer. One day the calendar man was sick and the overseer came around and asked me if I thought I could do the calendar job. I said I was pretty sure I could, so he tried me out and in a few days he told me the job was mine. I felt I was up in the world. I could always wear a clean shirt, you know, and a tie. I put a pencil

behind my ear too. Mother and Father were very
proud of me.

"I'd already started goin' to night school. I was
seventeen years old and it was during this time the
World War in Europe broke out. I'm puttin' this in
to show the scarcity of labor and the boss's attitude
toward labor. There wasn't any too many workers then
and I remember if I was sick the boss would come around
to the house and ask me how I felt and want to know
when I could get back on the job. Well of course I'd
try hard to get well then. And during the war, every
once in a while, they paid us a double-ticket—just
twice as much money as we actually earned. This was
to make us feel good and stay with 'em, and also, I
guess, because they were makin' so much money. And
they'd give us a bonus at Christmas time too. It was
a special check with holly leaves and berries on it. I
still remember them.

"Mother had been tradin' with a department store in
Eastland, Georgia, and they always sent a salesman
around on Saturday or Monday. It was owned by
some Jewish fellow. Well one time he came around
with his collector on that route and he must have seen
me because he told my mother they needed a salesman
and he liked my appearance. You see I was younger
then and I looked better than I do now. So I decided
to go to work for him. When the mill found out I was
quittin' the boss came around and begged me to stay
on. He says, 'You're next in line for a second-hand
job.' A second-hand job was the job next to the overseer of a department in the mill. Well I investigated
and I found out that another calendar man had been
workin' on the same job for five years or more and
they'd been promisin' him a second-hand job all along.

So I figured the boss was just talkin' and I went with the store.

"I got fifteen dollars a week and could buy the things I needed from the store at cost. I liked it 'cause I could stay dressed up all the time. I sold furniture and delivered it in a truck and then went around collectin' every Saturday or Monday. Sometimes I'd collect as much as five hundred dollars and I felt real proud that they'd trust me with so much money. I'd better tell you, too, that they ran an undertakin' parlor along with the rest of the business. It was on the second floor. I worked in there too. My duties were to handle the fluids while they were embalmin'. I had to go out to the cemetery with a Negro too and supervise the diggin' of the grave and settin' up the chairs and all that. It had an awful depressin' effect on me. I never have cared about dyin' since then. I always thought how awful it would be to be buried. I was scared to think about death for a long time after that job. To show I had superstitious traits, I remember I had to go up to that floor one dark winter afternoon and sweep out the room where the coffins were stored. I didn't want to do it, but I kept arguin' with myself that dead people couldn't hurt you. Well I was sweepin' with cold chills runnin' up my back and somehow I upset a stack of empty coffins and one of 'em fell over and struck me on the head. It was one a convict had been in. Years later I had an auto wreck and struck my head in the very same spot that coffin hit me. It was quite a coincidence.

"Well I worked there till 1920. I was nineteen years old then. In 1920 the flood came. The Chirpalikkee River overflowed its banks and covered the entire business district of Eastland. We stacked up the goods;

piled them up on the counters and anything that was high enough to escape the water. We had to spend the night in the store. It just come up so sudden we didn't have a chance to get home or anything. We all slept on cloth in the storeroom. Next mornin' the water broke through the store windows; the pressure was so great, y'know. I wanted to get out. I was afraid the buildin' would collapse from the pressure or by bein' undermined. So you know what I did? I tied bolts of cloth together and swung down out of the window to a bateau. There was bateaus all around in the water rescuin' folks.

"I came back several days later after the water had receded. It'd left slime and silt all over the first floor. We had to clean it up. We had on rubber boots shovelin' up the stuff and the boss comes over to me and says, 'By God, get to work and clean this up!' Just because I'd been standin' around doin' nothin' for a few minutes. I lost my temper and told him to go to hell. I said I wasn't hired to do any dirty work like that and that I didn't have to work for him. So I lost my job.

"Then I got a job as a soda-jerker. I think you oughta call that a soda-clerk; it sounds better. Besides, I waited on people for all sorts of things; not just drinks. Yeah, I got the job easy although I'd never made drinks before. Labor was short in those days and it was no trouble to get a job. I always figured I didn't have to do anything I didn't want to do. And I didn't then. But I've got more sense now, had some of that knocked outta me. Well I made seventeen dollars a week there. You notice every time I quit one job and went to another one I gotta raise. Maybe that's one reason I quit so many. Of course the

accusation might be raised that if I'd stuck to one job
I would have made more of a success. Well I worked
at this drugstore two years. Had charge of the whole
store. This added to my feelin' of egoism, you might
call it. Then I had a fallin' out with the manager.
One day I was writin' a letter to a girl and I had to
stop to wait on a customer. Well while I was waitin'
on the customer the delivery boy started readin' my
letter. There's nothin' makes me madder than that.
I told 'im I'd kill 'im if he didn't stop. Well he didn't,
so I took the heavy glass top from a big pineapple jar
and threw it at him and broke a showcase. I remember
it nearly scared hell out of the customer and she—she
was a woman—ran out of the store. When the manager
came back we had some words and I got mad again and
said somethin' and he fired me.

"So then I went to work for an electrical contractor
who was puttin' in conduits in the mill there. I was an
assistant's helper gettin' eighteen dollars a week and
board. Another raise, you see. Well I worked for
them till the job was completed. In the meantime my
people had moved to LaPlant . . . I forgot to tell you.
Father had got a job in a mill there. So after this job
I went to LaPlant. There was a minister holdin' an
Episcopal revival service there and I didn't have anything better to do so I started goin' to the meetin's.
I got to know the evangelist. I'd help him put up the
tent and after a while he started takin' me around the
countryside with him in an ole T-model Ford. I'd help
him set up the things for the meetin'.

"One day he said to me. 'You know, son, the ministry's a great service to humanity. How would you like
to go into it?' Well I said I had no education, but he
said he'd take care of that. So I thought it over for

several days and finally I said yes. The first thing he did was give me a prayer book and make me learn the catechism. He said he'd see the Bishop and arrange my startin' to school. Well the Bishop came down and confirmed me.

"I took a special examination and entered the eighth grade. The preacher in the meantime had gotten me a room with a man and his wife who worked in the mill so I wouldn't be a burden on my people. He gave the people some food and I took care of the house in return for my bed and board. I'd sweep and make the beds and cook up their lunch for them before I left for school, and then I'd run home later and warm it up so I'd have it hot for them by the time they got there. Yeah, I can still cook. Good, too.

"Later I entered the LaPlant High School and went to live with the preacher. He had a big library—lots of books on theology, and I read 'em. On Sundays I was a lay-reader and I taught a Sunday School class. Well I completed high school and then moved to Steward with the minister. I entered Dell Academy there and got my diploma. Then I went to Derby College at Terrapool, Florida. I studied to get an A. B. degree. I went there two years. While there I met some Jewish and Spanish students who influenced my ideas of religion and I began doubting whether any one religion was better than another, and I didn't feel I should enter any particular ministry until I was sure I was teaching the Truth.

"Well the preacher was very nice about it when I talked it over with him. He helped me justify my position although both he and the Church had been supportin' me and sendin' me through college. He had said all along that all the Church expected of me was to pass along to the world—to humanity—what I'd learned.

"In addition to my changin' thoughts on religion my old habit of masturbation was still troublin' me and interferin' with my spiritual thoughts. I was strugglin' within myself and couldn't somehow feel right about it all in my mind. Try as I did I couldn't be what I wanted to be and I was gettin' very unhappy. So the upshot of it all was I left college and went back to LaPlant. I was there only a short time when I got a letter from a friend of mine who I'd known at college. He'd left before I did and gone to Boston and opened a candy store. He wrote and asked me if I wanted to work for him that season at Coney Island and later go on to California with him. He asked me to wire him an answer. So I wired him and said yes and he wired me some money back that afternoon and I left LaPlant the next morning. Well I worked that summer at Coney Island. I learned to make candy and they sold it in the front of the little shop. I was twenty-five years old then and makin' at least forty dollars a week and sometimes one hundred dollars a week.

"I married my first wife there. She was workin' in the candy kitchen, or, rather, she stood out front and gave away samples. She borrowed some money from me; that's how I really got to know her. She was broke and couldn't pay her rent and I just sympathized with her and lent her the money. And then I got started goin' around with her a little and in a few weeks we got married. She was an Americanized girl of Russian ancestry and she came from the coal-minin' district of Pennsylvania. She was a Roman Catholic, too, and when we got married we went first to a priest, but he wanted the children to be Catholic. I wouldn't have

that, so, me bein' an Episcopalian, we went to an Episcopal minister.

"Well we rented a furnished apartment and she
stopped work. We lived together about a month and
then she decided to go to Chicago to visit some friends.
She came back in two weeks and stayed until I was
ready to go to California with this fellow. He'd saved
about ten thousand dollars and the season was closin' at
Coney Island and he wanted to leave right away. So
we went by way of Chicago and I left my wife there.
I gave her one hundred dollars to take care of her until
I could get settled in California. She'd already been
promised a job in Chicago when she went to visit her
friends. It wasn't exactly a job yet, but she was to get
a small salary while learnin' the trade of beautician in
a beauty shop, one of a chain throughout the country.

"I stayed one night in Chicago with her. I remember
we went to a theater and saw Gilbert and Sullivan's
'Mikado.' Then we went to some restaurant and I
spent seven dollars for supper. I didn't know it was
gonna be so much, but the waiter kept bringin' on food.
As fast as we got through with one thing he'd bring
on another and when the man at the door gave me the
check it was seven dollars. I spent forty dollars altogether that night. I don't know what on.

"I left the next day with my friend and drove to
Springfield, Mo., where we stayed three days. My
friend had a brother there who was married and had
a little girl seven years old. Well when he heard we
were goin' to California he decided to go along with us.
So he picked up another woman he was in love with
and left his wife and child and came along in his car
with us. We drove out over the Santa Fe Trail and
just took our time. We stayed three days at the Grand

Canyon. On the way out this woman with my friend's brother became dubious about livin' with him without bein' married to him, so they asked me to read the marriage service to them since I was a lay-reader. Well I slipped into an Episcopal church in some town—I forget where—and purloined a prayer-book. You know how they have them layin' all about in the church. So I got one and read them the service and she felt better about it. I forgot to tell you that she had a boy friend of her own and when he heard we'd brought her along with us, he jumped in his car and followed us. He caught up with us in Ashfork, Arizona, but we got away from him. Then, to throw him off the track, we bought some gray calcimine and painted over the red trimmin' on the car. We didn't do a very good job of it and part of the red showed through, and the cops stopped us because they thought it was a stolen car. We had a hard time convincin' 'em some kids had done it on Halloween.

"Well we arrived in San Diego on Christmas Eve. Me and my friend got an apartment. My friend's brother had done a lot of readin' on psychology and psychiatry and stuff and so he decided to be a psycho-analyst and on the trip out we planned that I was to be his secretary. I was carryin' all his money for him— five thousand dollars that he'd drawn out of the bank back in Springfield. He let me carry it because he said I didn't look like I had money and nobody would try to hold me up. When we tried to deposit it in the bank at San Diego they called the cops and he had to prove the money was his. Well, anyway, his plans about bein' a psychoanalyst didn't pan out. He tried to get an office right at first, but because he couldn't get the one he wanted, he gave up the idea. The truth was, he was too infatuated with his woman to give any time to business. I don't know what became of him, but that sort of stuff goes over big out on the West Coast. I mean the psychoanalysis.

"I lived with my friend a short time while lookin' around for a job. Finally I got one sellin' subscriptions for a newspaper. They paid me seven dollars a week and I got one dollar for each subscription. Well I couldn't make enough money on that to save any to send for my wife, so I borrowed some equipment from my friend and set up a candy place. I set the equipment up in the backyard of the apartment where I lived. I made candy in the mornin' and then went out in the afternoon and peddled it. I'd sell about one hundred bags and average eight or nine dollars a day. This was durin' the cold season. Well when the warm season came on people wouldn't buy candy and so I had to give it up.

"Then I got a job selling furniture polish from office to office. The second day I was on this job I was trying to sell to a man. He said he wasn't interested but we talked a while and he said he was gettin' ready to go into the candy business. He was goin' to pack it specially in tin cans to keep out the moisture, you know. He was all ready to go, but said he didn't have a candy-maker. I said, 'Well, brother, I'm your man!' So he opened up a place and I went to work makin' candy again. It's funny that I'd just gotten out of the business and then ran right into him. Well, he paid me thirty dollars a week and when I'd saved a hundred and fifty dollars I sent for my wife.

"She came right out and, to show you how she'd changed, I remember when I went down to the station to meet her, she wouldn't even kiss me. I guess her love had cooled in just those few months. I figure now she just wanted to get to California and she didn't give a damn about me after she got there. Was just usin' me for a good thing.

"She had become a professional beautician by then and was workin' regularly in the beauty shops. Well as soon as I met her she told me that the owner wanted her to go on to the Los Angeles shop and she gave me orders to go on with her. You know, they'd switch 'em around from one shop to another, if they was good. Well she gave me orders to pack up and go with her. Mind you, all this was before we even got home from the station. Well I didn't want to go, but she insisted that I give up my job and ordered me to go on with her.

"Well I loved her and so I gave up my job and we left the next day for Los Angeles. But on the train she told me that in a business like that it was better for a woman to remain single. She said it was better for her career. So she insisted that we must not live in the same place in Los Angeles. I didn't like it a little bit, but there was nothin' I could do at this time. So the first night in Los Angeles she went to the YWCA and I got a room somewhere. The next day she got a furnished apartment and began workin'.

"Well I had to get a job right away, so I looked around and took the first thing I could find—a job with the Prudential Life Insurance Company as a contact man. I worked for a man who was an insurance broker, y'know. My wife was makin' thirty-five dollars a week and I was makin' twenty-five dollars a week and commission.

"The only way I could see my wife was to go callin' on her like a sweetheart and set about her apartment

at night and tryin' to get her, you might say, to perform her duty as a wife. She was a very cold woman,
though, and had no apparent desire for sex. I realize
now that she'd just been caterin' to my desire when she
had indulged formerly. Well I didn't like it at all.
Here she was my wife and I wasn't gettin' anything out
of it at all. We'd fuss all the time and that kept me
upset and then I wasn't gettin' any relief and that
didn't help any. I kept after her and finally I persuaded her, you might say, to let me move in with her.
So I did, but we didn't get along so well because of
those ideas of hers. She still didn't want to give in,
and she wanted twin beds and all that sort of thing.
I didn't like that; I believe a man and his wife should
sleep in the same bed. But she wouldn't have it, and
she wouldn't have any sex either. The truth was she
was afraid she'd get pregnant and it'd hurt her business. She didn't want to spoil her figure either. She
didn't know anything about birth control and I didn't
either at the time. Well things got worse and worse
and we was scrappin' all the time and finally we had a
break-up.

"She moved downstairs in the same buildin'—got another apartment—and I stayed upstairs. It was bad.
Because of my religious trainin' I felt that I shouldn't
step out on her . . . shouldn't go out with other women
to satisfy myself. Even if she wouldn't be a wife to me
I felt I couldn't go back on my vows I'd made in church.
Well I couldn't satisfy myself and I'd nearly go crazy.
Some nights I'd just go out of my head and I'd go
downstairs and beat on her door beggin' her to let me
in. One night I just had to break her door right in
and we had a big fight. I don't mean I exactly beat her

up—I was just wild—and you might say I raped my own wife, just took it away from her.

"Unluckily, shortly after that night, she announced she was pregnant. Well there was nothin' for it but to have it out, so she took fifty dollars I gave her and went to a doctor and had—what do you call it?—yeah, an abortion. From that time things grew worse and worse and I finally decided we couldn't live together. So I divorced her and came back East, to LaPlant.

"My father was still workin' in the mill. While I was gone my next oldest brother had become afflicted with some sort of rheumatism that paralyzed his arms and legs. But he always had a good mind and so he and my mother had opened up a small store there in LaPlant. She did the work and he managed the business end. Between my father's salary and the income from the store they were livin' comfortably. The family, in the meantime, had increased to one sister and five brothers.

"Well I got a job as a reporter on a newspaper. In fact, you might say I was a reporter, business manager, editor, and everything else. I forgot to tell you that I'd done some reportin' in Eastland and had had some experience. The paper was started by a couple of friends of mine. We had it printed over at Cold Springs, but there was no money in it. It went broke.

"After that I got a job soliciting for a dry-cleanin' company. I made good money at that. In the meantime I'd met another girl—my present wife. We married shortly thereafter. She worked in a factory there. I just forgot the other woman entirely.

"Oh she was born in south Alabama on a farm. She went through the sixth grade. Her father was a tenant farmer like mine had been. He died when she was four-

teen years old. Then her mother had decided they
could do better if they moved to town. They had
relatives in Phoenix, so they moved there—she and her
mother and an older brother. Both of them, her and
her brother, worked in a factory. But her mother died
in a year and then she went to LaPlant to live and that's
how I met her. See, her mother had a sister in LaPlant
and she came down to Phoenix to see about the funeral
and she brought her and her brother back with her because they were so young and there was nobody to look
after them.

"When I married her she was nineteen, and our first
baby, a girl, was born in the shortest period of time
which could elapse between marriage and havin' a child.
We were married in January and she was born in October.

"Well, in two years we went to Phoenix to live. The
depression drove me out of the dry-cleanin' business.
No commissions any more. I thought I could do better
in Phoenix but the only job I could find was back in
the mill. I had to learn the job on my own time. I was
a battery-filler. I'd wind the thread on the battery before it went to the automatic loom. I made seven dollars and fifteen cents a week.

"We lived in a furnished room, the three of us;
cooked, ate, and slept in it. Soon I left the mill and
went into the insurance business. I'd already done
some of it in Los Angeles, y'know. I built up a debit
and averaged fifteen dollars a week. Well pretty soon
the company cut my commission, so I quit 'em.

"Then I went back to the mill, in the weave room as
a cloth doffer. I stayed in the mill three years off and
on. It was during this time our second girl was born.

This was three and a half years after the first one. I'd learned somethin' about birth control, y'see.

"Well in the meantime I'd joined a labor union. It was the United Textile Workers of America. Yeah, A. F. of L. I was very active in the union work. I'd never thought much about unions before, but I took right to it. I did a lot of studyin', readin' and speechmakin'. And I held offices.

"Somehow the management found out about it—I hadn't been keepin' it any secret—and the superintendent called me in the office one day and began tellin' me how much they thought about me, and he said if I'd give up the union why they'd find me a better job. And they did. They gave me a timekeeper's job and I wore my best suit and white collar on the job. But I didn't promise nothin', see?

"Well I held the job all right; I could do the work, but I didn't give up my union activities. So they demoted me back to a 'learner-weaver.' It was just about that time a union organizer asked me if I'd take a trip with him for two weeks. He'd heard I was a good driver and he wanted me to drive him around the country. He'd pay the expenses. Well there wasn't much I hadn't learned about a car on that trip to California, so I went to the boss and asked him to let me off for two weeks. I didn't tell 'em for what purpose, y'understand, I just made up some excuse, I don't know what.

"Well they let me off and I went with the organizer. We went through Alabama, me makin' speeches with him. He always introduced me as an official of the union, but the truth was I wasn't holdin' any office just then. We organized several towns and then we came back to Phoenix.

"As soon as I reported at the mill the overseer fired

me. They'd heard about what I'd done and he said I
didn't need the job because they understood I had another one. Bein' sarcastic, y'know. Well I got mad
and I cursed him. I told 'em they couldn't starve me to
death and God-damn 'em sometime I'd get even with
'em. Losin' that job didn't matter so much, but they
blackballed me from all the other mills. I'd get all
kinds of promises for jobs because I was known as a
good worker. I'd fill in applications, y'know, and
they'd say they were pretty sure they'd put me to work
in a day or two, and then when I'd come back they'd tell
me they didn't need me.

"Well there was nothin' to do but apply for relief.
I did, and finally got a job on the WPA. Worked on a
labor project; dug ditches, rolled wheelbarrows, and
things like that. I did all sorts of temporary jobs between the WPA work. One time I manufactured my
own roach killer and peddled it from house to house.
And I kept up my union activities. I became secretary
of an Unemployed Workers' Union. Yeah, it was a
WPA union.

"Oh! I forgot to tell you about the strike at the mills
in 1934 and how I got jailed. I was walkin' down the
street one day and I had a pair of spy-glasses with me.
Well I looked through 'em and over on a hill about a
mile away and saw a group of men standin' around on a
road. Well I thought there'd been an accident, so I
walked on over there and found out they were armed
with clubs and all sorts of weapons. They said they
were gonna beat up some Negroes who were scabbin' on
the job. They told me to take my glasses and look
down the road for the trucks which were bringin' the
Negroes to the mill. Well I watched for the trucks
and pretty soon I saw 'em comin' 'way off, y'know.

But the trucks didn't only have niggers in 'em but they were loaded down with soldiers too—the national guard.

"Well I told the men what I saw comin' and they all dispersed—ran away. But I stayed there. I didn't see why I should run; I hadn't done nothin'. Well the trucks came on up the road and when the soldiers saw me with the glasses they jumped out and arrested me. They put me in jail and I stayed there eight days. They put me in a filthy old cell. It was just about six feet long and not that wide, and the cot had a dirty old mat on it so full of bugs that I had to sleep on the floor. The jail was owned by the mill. You see, the mills just run the whole town and they could do what they liked.

"For a couple of days my wife and children didn't know where I was. But about the third day some of the soldiers went over to see my wife and told her they'd jailed me. They tried to pump her, but they didn't get anything out of 'er. There wasn't anything she could tell 'em anyway; I hadn't done nothin'. Well they kept me shut up there and asked me a lot of questions. They didn't do nothin' to me except to threaten me. They told me they'd heard a lot about me and the things I'd been doin' in the union. I wish I'd done half as much as they said I did. They told me if I didn't lay low and stop my union activities, they'd put me away for good. Then they let me go.

"As soon as I got out I went right down and got a job on the picket line picketin' the mill. I worked three months picketin' and got two dollars a day. Sometimes forty-five cents an hour.

"After that I did all sorts of odd jobs and worked on the WPA again. Then I heard about the Adult Education Program. I'd already organized a class of

workers on my own—I didn't know there was any such
thing as an Education Program. Well I told the WPA
office I was interested in that kind of work, so when the
supervisor came down from Huntington he said he'd
take me on the program. I didn't tell him much about
my past, not that I had anything to hide, but people
act so funny if they know you're for the worker. He
was a nice fellow and he was very careful to tell me that
I wasn't to do any organizin' or anything like that.
He said my job was to teach, just that and nothin'
more. If the workers wanted me to tell 'em about
unions then it was all right, but I wasn't supposed to
encourage 'em or discourage 'em about the unions. I
figured it out that what he meant was that if the workers were gonna organize they were gonna organize and
there was nothin' we could do about it except to try to
educate them so they wouldn't run wild once they got
some power.

"I was assigned to the program in a few days and
told to report to Huntington. I got there on March
15, 1938. In the meantime my wife had had another
baby—a boy. I took a trainin' course there in Huntington in the subjects I was to teach and then went back
to Phoenix. I started classes with the textile workers
and plunged into a lot of readin' and studyin'. I'd
read some of these things in the past, of course. I'd
read Robinson's *Mind in the Making* and things like
that. I'd also read *Merchants of Death*. I was always
particularly interested in the munitions manufacturers.
In fact I'd done some columnings on these subjects in
a Phoenix newspaper. I'd read *The Robber Barons*, a
history of John D. Rockefeller and the Astors and
other financiers. So to be paid for doin' the sort of
thing I'd always wanted to do anyway was wonderful.

"I've always had an ambition to save the world. Maybe it's a—what do you call it?—yeah, a Messianic complex. My real ambition is to be a writer and show people what's right. Give 'em truth. Oh I'd write on any subject; anything to teach the people why we're here, the purpose of life. As to what I actually *will* do in life—well, brother, who knows?

"Why tomorrow I may be myself
With several thousand yesteryears."

"My philosophy now might be:

"A loaf of bread, a jug of wine, and thou
Beside me in the wilderness;
O wilderness were paradise enow!"

"I'm interested in poetry. I particularly like Omar Khayyam. I tried to write some poetry once; had some published in newspapers. Sent some to the *New Masses*, but they sent it back. It must have been punk. But I like those kinds of publications; they tell the truth and that's what people need.

"That's the trouble with schools and universities today. They don't teach the truth. They're run with the idea of maintaining the 'status quo'—maintaining the capitalistic system. Of course I'm not sayin' that the capitalistic system shouldn't be maintained, but it should be maintained with a more equitable distribution of wealth. Oh yes, in spite of that I want my children to be educated all they can; at least up to the extent that they'll know what's goin' on in the world. I want 'em to see what's underneath and behind our social system so they won't be fooled. I hope they can go through college, but I don't know. Don't see any way

for it now. I know they won't get what they need in
college but I'll tell 'em the real inside dope myself.
You need a college degree to get on the WPA now.
Sure you do. It's a damn dirty shame but that's the
way the world is. I've been interviewed by social workers that haven't had sense enough to get out of a shower
of rain. They haven't got any real feelin's, but because
they've got a college education they give 'em the jobs.
I wish they had to get out and deal with these workers'
classes; they wouldn't get to first base. It'd learn 'em.

"Not on your life, brother, I don't want any more
children. There's five of us now havin' to live off of
eighteen dollars a week. We don't have anything; no
furniture, no car, nothin'. All five of us eat, sleep, and
do everything else in one room. I'm 'way in debt.
Owe one hundred dollars and don't know how I'll pay
it. Doctor's and grocery bill. When any of us have to
go to the hospital it's just straight charity. We had
the baby in the hospital just a little while back. He had
an infection from an injury to his chin which came
about from havin' to live in a tenement. It all goes
back to this rotten social system. Well maybe they
don't call 'em tenements there in Huntington but if
landlords thought more about fixin' up their places
instead of makin' all the money they could out of 'em
that porch woulda had banisters and he wouldn't have
fallen off. Yeah, the second story. My wife's always
sick. She needs to be diagnosed for various things now.
We all need dental care because of lack of proper diet.
Especially the children, because my wife didn't have
the proper kind of food to provide calcium for them
while she was pregnant. I've made a special study of
diet and I know what kinds of food we oughta have but
I can't afford it. No, I'm seldom sick myself. Last

time I was in the hospital was in 1924, when I got drunk and wrecked a car.

"I figure I need exactly two hundred dollars a month to live on. Every bit of it. Anybody with a family does. That's why I'm for the union. I don't care if people do say they're always belly-achin' and wantin' more. Sure they want more, why shouldn't they? Everybody in the world should have two hundred dollars a month, especially men with families. Is it right for me to try to live on eighteen dollars a week when I know that eighty percent of the wealth of this country is controlled by five percent of the people? Is that fair? Hell, no!

"And that brings up another thing. Do you know I've never voted in my life, never been able to exercise my right as a citizen because of the poll tax? I've had to eat and sleep and I can't pay a poll tax, can't have a voice in my own government. You quote me as sayin' I'm very interested in some means to remove the poll tax. Sure I'm for this administration. I'm with Roosevelt right up to the hilt. I don't know whether Roosevelt'll have a third term or not, but if he doesn't . . . God help this country! I'm dealin' with the workers every day and I know what they say. They've got more from this administration than ever before and they're not gonna stand for anybody takin' it away from 'em.

"Religion? I'm not sure what I think along that line any more. I know religion doesn't influence my morals. I'm moral for morality's sake . . . because of the effect it might have on me physically and mentally to indulge my lower desires. I think the average church is just a racket. They don't really give the people anything. Understand, I don't mean I'd do away with the churches. But I don't have anything to do with 'em. I've found my own philosophy. It may change every day, but I'm findin' it. I've just come to the conclusion that most churches are not interested in humanity for humanity's sake. I might go for the sake of contacts, but there again I'm not financially able to dress as I should, so I don't go.

"No, we don't do anything in the way of recreation. We can't afford to on eighteen dollars a week. We listen to an old piece of a radio I've got. I especially like to hear Walter Damrosch's dissertations on music, and I like Gilbert and Sullivan. Never go to a movie. I read a lot, especially poetry.

"Well, I'm beginnin' to ramble now. I guess you've got all the story you want. Anyway, that's all there is of it. Come back in another year and maybe I'll have added somethin' excitin' to it.

"By the way, I want a copy of whatever you're goin' to write. I'd like to have it for my children to read some day. Let me know when it's published, hear?"

MAURICE RUSSELL

Weary Willie

MILLARD KETCHUM HAD JUST COME IN FROM HIS day's work in the field. He was still in his blue CCC work uniform. "This is better clothes than I ever had at home," he said, "before I got to the CCC. You see, at home they was so many of us, we couldn't have much clothes to wear and in summer time we jist didn't wear no shoes, and no shirts much, nor nothing else much."

"Let me git you some where to set if you want to talk a while. Hey, Sarge! kin I git a few minutes off to talk here to this lady here? Okay, Sarge."

When asked about his family, he said, "Well, my mama she come from Bundy County. She was a Dunlap. My papa, he come from Chester County, over here nigh Henderson. They live at Zama now and been there about two year. I ain't got so big a family to keep up, not so big as lots of the boys has. I jist got five brothers and one sister. I'm the oldest and I ain't but nineteen year old.

"My brothers, they's named Winston Gormer, Jim Ables, Luther Crocker, Ray Slowey, and Jonathan Junior. My sister she's named Pearlie Jo and she's thirteen.

"We's farmers and renters. Ain't ever owned no home as yet. We lives at Zama now with a Mr. Lew Truitt. We've got two big houses on each side of us and they's shore pretty, too. We ain't got so big a house to live in—jist a small house, but my mother she's a good housekeeper and keeps everything spick and span. Ain't much trouble, you know, with a little house to keep it clean. We ain't got so much in it neither. Jist enough to make it comfortable for us. We got plenty of beds, though, arn bedstids, and all. You know jist like most any pore farmer's got, but enough to do us all.

"I ain't never been much to school. Jist went to the second grade, that's all, excepting what I learned here in the CCC. I could have gone, I guess, but for some reason didn't keer nothing about it. Jist didn't want to go. I would have went if I wanted to. They didn't make me not go. We jist didn't none of us go. I got one brother that went to the second grade, too, and my sister she went to the first. Then she quit. We jist wasn't a family that like school.

"I quit that old second grade when I was fourteen. I left home and went to work. Been on my own ever since. I went down here to Woolard and went to work on a farm. The man he was sick and not able to work and had to have somebody to help him. That's why I got to work so long, and even got the job at all. Got twenty dollars a month."

I asked. "Would you go on to school and finish now if you had the chance?"

"Don't know whether I could or not. I would really like to learn." He flushed and scowled. "The boys they make fun of us when we can't read the funnies nor nothing. I look at pictures in books, and things like that in the recreation hall, so they won't laugh at me. I wish I had gone on to school now and would go as far as I could if I git the chance. Guess I couldn't git much learning now though, could I? I'm too old most to learn now."

I asked if he wanted to stay with the CCC.

"Yes'm, as long as I kin, because I git plenty to eat here. I didn't always at home, not the same kind of stuff, anyhow. Guess we had plenty, such as it was, at home, but it jist wasn't good like this, nor enough of it for the kind it was. I git to go more, git to see more. I'm learning too. I watch the others, and then, I have more clothes and can keep cleaner too.

"You see where we is at home they don't go to school. None of them has gone any since they moved to Rivers County. They's three at home now to go to school, but they ain't went none and guess they won't ever. I got higher'n any of 'em. My littlest brother, he three year old now. I git thirty dollars a month and send twenty-two of it home to them. They need it! My papa he don't make enough to do for all, jist renting and farming like he does.

"You see, my pap drinks some. Not all the time, but he gits drunk at times, and that makes it hard on mama. I got drunk a few times. First time I jist all at once didn't know what was wrong. I jist couldn't walk, so I set down and went to sleep. I don't drink now. I quit since I got in the C's which I've been in nineteen months now.

"I ain't never voted yet. Ain't old enough and don't think I will till I git old enough, neither. My papa, he's a 'Publican, but I'm going to be a Democrat myself. He don't vote in every election neither. But I'm going to when I git old enough. I'll take them all in as they come.

"Do I go to church?

"Well, no'm. Not now. But while in the C's I do.

The chaplain preaches to us two times a month, and I like to hear him. He makes tears come in my eyes, too. I quit drinking all on account of him. I'm a good boy now. I don't go to church at town much because I'm afraid they'll laugh at me. My mother she's a Baptist, but I jist go to any of them. I always give some money when I have it to give.

"Down home it's different. I've rambled all over that place and they ain't got no churches down there. I been there two years and ain't ever seen no church yet. Some of my little brothers ain't never seen no church yet.

"No'm. Ain't ever been sick to speak of. Ain't never had nothing but measles and 'pendicitis and had them both in Camp and got my bills paid. If I'd been at home, I wouldn't had no operation, couldn't have paid for it. I skipped all other sorts of being sick. I ain't never had pneumonia sickness yet. I jist about got all the doctor bills at home paid up now because I sent my whole check home and done without going to shows or smoking and everything to git them all paid up. The family's sick lots."

"Are you ever homesick?"

"Yes, heck! I have enough to eat, but by gosh, when the rest gits to raising cane to go home, sometimes it makes me homesick, too. I don't git there much because I can't pay my way. I like to see my mother though. You see, at home we have peas with bugs and weevils in them. We have sweet potatoes and I don't like peas, and sometimes we have pudding and meat when Mama has time to make pudding for us.

"You ought to go to my house some time. We got a pump, and the water ain't much good. But Mom she's clean. They jist don't make them no cleaner than my

ma. And I got a girl at home. She jist lives half a
mile of me. We go walking every time I go home, because we ain't got no car. We go boat riding sometimes, but I don't like swimming. I can't swim and,
anyway, I don't want to see my girl in swimming and
nearly naked like most of them goes. I ain't going in
for anybody looking like that. I kissed her last time I
was home, but didn't do that till after dark. I ain't
never asked no girls here at Belgrade to go with me
nowhere. I'm afraid they won't. Anyhow, I'm going
to marry some day when I git a good job to keep her
up. It would be too many children to keep up on what
I make now. Mama needs what I make for the ones
at home."

"What does you father do?"

"Blame if I know. Nothing. Jist sets around the
house after he gits off work at night. You see, he
farms. After the crop is laid by, he don't do nothing
much. Jist sets around. He might go out to the
stores some. They's three or four little stores around
there, about half a mile apart. He won't let me go
off in a car. I went riding in an auto one time with my
girl and a whole lot of us. It runned off in a ditch and
I ain't got in none of them no more. I jist ain't going
no more. I'm afraid.

"I git up about five in the morning, eat breakfast, go
to morning classes, then go to the field. I don't work
nearly so hard in this as I do in the field at home. I
git to be with lots of boys that I wouldn't at home.
They help me lots, show me how to do things I wouldn't
have never knowed about. I like all my bosses and I
like all the fellers. They tease me sometimes, but they
like me, too.

"They call me Weary Willie. I guess it's because I

look so sleepy-headed. I go to the shows some and I guess I make much as I need. I spend every blame penny I git my fingers on. I get eight dollars a month to spend. I sure do run through with it. Bet I could spend twenty dollars without half trying."

NELLIE GRAY TOLER
JAMES R. ASWELL

Instructions to Writers

1. Materials are to be collected on tenant farmers and their families, farm owners and their families, cotton mill villagers and their families, persons and their families in service occupations in towns and cities, and persons and their families in miscellaneous occupations such as lumbering, mining, fishing, turpentining. Samples showing the nature of the materials to be collected are attached hereto.

2. The life histories may range from approximately two thousand words to ten or fifteen thousand words, depending upon the interest of the material.

3. An outline is attached hereto. This outline shows the nature of the subject matter which should be covered in the life history. However, it is not desired that each life history or story follow this outline in a rigid manner. The stories will not be useable if they are constructed on a rigid pattern. For instance, the writer may reverse the order of the outline, he may begin with any item which he considers of special importance in the case under consideration, he may follow the whole outline or limit himself to a part of it in any particular story. It is immaterial whether the stories are written in the first, second, or third person. Insofar as possible, the stories should be told in the words of the persons who are consulted. The effort should be made to get definite information. Avoid generalities such as "those who are industrious and ambitious can do well," "had not made good use of opportunities"— wherever possible expand such wording to give detail, that is, exactly what industry and ambition might have done or what the opportunities were that could have been used. In general

avoid the expression of judgment. The writer will, of course, have to exercise judgment in determining the course of a conversation through which he gains information, but aside from this, he should keep his own opinions and feelings in the background as much as possible. For instance, if he sees people living under conditions which he thinks are terrible, he should be most careful not to express his opinion in any way and thus possibly affect the opinion of the person to whom he is talking. He must try to discover the real feeling of the person consulted and must record this feeling regardless of his own attitude toward it. Any story in which this principle is violated will be worthless.

4. Writers should not limit themselves to the types of stories shown in the samples. It is hoped that original modes of presenting the material will be developed. The criteria to be observed are those of accuracy, human interest, social importance, literary excellence. It may not be possible to combine all these in any one story. However, accuracy and literary excellence should be present in all. A story of some very exceptional family may be of great human interest but of minor social importance. The best stories will be those which combine all these elements. (By accuracy, it was explained in conferences, is meant simply write what you smell, see, hear. Writers cannot check on the accuracy of what is said. Get in the subject's own words what he has done, felt, and thought. If the subject's head is filled with wrong notions, foolish thoughts, and misinformation, if this kind of material comes out in conversation, record it. Let the subject's mind speak for itself.)

5. While the majority of stories should be about families and should attempt to include information on all the points listed in the attached outline, it may be best in some instances to write about a section of a village or a community dealing with all the families in that section or community; or a story may be written about any one of the items in the outline, such as, for instance, the size of the family, the coming of children and the effect their coming has on the fortunes of the family.

Any town, community, village, or open country from which a number of stories are secured should itself be described in a separate story.

6. Some topics of importance may come up which are not covered in the outline. It will be best to go ahead and treat such topics and not wait to ask for permission to deal with them. However, no state director should allow writers to abandon the outline and sample stories to such an extent as to change the nature of the work.

7. All the stories do not have to be solemn and packed with information. If an amusing incident reveals the attitude of a family towards some important problem then this incident should be related.

8. The purpose of this work is to secure material which will give an accurate, honest, interesting, and fairly comprehensive view of the kind of life that is lived by the majority of the people in the South. It is extremely important that families be fairly selected, that those which get along well or fairly well be selected for stories as well as those that make a less favorable impression. The sub-normal, the normal, the above normal, all should have stories written about them. As the work gets along, it will be necessary to expand it in order to include other important groups, but insofar as possible, a beginning should be made with the groups indicated above. In those parts of the South where cotton textile manufacturing is unimportant, and other industries dominate the scene, these other industries should be selected for treatment. For instance, in and around Birmingham, Alabama, both families in textile manufacturing and families working in coal and iron industries should be treated.

9. Each story should carry on the first page the date when the first version is written, the name of the writer and the name and address of the family written about. This information needs to be given for purposes of verification. Names will be changed in any material that is published.

10. It is hoped that out of this material four or five volumes will be secured which can be published under a series name

such as LIFE IN THE SOUTH with individual names for each volume.

OUTLINE FOR LIFE HISTORIES *

I. Family

    1. Size of family.

    2. Effect of family-size upon financial status of family.

    3. Attitude toward large families.

    4. Attitude toward limitation of family.

    5. Occupational background of family.

    6. Pride in family, including ancestry.

II. Education

    1. Number of years of school attendance.

    2. Causes of limited education.

    3. Attitudes toward education.

        a. Educational advantages desired for children.

        b. Whether worker believes school training is economic advantage.

        c. Evaluation of school system.

        d. Ambition, ideals. Idea of good life. Which comes first owning home or owning car. Does family own car?

III. Income

    1. Comparison of present income with first weekly or annual income.

    2. Actual needs to be covered by income.

    3. Extent to which income covers actual needs.

    4. Sense of relative values in expenditure of income.

    5. What person consulted considers an adequate income.

IV. Attitudes Toward Occupation and Kind of Life

    1. Pride or shame in work.

    2. Influence of attitudes of others.

    3. Basis of objections to or satisfaction with life.

    4. Attitudes toward owners.

    5. Advantages or disadvantages of present life in comparison with other types of life, e.g., working in mill compared with working on farm, life in town with life in country.

V. Politics

    1. Extent of voting.

    2. Degree of independence in casting ballot.

* Prepared by Ida Moore.

3. Preferences in choice of candidates.
4. Party consciousness.
5. Consciousness of changing trends in thought.

VI. Religion and Morals

1. Influence of religion on morals.
2. Attitudes toward various forms of amusements.
3. Relations to churches.
   a. Contributions.
   b. Attitude toward aid from churches.
   c. Attendance.

VII. Medical Needs

1. Money expended for hospital and doctor bills.
2. To what extent health has been protected through adequate medical care.
3. What effect work has had upon health.

VIII. Diet

1. Knowledge of balanced diet.
2. To what extent knowledge is applied.
3. To what extent it is possible to have balanced diet on wage earned.

IX. Miscellaneous Observations

1. Cleanliness and order of house; number of rooms.
2. Cleanliness of person.
3. Furnishings in house.
4. Sleeping accommodations.
5. Bathroom facilities.
6. Pride in possessions.

X. Use of Time

1. Annual routine.
   E.g., preparation of soils for planting—planting—cultivation—laying by—occupations and amusements during interval between laying by and harvesting—harvesting—settlement—moving.
2. Daily routine during the different periods indicated above.
3. Amusements, visiting, courting. Where do courting couples go?
Where do men spend their leisure hours?

George F. Kennan   *Realities of American Foreign Policy*   N320

Gabriel Kolko   *Railroads and Regulations, 1877–1916*   N531

Howard Roberts Lamar   *The Far Southwest, 1846–1912: A Territorial History*   N522

Peggy Lamson   *The Glorious Failure: Black Congressman Robert Brown Elliott and the Reconstruction in South Carolina*   N733

William L. Langer   *Our Vichy Gamble*   N379

William Letwin, Ed.   *A Documentary History of American Economic Policy Since 1789* (Rev. Ed.)   N442

Richard P. McCormick   *The Second American Party System: Party Formation in the Jacksonian Era*   N680

William S. McFeely   *Yankee Stepfather: General O. O. Howard and the Freedmen*   N537

Robert C. McMath, Jr.   *Populist Vanguard: A History of the Southern Farmers' Alliance*   N869

C. Peter Magrath   *Yazoo: The Case of Fletcher v. Peck*   N418

Donald R. Matthews   *U.S. Senators and Their World* (Rev. Ed.)   N679

Burl Noggle   *Teapot Dome*   N297

Douglass C. North   *The Economic Growth of the United States, 1790–1860*   N346

Arnold A. Offner   *American Appeasement: United States Foreign Policy and Germany, 1933–1938*   N801

Robert E. Quirk   *An Affair of Honor: Woodrow Wilson and the Occupation of Veracruz*   N390

Robert E. Quirk   *The Mexican Revolution, 1914–1915*   N507

Robert V. Remini   *Martin Van Buren and the Making of the Democratic Party*   N527

Bernard W. Sheehan   *Seeds of Extinction: Jeffersonian Philanthropy and the American Indian*   N715

James W. Silver   *Confederate Morale and Church Propaganda*   N422

Kathryn Kish Sklar   *Catharine Beecher: A Study in American Domesticity*   N812

John W. Spanier   *The Truman-MacArthur Controversy and the Korean War*   N279

Ralph Stone   *The Irreconcilables: The Fight Against the League of Nations*   N671

Ida M. Tarbell   *History of the Standard Oil Company*   (David Chalmers, Ed.)   N496

George Brown Tindall   *The Disruption of the Solid South*   N663

Frederick Jackson Turner   *The United States 1830–1850*   N308

Richard W. Van Alstyne   *The Rising American Empire*   N750

Harris Gaylord Warren   *Herbert Hoover and the Great Depression*   N394

John D. Weaver   *The Brownsville Raid*   N695

Arthur P. Whitaker   *The United States and the Independence of Latin America*   N271

Joel Williamson   *After Slavery: The Negro in South Carolina During Reconstruction, 1861–1877*   N759

Bryce Wood   *The Making of the Good Neighbor Policy*   N401

Howard Zinn   *LaGuardia in Congress*   N488